PRAGMATICS

MODERN LINGUISTICS SERIES
Series Editor

Professor Maggie Tallerman
University of Newcastle

Each textbook in the **Modern Linguistics** series is designed to provide an introduction to a topic in contemporary linguistics and allied disciplines, presented in a manner that is accessible and attractive to readers with no previous experience of the topic. The texts are designed to engage the active participation of the reader, and include exercises and suggestions for further reading. As well as an understanding of the basic concepts and issues for each topic, readers will gain an up-to-date knowledge of current debates and questions in the field.

Titles published in the series

English Syntax and Argumentation (3rd edition) Bas Aarts
Phonology Philip Carr
Pragmatics Siobhan Chapman
Linguistics and Second Language Acquisition Vivian Cook
Sociolinguistics: A Reader and Coursebook
Nikolas Coupland and Adam Jaworski
Morphology (2nd edition) Francis Katamba and John Stonham
Semantics (2nd edition) Kate Kearns
Syntactic Theory (2nd edition) Geoffrey Poole
Contact Languages: Pidgins and Creoles Mark Sebba

Further titles in preparation

Modern Linguistics Series
Series Standing Order
ISBN 0–333–71701–5 hardback
ISBN 0–333–69344–2 paperback
(outside North America only)

You can receive future titles in this series as they are published by placing a standing order. Please contact your bookseller or, in the case of difficulty, write to us at the address below with your name and address, the title of the series and one of the ISBNs quoted above.

Customer Services Department, Palgrave Ltd
Houndmills, Basingstoke, Hampshire RG21 6XS, England, UK

Pragmatics

Siobhan Chapman

First published 2011 by
PALGRAVE MACMILLAN

Palgrave Macmillan in the UK is an imprint of Macmillan Publishers Limited,
registered in England, company number 785998, of Houndmills, Basingstoke,
Hampshire RG21 6XS.

Palgrave Macmillan in the US is a division of St Martin's Press LLC,
175 Fifth Avenue, New York, NY 10010.

Palgrave Macmillan is the global academic imprint of the above companies
and has companies and representatives throughout the world.

Palgrave® and Macmillan® are registered trademarks in the United States,
the United Kingdom, Europe and other countries.

ISBN 978–0–230–22182–6   hardback
ISBN 978–0–230–22183–3   paperback

This book is printed on paper suitable for recycling and made from fully
managed and sustained forest sources. Logging, pulping and manufacturing
processes are expected to conform to the environmental regulations of the
country of origin.

A catalogue record for this book is available from the British Library.

A catalog record for this book is available from the Library of Congress.

10 9 8 7 6 5 4 3 2 1
20 19 18 17 16 15 14 13 12 11

Printed and bound in Great Britain by
MPG Books Group, Bodmin and Kings Lynn

Contents

Preface

Pragmatics is an exciting and fast moving field of present day linguistics. The aims of this book are to describe both early and recent developments in pragmatics, and also to show how pragmatics relates to the study of language more generally. It is suitable for those who are just starting out in pragmatics, since it assumes no previous knowledge of the subject. However, it does more than provide an introductory overview; it encourages the reader to engage with some of the fundamental issues faced by pragmaticists, and to appreciate the current controversies and debates in which they are engaged. It is therefore aimed primarily at students taking undergraduate degree level courses in pragmatics or in linguistics more generally, but it should also be of use to postgraduate students in these areas and to researchers in linguistics and related disciplines who want to find out about what is currently going on in pragmatics.

The focal part of this book is the two large Chapters 4 and 5, which set out the main theories, terminologies and mechanisms of pragmatics. It is therefore these two chapters that conclude with suggested exercises and discussion questions, designed to help readers practise their understanding of the content of the chapters and also consider the wider implications of the different theories discussed. The other chapters put the central theories of pragmatics in context. The early chapters explain something of the nature of pragmatics, including the types of data it is centrally concerned with and its relatively recent emergence as a field of inquiry in its own right. The later chapters extend the scope of the discussion by considering how pragmatic theories have interacted with, and had an impact on, the study of a wide range of phenomena relating to language use.

Like most specialist fields of inquiry, pragmatics has developed a range of technical terms that can prove daunting to those new to the discussion. For this reason, this book concludes with a glossary of some of the main technical terms that readers will encounter, to provide a quick point of reference. Those terms that are included in the glossary are printed in SMALL CAPITALS when they first appear in the main text.

It has become standard practice in pragmatics to use the pronoun 'she' to refer to the speaker of any utterance under discussion, and 'he' to refer to the hearer, and this is a practice that will be adopted in this book. It avoids the stylistic or grammatical awkwardness of using either 'he or she' or 'they' on each occasion. Since one of the things we learn from pragmatics is that both speaker and hearer have a vital and active part to play in the collaborative creation of meaning in context, it privileges neither the female nor the male protagonist.

I am grateful to Kitty Van Boxel and the editorial team at Palgrave Macmillan for their encouragement, enthusiasm and patience during the writing of this book, and to my family for putting up with my even more gloomy than usual predictions about whether it would ever be finished. Maggie Tallerman and two anonymous reviewers made very helpful comments and suggestions on the first draft, for which I am very grateful. I am also grateful to the students who took my second year 'Pragmatics' module at the University of Liverpool during the academic year 2009–10, for serving as unwitting guinea pigs for the material presented here, and for keeping smiling through all the pragmatic theory that I could throw at them.

SIOBHAN CHAPMAN

Introduction

Some statements about pragmatics are easy to make and are not likely to prove too controversial. Pragmatics is one component of the study of human language, and can therefore be described as a branch of the academic discipline of linguistics. It has emerged relatively recently, certainly within the last half century, but is now an important and thriving area that continues to expand and develop. Concepts, theories and approaches developed within pragmatics are being used by those working in many other areas: both in other branches of linguistics, such as sociolinguistics, stylistics and psycholinguistics, and in different disciplines, such as artificial intelligence, clinical psychology and even law.

Once we get beyond such general statements, however, we get into more disputed territory. More precise and specific statements about pragmatics tend to be prefaced with comments such as 'some linguists argue that...' and 'it could be said that...'. Perhaps surprisingly, this includes definitions of what pragmatics actually is. In other words, pragmaticists (the term generally applied to those working in the field) don't all have the same ideas about what they are studying. Everyone agrees that pragmatics is concerned with the study of meaning. But beyond that there are a lot of different possible ways of defining precisely what aspects and types of meaning are the particular subject matter of pragmatics. Quite a good short description, one that is useful for explaining to people what you are studying and that steers clear of many of the major controversies, is that it is concerned with 'meaning in context'. However, as you read around the subject you will come across definitions that range from the informal ('it's about what people mean rather than what they say') through the more precise ('it concerns meaning in use rather than literal meaning') to the highly technical ('it is the study of meaning minus truth conditions').

There are two main reasons why pragmatics currently accommodates such varied and diverse definitions. The first is simply that it is itself a varied and diverse field of study, which covers many aspects of the relationship between meaning and context. There is, as we will see, something to be said in favour of all the definitions suggested above, as well as others that you may come across, even if none of them in isolation tells the whole story. The second reason for all the different definitions is that the various models, theories and schools of thought that make up pragmatics each have different ideas about what are the appropriate terms of the discussion. For instance, not all pragmaticists would agree that 'literal meaning', a concept that is central to one of the definitions above, even exists. Some would deny that it is legitimate to distinguish between pragmatic meaning and 'TRUTH CONDITIONS' as the third definition proposes. We will consider these differences of opinion, and others, later in this book.

Before we can get involved with the particular implications of these different definitions, we need to begin thinking about what might be involved in studying the relationship between meaning and context. This relationship is important every time anyone uses language to communicate, so we could take just about any instance of something that someone has said or written, but let's start with the following spoken example:

1. Towards the end, with the light, it was tough.

A very natural first reaction to this example might well be that it is clearly taken out of context, and that without some background information it is impossible to work out what is being communicated here. This reaction illustrates our awareness that meaning is closely bound up with context. If you are used to analysing examples in terms of their grammatical structure you might spot that this is a complete and grammatical sentence. So the problem with interpretation can't be that the example is in some way incomplete in itself or is just a fragment. The sentence may be complete but it doesn't contain sufficient information within itself to tell us what is being communicated. For many aspects of what is being communicated we need some further particulars of the context in which this example was spoken.

Note, however, that even without any such particulars there are some things that we do know about the meaning of this example; we are not totally at a loss as to what we can understand from it. For instance, we know that someone is describing an event or situation that took place at some point in the past. We can also form some general ideas about what types of things might be described by words such as 'end', 'light' and 'tough', although even these ideas will have to remain both vague and tentative. We know these things simply because we are speakers of the English language. That is, our knowledge is based on what we have learnt, either as little children or more recently, about the vocabulary and the grammar of the language. One way of putting this is to say that this knowledge is part of our knowledge of the SEMANTICS of English. We will consider semantics, and in particular its relationship to and difference from pragmatics, in more detail in the next chapter.

Even if we are fully competent in the English language, there are many questions about example (1) that we simply can't answer. We can't say, for instance, when the situation in question occurred, what particular light is mentioned, or what the pronoun 'it' refers to. Furthermore, without knowing what 'it' refers to we can't be sure what exact properties are being described by the adjective 'tough'. There are many different ways in which we use 'tough' in our everyday language. A pair of trousers, a maths problem, a decision and a piece of beef can all be described as 'tough'. All these aspects of meaning, and more beside, can only be settled once we learn some more about the context in which the example was spoken.

In fact, example (1) is a quotation from an interview with the tennis player Roger Federer on 6 July 2008. He had just lost the men's singles final at Wimbledon to the relative newcomer Rafael Nadal in a hard-fought match that had continued into the evening when it was almost dark. This amount of information, which would of course have been readily available to the original audience of Federer's remark, immediately fills in many of the blanks in our understanding of what was being communicated in example (1). We now know, for example, that the past tense verb 'was' relates to an event that occurred just a little time before Federer was speaking, that 'the light' referred to was the ambient daylight in the late evening on a July day in south-west London, that the pronoun 'it' refers to a particular tennis match, or perhaps to Federer's experience of playing in that match, and that 'tough' is being used in the sense of 'difficult or arduous' rather than 'stiff and resistant'.

Pragmaticists have concerned themselves with all these different types of context-dependent meaning, and we will look at them in turn during the course of this book. However, there are further aspects of what might generally be described as the meaning of example (1) that we have not touched on yet. These are not so straightforwardly identified by looking at the particular words that Federer used and then thinking about what the specific context can tell us about how to understand them. They are concerned with why Federer chose to use these words on this occasion, with what particular point he was making in using them, or with what we might informally describe as what Federer meant by what he said. A natural interpretation of what Federer meant, so natural that you are hardly likely to pause to think about it much, is that his experience towards the end of the game was tough because of the light, or more specifically because the light was failing. But notice that all that he actually said was that the toughness occurred 'with' the light not 'because of' it. Our perfectly natural assumption that he meant that the light was a cause of the toughness comes from certain types of knowledge that we have acquired as users of the language, but it doesn't come from our knowledge of the language itself; we know perfectly well that 'with' and 'because' have distinct meanings. We might say that Federer didn't literally say that the light caused the toughness but he certainly very strongly implied or suggested it. A major concern of pragmatics is what it is about our knowledge of how language is used that helps us to understand implications or suggestions of this type. Later in the book we will look at various different explanations of the rules or principles of interpretation that allow us to understand meaning in context beyond literal meaning: in effect, the rules that get us from 'with' to 'because of' in example (1).

There is still more to be said about what Federer meant by example (1) in terms of what he might have been implying or suggesting beyond the literal meaning of the words he used. On the face of it, example (1) is a simple description of an event or of one person's experience of an event. But a number of commentators suggested at the time that Federer might have intended it as an implicit criticism of the umpire for not halting the match on the grounds of poor light or as an indirect suggestion that Nadal's victory was not entirely fair. We would of course need much more than knowledge of English and of the basic details of the context to evaluate suggestions of this sort. Even if we have access to many other factors, our claims about what Federer really meant would have to remain tentative. Nevertheless, this type of implicit or indirect meaning is interesting precisely because it shows how far what is communicated in context can be from basic semantic meaning. It is a central and pervasive concern of pragmatics, and is a type of meaning that will be a major concern throughout this book.

1.1   Types of pragmatics

We have begun to think, so far in very general and non-technical terms, about the sorts of features of communication, and the types of meaning, that are the subject matter of pragmatics. Like the various other branches of linguistics, pragmatics forms one part of our attempts to find out about human language and communication. As such, it is of obvious importance and interest; it is one aspect of the much wider human endeavour to discover what we can about ourselves. Indeed, many linguists would argue that in studying language we are studying something that makes us distinctively and uniquely human. But in pragmatics, language is not studied in isolation or as a closed system that can be straightforwardly identified and then analysed. Rather, as we have seen, pragmaticists start to get interested when language can be studied in relation to the context in which it is produced or the ways in which people use it in their everyday interactions. Pragmatics is concerned not just with who we are as human beings, but with how we use language to do all the various things that enable us to relate to, understand and possibly influence other people: describing the world around us, learning about how others feel about things, getting other people to do things for us, as well as many other examples.

In the next section of this chapter we will look at how pragmatics connects with linguistics and how it relates to but remains recognizably distinct from other branches of the discipline, particularly those that deal with meaning or with aspects of context. These other branches might be said to define the borders of pragmatics, or to give an indication of what is the subject matter of pragmatics and what belongs in other areas of study. At one extreme we have semantics, which for now we can loosely define as being the study of the meaning of language without any consideration of contexts of use or as the formal study of linguistic meaning. The relationship between semantics and pragmatics is so intricate, and so important to a full understanding of pragmatics, that it forms the subject of the whole of the next chapter. At the other extreme, at what we might call the 'contextual' end, we have branches of linguistics that are concerned only with instances of language as it is actually used and generally have little time for any discussion of 'linguistic meaning' as something distinct from meaning in context and worthy of study in its own right. Such branches are often concerned with fairly long stretches of language use or with the ways in which language use relates to broader social and cultural systems. They include discourse analysis, conversation analysis and sociolinguistics. Pragmatics occupies the space between these two extremes. Some pragmaticists have a lot in common with semanticists in terms of their interests, subject matter and methods. Others have a lot in common with sociolinguists or discourse analysts. This suggests a wide range of activities and types of study going on within a single branch of linguistics, and pragmatics is indeed a very broad category, with various identifiable versions and subdivisions. It is as well at this early stage for us to get a clear picture of what type of pragmatics we will be concentrating on in this book.

At first glance the range of different work to be found in a publication such as the *Journal of Pragmatics* could be bewildering to anyone trying to find out about what pragmatics is and how it is practised. This is a major forum for many researchers to publish their work and, as the title suggests, all these researchers would consider themselves to be doing pragmatics. But in one issue, chosen more or less at random, we can find: an article on how best to account formally for the differences between pairs of 'belief sentences', that is sentences that are used to assign beliefs and thoughts to other people (Capone 2008); a study of the intonational choices of teachers (Riesco-Bernier and Romero-Trillo 2008); an analysis of some taped conversations between female friends focussing on disagreement and humour in cross-cultural communication (Habib 2008); and a brief discussion of the relationship between language and logic (Fulda 2008). These four articles all have very different preoccupations and emphases from each other, all use different types of data, and all have different working methodologies. Beyond a focus on the very broadly defined topic of 'meaning in context' suggested at the start of this chapter, it is difficult from this range of work to get very far in describing what pragmatics is and how it is done.

The picture can be clarified a little if we draw a rough and in some ways not entirely satisfactory distinction between two different types of pragmatics currently being practised. We might describe these as 'theoretical pragmatics' and 'social pragmatics'. The former concentrates on the analysis of particular aspects of meaning, and on how these might be explained within more general formal accounts of language use. The latter focusses on various aspects of the relationship between language use and more general social and cultural factors. Yan Huang (2007: 4) identifies the split in pragmatics as being between 'Anglo-American' and 'European Continental' schools of thought, reflecting the fact that these two approaches are generally associated with different geographical locations and traditions of thought. Each has an identifiable and distinct history that reveals something of the influences that have gone in to making up present day pragmatics. Theoretical pragmatics can trace its beginnings to the Anglo-American tradition of the philosophy of language, and still has much in common in terms of approach and outlook with that tradition. Social pragmatics developed out of work by anthropologists and sociologists that had a particular emphasis on communication. Looking again at the four articles from the *Journal of Pragmatics* mentioned above in the light of this general division of pragmatics into two separate types, the first and last could be classified as belonging to theoretical pragmatics, and the second and third as belonging to social pragmatics.

This book will focus on theoretical pragmatics of the Anglo-American tradition. It will consider the main types of context-dependent meaning and the principal assumptions and methodologies that constitute pragmatics as a separate branch of linguistics. It will also trace the development of theoretical pragmatics from ideas that originated in British and American philosophy of language through to being an established field of study in its own right. We will not be ignoring other types of pragmatics altogether. In fact, one of the aims of this book is to show just how important pragmatics has been in terms of its relationships with and influence on other types of language study, both within linguistics and beyond. But theoretical pragmatics will be the main topic of this account of the subject. Unless otherwise specified, the term 'pragmatics' can generally be read here as convenient shorthand for 'theoretical or Anglo-American pragmatics'.

One of the most striking differences between theoretical pragmatics and social pragmatics, and one that is very telling about their different aims and emphases, is the difference between the types of data they use. To put it another way, the two different types of pragmatics demonstrate different ideas about what counts as the appropriate type of examples to be discussing, analysing and seeking to explain. If you look through an article from theoretical pragmatics, such as the one on belief sentences mentioned above, you will notice that it includes discussion of examples such as the following:

2. Alexander believes that Cicero was a great orator of the past.
3. Alexander does not believe that Tulius was a great orator of the past.
   (Capone 2008: 1023)

It isn't necessary for the author of the article to provide details about who said these things when, or who they were talking to. In fact, it's not even necessary that they must have been things that anyone ever actually said or wrote, other than for the purposes of pragmatic analysis. The examples used in theoretical pragmatics are chosen because they are illustrative of certain features of language use and interpretation that are potentially interesting and in need of systematic explanation. In this particular case, once you know that 'Cicero' and 'Tulius' were in fact two different names for the same person, examples (2) and (3) raise the interesting point that these two statements can both be made, and be made sincerely, even though they would seem literally to be incompatible or contradictory with each other. If Alexander doesn't know that 'Cicero' and 'Tulius' refer to the same person, then both (2) and (3) can be true. This observation raises various questions about the effect and behaviour of the expression 'believes that…', questions that theoretical pragmaticists are interested in exploring further.

On the other hand, readers of the article on disagreement and humour will be struck by lots of examples such as the following:

4.
Dee:... I said. Well, I said if you decide not to do this, I'll give you the twenty hundred dollars... You know, I mean the level of stress is. Natalie is just like Stan, everything is negative and everything is stressful and.
Altina: = =but why don't they get the house, I mean (continues to say something which is unclear because of the overlap)
Beatriz: [<u>why does it have to be so expensive or so big</u> or?
Dee: (   ) the family well they have to reinvest.
Annabelle: That is th-the family.
    ((3-second pause))
Beatriz: It is the expectation of (   ) (Habib 2008: 1127)

The differences between example (4) and examples (2) and (3) are many and obvious. To start with, example (4) is much longer. Unlike the single utterances in (2) and (3), the example to be analysed in (4) stretches over several turns in a conversation. Secondly, the individual speakers are identified. In fact, earlier in the article we are given some brief details about them, such as their age, nationality and educational status. In this case, unlike in the case of examples (2) and (3) above, it matters to the analysis who was speaking and in what context. Perhaps most strikingly, example (4) is an extract from the careful transcription of a natural conversation that really did take place between a group of speakers at a particular point in time and space. It is presented complete with the hesitations, pauses, false starts and errors that are characteristic of everyday language use. For the purposes of this study, the authenticity of the data is crucial. The article from which the example is taken is concerned with questions about the role of disagreement and humour in cultural learning in cross-cultural communication. It is possible to investigate such matters only by looking at how real people actually behave in particular settings. It's also worth noting that this article belongs to a particular type of social pragmatics known as 'cross-cultural pragmatics', which is concerned specifically with how communication operates in different cultural and language settings, and also between speakers from different cultural and language backgrounds. Cross-cultural pragmatics will not be a major topic in this book because of our focus on theoretical rather than on social pragmatics. However, it will be mentioned again when topics that are covered in this book have been discussed, evaluated or criticized in relation to cross-cultural features, for instance in the case of Gricean IMPLICATURE and of politeness theory.

Theoretical pragmatics might seem to be laying itself wide open to the criticism that if social pragmatics works with authentic recorded data then it should too. Indeed, people from outside the discipline sometimes express surprise or even disapproval when they are told that pragmatics is concerned with meaning in context and then open a book or article on pragmatics to find it full of isolated, invented examples. It would be an exaggeration to say that theoretical pragmatists never deal with authentic data. And, as we will see later in this book, the theories developed within theoretical pragmatics have been applied to a wide range of 'real life' data and situations. Nevertheless, pragmatic theories are generally developed, and initially at least explained and discussed, using invented examples. The reason why theoretical pragmatics uses a different type of data from social pragmatics, and why this use is justifiable, is that it isn't asking the same types of questions or looking for the same types of explanation. Theoretical pragmatics isn't centrally concerned with describing and analysing what people do in specific communicative situations. Rather, it's concerned with the question of how meaning can in general be communicated between speakers and hearers, given the finite resources of a language and the vagaries of context. It is concerned not with building up a picture of what individual speakers do in particular types of circumstances, but in establishing what are the general rules or principles that operate when language is used. Theoretical pragmaticists are concerned, for instance, with determining how it is that a single word or string of words can communicate an array of different meanings on different occasions of use, and with looking into the precise distinctions between linguistic meaning and general features of language use that must be involved.

In order to address these questions, theoretical pragmatics deals with certain types of expression or areas of meaning. In doing so, it may sometimes draw on examples of things that have really been said, as in the case of the quotation from Roger Federer in (1) above, but such examples will be carefully chosen for the purpose, and any context they are presented with will be selected and simplified. Large stretches of recorded conversations are of little use to theoretical pragmaticists; at best they would have to trawl through them looking for relevant examples of the type of meaning under investigation. Authenticity matters in theoretical pragmatics not in that every example must be an accurate transcription of something actually said in a certain time and place, but in that the examples must make sense and suggest an intuitive interpretation to ordinary speakers of the language. Intuitions about examples provide the starting point for much work in pragmatics.

As just one example of this process, consider our everyday understanding of words representing numerals: words such as 'one', 'two', 'twenty-seven', 'sixty-five' and so on. At first glance there might not seem to be much to be said here. We know the meaning of these words because we know about the mathematical numbers they relate to. We are not at a loss to explain exactly what might be conveyed when an example such as (5) is used:

5. Jane has written three books.

If someone says this to us sincerely we don't expect later on to discover that Jane has written only two books or that she has written four or more. But in some contexts, it is perfectly possible for a statement such as that in (5) to be compatible with the fact that the exact number of books Jane has written is different from three. This might at first appear to be an extremely odd claim to make, but consider the following example:

6. [*Context: if you have written three books you are eligible to apply for a professorship*]
   Jane's friend: 'Jane should certainly consider applying for that professorship because she has written three books; in fact she has written four!'

Note that in the particular context specified in (6), Jane's friend need not be accused of saying something contradictory or even misleading in stating that Jane had published three books and then immediately stating that she had published four. What Jane's friend meant, we understand, was that Jane is eligible to apply; she has published at least three books.

However, while saying 'three' turns out in some contexts to be compatible with saying 'four', it isn't compatible with just any other number. It doesn't seem to be compatible with a lower number. Imagine that a different candidate, Mary, gets as far as the interview stage for the professorship and that the following exchange takes place:

7. *Interviewer*: 'How many books have you written?'
   Mary: !'I've written three; in fact I've written two.'

Mary's answer really isn't very satisfactory. The exclamation mark before the example is a conventional way in pragmatics of marking that there is something distinctly odd or abnormal about it. It's not actually ungrammatical (conventionally, ungrammatical examples are marked with an asterisk in front of them, such as *'I written have three') but it doesn't really work as far as conveying a coherent meaning is concerned. We are forced to say that Mary has contradicted herself, or perhaps more realistically that she has changed her mind while talking and decided to come clean about her publications. Certainly, saying 'two' in this context is not compatible with just having said 'three'.

Pragmatics doesn't just leave it at that. Having made these observations, and agreed on these intuitions about what can and can't be said coherently, pragmaticists seek to go further and to explain how all this works. One solution, but a very unsatisfactory one, would be to say that after all the numerals don't have such clear-cut meaning as we first thought. For instance, 'three' can mean 'exactly three', and it can also mean 'more than three' but it can never mean 'less than three'. This is unsatisfactory because it doesn't offer any explanation of what is going on here, and also it opens up the possibility that it might never be possible to say anything very definite about meaning. Such an account of the meaning of 'three', and therefore by extension of all the numerals, is no more than saying 'sometimes it means...' and 'other times it means...'.

Pragmaticists attempt to say what it is about how we use and understand language that can account for these apparent differences in meaning. A good pragmatic account is one that not just observes a systematic set of interpretations such as those of the numerals, but also explains these interpretations. A really successful pragmatic account is one that relates this explanation to interpretations of other types of words in different contexts, and therefore to possible general rules about how we use and understand language.

We have seen that examples that appear together with a description of their context are typical more of social than of theoretical pragmatics. Social pragmatics, in common with fields such as conversation analysis and discourse analysis, typically studies stretches of language use that go beyond a single utterance or a single turn in the conversation. But as we have just seen in our consideration of numerals, particular details of context can often be extremely relevant to observations and explanations in theoretical pragmatics. On such occasions, pragmaticists tend to describe a very specific context for an example, such as the brief account of context in square brackets in example (6), or the description of context and then the contextualizing question in example (7). Context is generally of course a much more complex thing than can be summed up in a single statement or accounted for by a single question. Conceivably, any fact about a person's previous life, experience, character, and so on, might be relevant to explaining what they say and what they mean by it. But in pragmatics, as in any other theoretical discipline, explanations have to deal with limited numbers of factors if they are to explain anything at all. A scientist, for instance, doesn't attempt to account for everything going on in a particular situation, but specifies certain factors to be explained, often in 'laboratory conditions' in order to reduce the variables to a manageable number. The scientist aims to idealize the data, almost to 'pretend' that many potentially relevant factors don't matter, in order to be able to offer a successful model of some aspect of a situation. In the same way, theoretical pragmaticists 'pretend' that all relevant aspects of context can be neatly described in a few sentences, in order to be able to get on with the business of saying something interesting and illuminating about the data.

1.2 Pragmatics and linguistics

We have seen that pragmatics deals with a particular aspect of human communication, namely the relationship between language and the contexts in which it is used, and as a result it is concerned with analysing and explaining particular types of data. It is often described as being a branch or field of linguistics; indeed, this is a description we have been using in this book. Categorizing it in this way makes a lot of sense. Linguistics is the academic subject that is concerned with the analysis, description and explanation of human language, and pragmatics contributes to this project by focussing on the interaction between language and context. But perhaps strictly speaking pragmatics should be described as outside of and separate from mainstream or 'core' linguistics. The 'core' components of linguistics, which together describe and explain human language, include phonology, morphology, syntax and semantics. These are concerned with the analysis of language as a formal, isolated and identifiable system in its own right, or with a specific linguistic component of knowledge.

Pragmatics stands apart from these because its subject matter is not, or not exclusively, language itself, but the production and interpretation of language in relation to contexts of use. That is not to say, of course, that pragmatics is of no interest to linguistics. On the contrary, determining what aspects of communication are dependent on context and how they are dependent on it can tell us a lot about those aspects that are purely linguistic, or explicable entirely in relation to the language. Pragmatics can perhaps be seen as an adjunct to linguistic theory; it is necessary for the adequate account of language that there should be a rigorous study of how language interacts with context – but that study is not in itself strictly a linguistic study. Pragmatics is distinguished from 'core' linguistics by being concerned not just with the linguistic component of the mind but with the much larger set of knowledge and cognitive processes concerned with the interpretation of communication in context.

In its early days, pragmatics wasn't always regarded very favourably by mainstream linguists for precisely these reasons. Any attempt to discuss language in relation to context or to the specifics of production and interpretation was seen as getting dangerously far away from the central concerns of linguistics. A phrase that became associated with this type of attitude was the description of pragmatics as the 'wastebasket of linguistics'. In other words, the major components of linguistics were expected to do the main job of describing and analysing language. Anything that couldn't satisfactorily be explained by these components was discarded, classified as in some way marginal to the concerns of linguistics, and ended up in pragmatics. The subject matter and therefore the data of pragmatics was therefore seen as made up of bits and pieces that could not conveniently be accommodated elsewhere. The odd-looking behaviour of the numerals, discussed in the last section, would be an example of this.

The term 'wastebasket' comes from an article by the philosopher and linguist Yehoshua Bar-Hillel, published in 1971. Bar-Hillel was complaining about what he saw as the then current tendency among linguists to try to explain in terms of established branches of core linguistics various phenomena that would much more appropriately be handled by the new discipline of pragmatics. What he actually wrote about the 'wastebasket' is the following warning to his fellow linguists: 'be more careful with forcing bits and pieces you find in the pragmatic wastebasket into your favorite syntactico-semantic theory. It would perhaps be preferable to first bring some order into the contents of this wastebasket as is' (Bar-Hillel 1971: 405). According to Bar-Hillel's analogy, pragmatics was not just like a wastebasket for off-loading troublesome pieces of linguistic data. It was also a storage receptacle from which such pieces of data could later be extracted for syntactic and/or semantic analysis. His argument was that the explanation of some aspects of communication simply belonged naturally within pragmatics and that these aspects had not yet been systematically identified and discussed.

Things have changed a lot since 1971, of course, and the subject matter of pragmatics is now in much better order and has been subjected to much more rigorous discussion. We will consider the precise subject matter in more detail in the next chapter, and concentrate on various discussions of it throughout the rest of the book. For some 'core' linguists, though, semantics and syntax are still where the main business of explaining meaning takes place.

This attitude may have a lot to do with the continuing influence of Chomskyan linguistics, or at least of one interpretation of Chomskyan linguistics, on present-day thinking in the discipline. Noam Chomsky rose to prominence with his theories about language in the late 1950s and 1960s. One of his ideas about language, and one that has remained remarkably pervasive in discussions of his work despite many changes and modifications in his own thinking, has been the distinction between 'competence' and 'performance'. Chomsky defined competence as a set of knowledge or a state of mind; it is what speakers know when they have acquired a language. Performance, on the other hand, is the observable behaviour of those speakers: the actual business of speaking and writing. Chomsky argued that the actual observable performance of speakers can be partly, but only partly, explained by their linguistic competence: 'to study linguistic performance, we must consider the interaction of a variety of factors, of which the underlying competence of the speaker-hearer is only one' (Chomsky 1965: 4). These other factors consist of a huge, baffling and complex array of phenomena including context, personality, physical state, social relationships and so on. Crucially, Chomsky identified competence as the appropriate focus of linguistic study. For him, language is primarily a mental structure, so true linguistic inquiry should concentrate on the nature of linguistic knowledge, rather than the distracting array of phenomena that get involved when people use language to communicate with each other. Furthermore, even if anyone were interested in studying performance, the task would be simply impossible because of the variety and the unpredictability of the factors other than linguistic competence that determine how people produce and interpret utterances.

It is perhaps not hard to see how pragmatics could have become identified in some minds as an attempt to study performance. It emphasizes the importance of contextual as well as linguistic factors in meaning. The 'speakers' discussed in pragmatics are conceived of as speaking and being interpreted in context, while Chomsky's 'speakers' are conceived of as being in possession of knowledge of a language, whether or not that knowledge is ever actually put to use in communication. Nevertheless, pragmatics has more in common with Chomskyan linguistics than it might at first seem to, and it's not by any means incompatible to work in pragmatics and also to subscribe to a broadly Chomskyan picture of linguistics. Pragmatics doesn't attempt to explain everything that goes on in an actual communicative situation. Rather, as discussed above, it aims to model certain aspects of context in order to learn something about general rules and principles of language use. As such it is very much in keeping with what we might recognize as a Chomskyan notion of idealizing the subject matter, not in order to obscure its true nature, but in order to be able to say something systematic about it. As Chomsky has argued in more recent work: 'in rational inquiry, in the natural sciences or elsewhere, there is no such subject as "the study of everything" ... we idealize to selected domains in such a way (we hope) as to permit us to discover crucial features of the world' (Chomsky 2000: 49).

Chomsky himself has seemed rather ambivalent towards pragmatics in his few published comments on it, at times regarding it as besides the point of true linguistic inquiry, and at times apparently relying on it to support his own accounts of linguistic structure and meaning. We will look at these attitudes further in Chapter 3, when we consider the history of pragmatics and how it has been viewed within linguistics. Certainly the formal nature of theoretical pragmatics that we considered in the last section, along with its reliance on intuitions rather than an insistence on authentic data, are very much in keeping with the Chomskyan programme. As the pragmaticist Asa Kasher (1998: 104) has commented, Chomsky's own work has largely been restricted to syntax, 'but its conception of objective, scientific methodology and philosophical foundations transcend syntax and lend themselves to interesting applications', including in pragmatics.

One of the aims of this book is to tell the success story of pragmatics. Far from being a 'wastebasket' to receive pieces of data and awkward examples not wanted in mainstream linguistics, it is now a central component in the study of human communication, with an identifiable and organized area of coverage and an established set of theoretical debates. It is important to linguistics not just in the way in which it does a specific job in the massive task of describing and explaining human communication, but also in the ways in which it has impacted on various areas of linguistic study. Its influence has reached beyond linguistics too, and has been influential in work in various other fields of inquiry and areas of study.

1.3 Structure of the book

This book focusses on the main features of language use and the types of examples that form the subject matter of theoretical pragmatics. In other words, it concentrates on the data of pragmatics. In the course of this book we will be discovering how different approaches and theories within pragmatics have explained these data. We will also consider some of the broader implications of these explanations for our understanding of human communication. These broader implications have informed work both within linguistics and in other academic disciplines and areas of study, but they all stem from ideas developed within pragmatics.

The chapters that follow, therefore, can be seen as divided roughly into three different groups, although the divisions are not strongly delineated and the groups don't function in isolation from each other. The first group, comprising Chapters 2 and 3, continues the definition and explanation of pragmatics that we have begun here. We will consider the complex and sometimes rather fraught relationship between pragmatics and the related but separate field of semantics, and then we will look briefly at the history and development of pragmatics as a separate branch of linguistics. The second group, Chapters 4 and 5, sets out some of the main theories and schools of thought that have emerged during the history of pragmatics. That is, they offer an overview of theoretical pragmatics. In the final group, Chapters 6 and 7, we look at the impact that the theories of theoretical pragmatics have had when they have been applied to the study of a range of different aspects of human communication, both within linguistics and beyond. We will also consider the relationships between pragmatics and some 'neighbouring' branches of linguistics; that is, types of language study that may be concerned with similar data to pragmatics, but analyse it in different ways or ask different questions of it. In these final two chapters we will necessarily look at some of the ways in which pragmatics has been relevant to the study of human society and at what happens when people use language to interact in conversations, but the focus will remain on theories developed in theoretical pragmatics; we will not be surveying work from 'societal pragmatics'.

Chapter 2 introduces some of the main concerns and most significant data of pragmatics under the title 'Semantics and Pragmatics'. The two branches of linguistics are both concerned with the study of meaning, and it's necessary to discuss semantics so early in the study of pragmatics because 'pragmatics' is defined, at least in part, by how its subject matter and its terms of discussion differ from those of semantics. The distinction between studying meaning as part of semantics and studying meaning as part of pragmatics, or what is sometimes termed the 'semantics/pragmatics borderline', partly defines the limits of pragmatics. Much of the controversy surrounding the definition of pragmatics can be described in terms of the general questions of its relationship to and its distinction from semantics.

Central to Chapter 2 will be the question of what counts as the distinctive data of pragmatics. As we will see, there are different possible answers to even this question; different theorists have different ideas about what falls within the scope of pragmatics and what within the scope of semantics, and even about whether the two are separate or overlapping categories. We will consider a distinction that many can agree is fundamental to the different territories of semantics and pragmatics: the difference between SENTENCES and UTTERANCES. The meanings of sentences are generally discussed in terms of truth conditions and compositionality. The meanings of utterances are generally discussed in pragmatics in terms of implicit meaning and context dependence. We will then consider a variety of topics that have provided the data for the discussion of semantics versus pragmatics, including: logic and natural language; MOOD; PRESUPPOSITION; and DEIXIS. These are topics we will be returning to later in the book when we look at different pragmatic theories and compare them in terms of what they have said about such linguistic phenomena.

Chapter 3, 'History of Pragmatics', steps back from the exposition of the data of pragmatics in order to give an overview of how pragmatics began and how it has changed and grown over the years. This offers another important aspect of the definition of pragmatics that is the main concern of this first part of the book. The story of how pragmatics, a relative newcomer, developed as a recognizable branch of linguistics, can tell us a lot about its status and scope. The serious study of language has always recognized the need to describe the relationship between meaning and context, but the specific foundations of present-day pragmatics can be found in the philosophy of language. In particular, the ideas of a group of mid-twentieth-century British philosophers, who became known as the 'ordinary language philosophers', proved particularly significant in the development of pragmatics. There is something of a 'happy accident' in the story of the birth of pragmatics. The ordinary language philosophers developed their ideas partly in response to various trends and approaches that were then current in the philosophy of language. But those ideas proved particularly appealing to some of those working on meaning in linguistics, because of what was happening in that separate academic discipline at the time. Since those days the general tendency has been for the data of pragmatics and the description of that data to become more systematized and, particularly in recent years, for pragmatics to become more interdisciplinary.

Chapter 4, '"Classical" Pragmatics', is concerned with theories of language use that developed within ordinary language philosophy itself. These set the tone for the debate in present-day pragmatics, and in many cases developed the terminology for that debate. These early theories have been found to be incomplete or in other ways inadequate in subsequent years, but they remain of central importance to the discipline. It wouldn't really be possible to understand present-day pragmatics without them, and aspects of them are still employed in current work in the field. In this chapter we will consider the theory of speech acts, as developed by the philosopher J. L. Austin and subsequently by others such as his pupil John Searle. This introduced the idea that has become absolutely central to pragmatics that there is a distinction to be drawn between what a sentence literally means and what it can be used to do, or to perform. The second major theory of classical pragmatics that we will study is that of 'implicature', a term coined and still most closely associated with Austin's colleague Paul Grice. This developed the idea, instantly and intuitive appealing but not previously investigated methodically, that what people say and what they intend to convey are often not the same thing.

Chapter 5, 'Modern Pragmatics', brings the survey of pragmatic theories up to date. The ideas discussed here all depend on and draw heavily on classical pragmatics, but all developed out of a dissatisfaction with some aspects of the earlier theories. We will look first at what has become known as 'neo-Gricean pragmatics'. This attempts to retain Grice's insights and basic approach but to refine many of the details of his theory, in particular in relation to how many separate pragmatic principles are considered necessary to explain the differences between literal and implied meaning. Relevance theory, another major trend in recent pragmatics, has attempted a more radical response to Grice's insights. Its aim is to develop an account of interpretation in terms of general human cognitive tendencies. Finally, a number of recent developments in pragmatics can be grouped around the discussion of the viability of 'minimal semantics' in the explanation of meaning. These are, in general, concerned with the question of how best semantics and pragmatics can be balanced in the process of explaining meaning. Discussion of this question has necessarily focussed on the nature of the distinction between semantics and pragmatics, and particularly on whether the two types of meaning can be seen as identifiably separate from each other.

As we have seen so far, the main ideas of theoretical pragmatics have largely been developed and presented using 'invented' examples of only one or two utterances at a time, and discussion has focussed on the success of different theories in explaining these examples. Pragmatic theorists have generally not shown much interest in applying their ideas to language in use or to processes of interpretation taking place outside of this rather closed discussion. But some pragmaticists have looked beyond pragmatics itself for support for their ideas and, increasingly, other researchers with a professional interest in language have turned to pragmatics for frameworks within which to describe and explain their own data. The last two chapters of this book, although drawing on ideas and theories discussed in the early chapters, are concerned with this type of work.

Chapter 6, 'Applications of Pragmatics', looks at some of the ways in which the ideas of pragmatics have been used to investigate a variety of different aspects of language use and interpretation. In each case, the particular application of pragmatics has brought it into contact with another academic discipline that is concerned with the study of language. For several decades pragmaticists have concerned themselves with the relationship between the production and interpretation of language in context and speakers' and hearers' awareness of the socially determined requirements of 'politeness' in their interactions. Pragmatic theories of politeness have drawn, in particular, on the classical pragmatic ideas about speech acts and implicatures. More recent versions have also been informed by ideas developed in sociology. Such newer versions of politeness theory continue to be a very productive source for explanations of linguistic interaction and particularly of the differences in patterns and expectations of interaction between different cultures and societies.

Pragmatic theories have been used in the study of literary texts, both in terms of analysing the texts themselves as examples of language in use and, more recently, in terms of considering what pragmatics can offer to attempts to define what constitutes 'literature' itself. Here pragmatics has interacted with literary studies, stylistics and critical theory.

The study of language acquisition has traditionally been associated with formal aspects of language, particularly the development of grammatical knowledge. However, researchers interested in how children learn to understand meaning have been interested in the differences between semantic and pragmatic meaning. In such studies, pragmatics interacts with developmental psychology. They have indicated that understanding of and ability in the two types of meaning may develop separately and at different stages. An exciting implication of this from the point of view of pragmaticists is that it suggests some independent, evidence-based support for the distinction between semantics and pragmatics. This is also the case with some work in the field of clinical linguistics, where pragmatics interacts with neuroscience. The evidence here comes in the form of physical data such as brain scans, as well as data about the performance of patients in various tests concerned with the production and interpretation of language. This evidence suggests that constructing and understanding meaning are complex and multifaceted tasks that involve many different areas of the brain. Pragmaticists have of course been keen to try to establish whether the identifiably different aspects of these tasks might correspond to the claimed differences between semantics and pragmatics.

Finally, experimental pragmatics, where pragmatics meets clinical psychology, has offered pragmaticists the chance to devise and conduct experiments to test their theories and, some claim, to compare the merits of competing theories in terms of how well they describe the psychological processes of language users.

The final chapter, 'Pragmatics and Language in Context', revisits and summarizes the current status of pragmatics with particular reference to its relationship to present-day linguistics more generally. We will look at some of the other branches of linguistics that study language in use. These in many ways overlap or share common ground with pragmatics, but they also help to define what makes it distinctive because they concentrate on different aspects of the subject matter and ask different questions about it. These branches of linguistics include conversation analysis, discourse analysis, sociolinguistics and corpus linguistics. In many instances pragmatics has provided useful models for interpretation and explanation in these diverse areas of language study. Such instances offer powerful arguments as to why pragmatics should be seen not as a marginal or specialist interest within linguistics, but as an element in the study of human communication that is of central and pervasive importance.

FURTHER READING

As might be expected in such a varied and diverse field, the various introductions to pragmatics currently available have different emphases and cover the different aspects of the subject in varying degrees of depth. Levinson (1983) offers an extended and in-depth discussion of many of the major branches and theories of pragmatics that had been developed by the early 1980s. It is quite technical and hard going, though. More accessible introductions include Thomas (1995) and Peccei (1999).

Many textbooks that are chiefly concerned with semantics include some discussion of pragmatics, concentrating of course on how the two fields relate to each other. See, for instance, Cruse (2004), Kearns (2000) and Hurford, Heasley and Smith (2007).

Some textbooks concentrate on the more formal and technical aspects of pragmatics: what we have been describing here as 'theoretical' pragmatics. Huang (2007) is an example of this type of textbook. Others, such as Cutting (2007), focus on the more 'social' aspects of pragmatics, in relation for instance to the study of conversation and of language in society. Discussions of intercultural pragmatics can be found in Scollon and Scollon (2000) and Gass and Neu (2006). Mey (1993) discusses the different aspects or versions of the field in some detail. Mey's coverage of what he calls 'micropragmatics' includes many of the major topics of 'theoretical' pragmatics, but he also deals in detail with 'macropragmatics', which includes the analysis of conversation and 'societal pragmat-ics', which overlaps with sociolinguistics. Cummings (2005) is an introductory textbook on pragmatics that explicitly argues that its significance can be appreciated only when it is considered in relation to a variety of other disciplines. Ariel (2010) is a more advanced survey of the subject that specifically tackles the problems of describing what constitutes pragmatics and the wide range of definitions that have been proposed.

Semantics and Pragmatics

2

In the last chapter we recognized that the study of meaning is the major concern of two branches of linguistics known as 'semantics' and 'pragmatics'. As mentioned then, the relationship between the two, and their specific roles in explaining meaning in language, are complicated and controversial matters. Nevertheless, we need to consider these matters in more detail before we can investigate and assess some of the specific approaches and theories developed within pragmatics. As we have seen, pragmatics is at least in part defined by how it relates to and what makes it distinct from semantics. So in this chapter we will continue our exploration of the nature of pragmatics by focussing on these issues.

The distinction between semantics and pragmatics can be illustrated most clearly in relation to certain types of linguistic examples. As we will see in later chapters, the development of different pragmatic theories, and debates between competing theories, are often conducted in relation to certain specific types of linguistic phenomena. It is a good idea to be familiar with the nature of these phenomena and the types of issue they raise before we go on to assess how they are handled by different pragmatic theories. In addition, it is important at this early stage to be familiar with the relevant linguistic phenomena because they tell us a lot about what pragmatics is and what it does. That is, they constitute the central topics in pragmatics, or the core types of data in need of explanation by pragmatic theories. We will begin, however, with a brief survey of the semantics/pragmatics borderline.

2.1 The borderline

If you read at all widely in this area of linguistics, it's a good bet that sooner or later you will come across mentions of the semantics/pragmatics borderline. Here are just a couple of examples of such mentions, which look ahead to some of the specific issues we will be considering in this chapter. Firstly, the editors of a recent collection of essays published in honour of the linguist Ferenc Kiefer commented on how his work on indirect speech acts shows 'his concern for the borderline between semantics and pragmatics, as is evidenced by articles specifically written on that issue' (Kenesei and Harnish 2001: vii). Secondly, a recent overview of pragmatics has described 'a radical literalist perspective, on which the semantics–pragmatics borderline should coincide with the borderline between saying and implicating' (Sperber and Wilson 2005: 479). It is a very pervasive, and also an appealing, metaphor. It suggests a picture of semantics and pragmatics as two separate but neighbouring countries, divided by a boundary that is identifiable but perhaps disputed, with each side laying claim to particular areas and maybe even with occasional skirmishes and readjustments taking place. There is certainly some truth in this analogy; as we will see in later chapters, there are constant discussions of the exact location of the line between semantics and pragmatics and suggestions that it might be redrawn in relation to some particular aspect of the data. The borderline, if it exists, is far from settled or universally agreed.

It wouldn't do to take the 'borderline' metaphor as a neat and entirely satisfactory picture of the relationship between semantics and pragmatics, however. Like just about everything else in this area of linguistics, its very existence is a matter of controversy. Some linguists working in the field argue that it is wrong to think of semantics and pragmatics as discrete areas of study that between them carve up the description and analysis of meaning. They dispute the idea that semantics does a particular amount of work towards explaining meaning, and that pragmatics adds further, separate aspects of meaning that relate to context and language use to arrive at a complete meaning. That is, they don't agree that some aspects of meaning are identifiably 'semantic', to be explained by semantic, therefore linguistic, rules, while some are clearly 'pragmatic', to be described by pragmatic, therefore context-dependent, principles.

So when we discuss the distinction between semantics and pragmatics, or the semantics/pragmatics borderline, as when we make any other general statement about pragmatics, we must bear in mind that what we say can't hope to cover every perspective on the subject, or even to be based on premises and assumptions shared by everyone working in the field. Of course if we were too cautious about making statements that might not sit comfortably with every single point of view or every way of defining the relevant terms then we would very soon be unable to say anything interesting at all. So we will continue our investigation of pragmatics armed with the assumption that much of the really interesting work in the field is concerned with identifying and defining the semantics/pragmatics borderline, and that pragmatic theories can be judged and compared in terms of how they place types of meaning and forms of explanation in relation to that line. The linguistic phenomena that we will be considering in this chapter are the ones most often referred to by those seriously engaged in establishing the nature of the relationship between semantics and pragmatics. The different pragmatic theories that we will consider in later chapters are those that have made concrete suggestions about the location of the borderline between the two. In the meantime we will turn to an issue that is central to the distinction between semantics and pragmatics, and is a good introduction to the different emphases and interests of these two types of study of meaning. That is the relationship between sentences and utterances.

2.2   Sentences and utterances

A useful general principle to bear in mind when thinking about the distinction between semantics and pragmatics, and one that we will stick to throughout this book, is that semantics is concerned with sentences and pragmatics with utterances. There are semantic facts about any language, concerning the meanings of its words and the ways in which they can combine together. These determine the meanings of the sentences of that language. Sentences are linguistic entities and any successful semantic description of the language in question needs to be able to explain their meanings. Pragmatic rules are not part of the language. They may vary between different cultures and societies (this is an issue we will look at later in this book) but they are essentially concerned with general properties to do with how people use language to interact with others, rather than with the language itself. An utterance is an instance of the production of a sentence or a fragment of a sentence. Since sentences are put together by linguistic rules it is possible to describe some strings of words as 'incomplete sentences'. But people often don't talk in complete sentences. Meaningful utterances may be productions of incomplete sentences but that doesn't mean that they are incomplete as utterances. An utterance is produced in an actual context by an actual speaker. It has certain linguistic properties, by virtue of the linguistic properties of the sentence of which it is an utterance. But it also has further properties that aren't shared by the sentence and don't belong to the language in question. This is best illustrated with an example:

1. I will see you here tomorrow.

Perhaps the most obvious differences between the sentence represented in (1) and any particular utterances of that sentence is that the utterances will have spatio-temporal and physical properties, while the sentence does not. So we could partially describe a particular utterance of the sentence by saying that it occurred at 11.40 a.m. on Monday 24 May 2010 in a lecturer's office, that it was spoken by Mary Smith and that she produced it in a low and quiet voice. We could say of another utterance of the same sentence that it occurred at 9.30 p.m. on Tuesday 24 August 2010 in the Red Lion pub, that is was spoken by Matt Jones and that he shouted it at the top of his voice. None of these types of description could be applied to the sentence itself, which is the same in each case.

The differences of meaning between the two utterances are also not shared by the sentence. So it is a property of the utterances that 'I' refers to Mary Smith in the first case and to Matt Jones in the second, that 'here' refers to Mary's office or to the Red Lion and that 'tomorrow' refers to Tuesday 25 May 2010 or Wednesday 25 August 2010. Furthermore Mary Smith may have said what she did intending it as an order to a troublesome student, while Matt Jones intended his utterance as a promise to his friend. Being an order or a promise is not a semantic property of the sentence in (1); it is a pragmatic property of the specific utterances of it.

According to the strict distinction between sentences and utterances that we will be working with in this book, any discussion of 'contexts' or of 'speakers' and 'hearers' is limited to descriptions of utterances. Sentences are abstract linguistic structures; they don't have contexts and they aren't produced by speakers or received by hearers. It is of course notoriously difficult to deal mentally with abstract, as opposed to concrete, entities. In this particular case, as soon as we are asked to consider a sentence we have a natural tendency to imagine it in use. But for the purposes of keeping in mind a clear distinction between semantics and pragmatics, we need to be able to keep separate in our minds our thoughts about a sentence and our thoughts about any particular or possible use of that sentence. In other words, in this book we are going to treat very seriously the distinction between sentences and utterances, and therefore the distinction between what semantics does in terms of explaining meaning that is communicated in context, and what pragmatics does.

Closely related to the distinction between sentences and utterances is that between 'GRAMMATICALITY' and 'ACCEPTABILITY'. These are two different types of judgements that it is possible to make: it is common to talk of the grammaticality or otherwise of a sentence and the acceptability or otherwise of an utterance. The distinction draws on the work of Noam Chomsky, who in his early work on syntax introduced example (2) which has become probably the most famous and widely quoted linguistic example of all time, together with example (3), to illustrate the point:

2. Colourless green ideas sleep furiously.
3. Furiously sleep ideas green colourless.

Chomsky's point was that although we might reject both these examples as 'equally nonsensical', we will still recognize that (2) is a grammatical sentence of English while (3) is not (Chomsky 1957: 15). That is, we judge (3) to be ungrammatical because the words in the string are not put together in such a way as to correspond to the grammatical rules of English. Example (2), on the other hand, does seem to conform to these rules; we can identify 'colourless green ideas' as a subject in which the adjectives 'colourless' and 'green' modify 'ideas', 'sleep' as the verb explaining what those ideas are doing, and 'furiously' as the adverb describing the manner in which the sleeping is taking place. The problem we have with it is not in recognizing it as a grammatical sentence, but in making sense of it, or of imagining any context in which it might be used meaningfully. In other words, in the case of (2) but not of (3) we are able to judge the example to be grammatical as a sentence, but unacceptable as a potential utterance.

Note that, because utterances are always related to specific contexts, what counts as acceptable can vary from one occasion to another. A judgement of grammaticality is not subject to variation. A string either does or does not conform to the rules of the language and, aside from specific historical changes in the grammar, will be consistently either grammatical or ungrammatical. Acceptability, however, is relative. Chomsky presents example (2) without any indication of context, safe in the knowledge that people will generally judge it to be unacceptable in any conceivable context in which it might be uttered. But some strings of words can vary in terms of their acceptability in relation to circumstances. Consider example (4):

4. I order you to be here by 9 o'clock tomorrow morning.

It is easy to recognize (4) as a grammatical sentence of English, and it is easy too to recognize contexts in which it would make an acceptable utterance. But note that certain specific types of contexts come to mind, involving certain types of relationship between the people referred to as 'you' and as 'I'. Example (4) would be acceptable in various contexts where 'I' is in a position of authority over 'you'. If the speaker and the hearer are equals, however, (4) would not really 'work' as an order and therefore would not be acceptable as an utterance. We will consider the relationship between acceptability and context, and specifically the particular conditions that have to be in place to make certain types of utterances acceptable, in more detail when we look at speech act theory in Chapter 4.1.

One final feature of the distinction between sentences and utterances, or at least of the way in which they are usually discussed, is worth noting before we move on to look at some of the specific types of data to which it is relevant. We have been discussing utterances in terms of 'speakers' and 'hearers'. Now of course not all uses of language involve speaking. Language is also used any time it is written and any time it is read, and pragmatic factors are just as relevant to explaining meaning on these occasions. Strictly speaking, our account of utterances should include reference to 'writers' and 'readers' too. But it is a standard practice in pragmatics to refer to producers of utterances as 'speakers' and receivers as 'hearers', and it is one that we'll generally stick with here. After all, the canonical situation for language use, the way in which it most frequently occurs, is in spoken exchanges. But bear in mind that writers and readers are language users too, and that written utterances are potentially just as relevant as data for pragmatics. One later section of this book will be entirely devoted to written language: that is Chapter 6.2 when we look at the application of pragmatic theories to the analysis of literary texts.

2.3 Language and logic

In the next chapter, when we look briefly at the history and the development of pragmatics, we will consider some of the claims that have been made about the relationship between meaning in language on one hand and logic on the other. For now, we can say, in general, that many prominent mid-twentieth-century philosophers of language saw logic as the best possible system for explaining how meaning works, including how meaning does or ideally should work in language. Pragmatics was in part motivated by the realization that there are many ways in which natural language operates, at least when it is used in context by speakers and hearers, that don't conform to the standard rules of logic.

So in some ways 'logical meaning' can be seen as an opposite of 'pragmatic meaning'. Nevertheless, some understanding of logic is important to anyone studying pragmatics. It tells a lot about how semantic meaning, itself central to the operation of any pragmatic theory, has been described. And it brings into focus the types of meaning that seem to call for a specifically pragmatic explanation.

Logic is concerned with the ways in which ideas relate to each other, can be combined together, and can be used to derive other, further ideas with confidence. Logicians tend not to talk about 'ideas', though; the basic unit of traditional logic is the 'PROPOSITION', a term which is also significant in discussions of meaning in linguistics. Propositions are not themselves sentences, although it can be easy to confuse these two different types of entities, since when we describe or discuss propositions we tend to do so by expressing them as declarative sentences. Propositions are the meanings that are expressed by declarative sentences; it is probably easiest to think of them as being the contents of thoughts. Consider the following examples:

5. Philip is a father.
6. The Tower of London contains the Crown Jewels.
7. Harold lives in Barcelona.

It is perfectly possible to speak of someone thinking, or believing, that Philip is a father, that The Tower of London contains the Crown Jewels, or that Harold lives in Barcelona. It is also, of course, possible to express these propositions in sentences, as in (5)–(7).

Examples such as (5)–(7) are a familiar type of data in linguistics, where the discussion of individual actual sentences is commonplace. In logic, however, it's more common to use symbols or 'logical variables' to stand in for the propositions under discussion. This is because logic is concerned chiefly with the properties of and relationships between propositions in general. It is common practice to use lower case letters, typically p, q, r and so on, to stand in for whole propositions. So the propositions expressed in our examples (5)–(7) above might be abbreviated in logical discussion to single letters: such that (5) is represented as p, (6) as q and (7) as r.

The propositions we have been considering so far are examples of what are known as 'simple propositions'. In effect, each could be the content of a single thought or represent a single fact about the world. Representing simple propositions by means of a single character enables logicians to show how they can combine together to form further, more complex propositions. For instance, we can indicate the negation of any proposition simply by adding the logical symbol for negation ($\sim$) to the symbol for that proposition. If we are using full sentences as our examples, we would have to express the negations of (5)–(7) as in (8)–(10):

8. Philip is not a father.
9. The Tower of London does not contain the Crown Jewels.
10. Harold does not live in Barcelona.

Using logical notation, once we have established what p, q and r represent for our current purposes, (8), (9) and (10) can be represented as $\sim p$, $\sim q$ and $\sim r$ respectively. We can also combine simple propositions in various ways to form complex propositions. For instance, if we wanted to combine (5) and (7) using a sentence we would need to express it as:

11. Philip is a father and Harold lives in Barcelona.

In logical notation, (11) is expressed as $p \wedge q$, where $\wedge$ is the symbol used to represent logical conjunction. Logical conjunction takes two or more propositions and joins them together to form a further, complex proposition. It also specifies the truth or falsity of the complex proposition on the basis of the truth or falsity of the propositions it conjoins. So if (5) and (7) are both true then their conjunction, (11), must also be true. But if either (5) or (7) or both are false, then combining them in (11) will produce a false complex proposition.

As well as showing how simple propositions can combine together to make more complex ones, logic has a way of describing and symbolizing the internal structure of propositions themselves. The examples we have been working with, (5)–(7), all consist grammatically of a subject noun phrase followed by a predicate verb phrase. We can think of the term 'subject' as referring to the entity that the proposition is about, and the term 'predicate' as referring to the property ascribed to that entity. So 'Philip', 'The Tower of London' and 'Harold' are subjects in our examples, while 'is a father', 'contains the Crown Jewels' and 'lives in Barcelona' are predicates. If logicians want to represent the structure of simple propositions such as these, they generally do so by choosing a capital letter for the predicate, typically F, and a lower case letter for the subject (logicians tend to use the term 'argument' rather than 'subject'), typically x, and then by presenting them in the order predicate-subject: Fx. If we want to be able to distinguish between our different simple propositions, we need to select different letters to stand in for each predicate and subject. So (5)–(7) could become Fp, Jt and Bh.

The logical meaning of simple propositions is determined by the principle of compositionality and is truth conditional. The theory of compositionality holds that the meaning of a whole is made up by combining together, by 'adding', the meaning of its parts. So the meaning of a proposition is composed of the meaning of the subject plus the meaning of the predicate. Semantics builds further on the principle of compositionality, so that the semantic meaning of a sentence is made up of the meanings of its constituent parts, the words and phrases that it contains, and is dependent on the syntactic structures by which these words are combined. Truth conditionality is central to discussions of meaning in logic and also in semantics. The truth conditions for any proposition are the specific circumstances that would have to be in place for the proposition to be true. In order for (5) to be true it would have to be the case that Philip is a father. Note that we can discuss the truth conditions of an example such as (5) without having any idea of whether it is actually true or false: that is, without knowing its truth value. Whether or not (5) is actually true depends on a very specific set of facts in the world. You don't need to know these facts in order to understand the truth-conditional meaning of (5); you simply have to know what would have to be the case in order for (5) to be true.

Thinking about the facts that would have to be in place in order for a particular proposition to be true makes it possible to talk about the relationships between different propositions and how they are connected in terms of truth. For instance, imagine that you discover that (12) is true:

12. Philip has a son.

Once you know that (12) is true, you can be confident that (5) is also true, since being a father follows (for a man) from having a son. To put it more technically, having a son entails being a father; a man can't not be a father if he has a son. The logical symbol for ENTAILMENT is →. Let us use Sp as the symbolic representation of (12). We then get:

13. $Sp \rightarrow Fp$

If we were to express this complex proposition in natural language, we would probably use a sentence such as (14):

14. If Philip has a son then Philip is a father.

We might be inclined to make the logical connection between the two propositions even clearer by saying something like:

15. Necessarily, if Philip has a son then Philip is a father.

Note also that the few logical relations that we have already considered allow us to talk about some of the relationships of truth that hold between propositions. For instance, if we have a complex proposition made up of two simple propositions, and if we know that that complex proposition is true, then it follows that any one of the simple propositions must be true. Logically:

16. $p \wedge q \rightarrow p$

The natural language equivalent is:

17. If Philip is a father and The Tower of London contains the Crown Jewels, then Philip is a father.

In this section we have been concentrating on some of the similarities between logic and language. There is certainly an appealing degree of correspondence between the two. There are various grammatical devices in the language available to combine simple declarative sentences together in ways that seem remarkably similar to ways in which propositions can be combined together in logic. We have been working, for instance, on the assumption that logical ∧ 'means the same as' natural language 'and', and that logical → 'means the same as' natural language 'if ... then'.

But note that this is far from straightforwardly the case. $p \wedge \sim r$ might be a convenient way of representing the propositional meaning of 'Philip is a father and Harold does not live in Barcelona', but it certainly doesn't seem to tell us everything about the significance of this sentence if it were used in an utterance. In particular, it doesn't allow for the fact that this would seem to be rather an odd thing to say, unless it were shared knowledge between speaker and hearer that there was some sort of connection or relevance between the two parts of the sentence. Similarly, $p \wedge q \rightarrow p$ may give us the logical form of 'If Philip is a father and The Tower of London contains the Crown Jewels, then Philip is a father', but we are still left with the feeling that this would be a very strange thing for anyone ever actually to say. Perhaps most strikingly of all, however, we have been working with the assumption that truth-conditional meanings of propositions can account for the semantic meanings of sentences. But there are some big problems with this assumption and for its implications for the nature of natural language sentences and the reasons why they are used in utterances in context. Even if we could put aside the contextual factors and questions of what is acceptable that we are obviously going to have to deal with, we would still need to account for the fact that natural language is used to do a lot of other things besides making statements about the world that can appropriately be judged to be either 'true' or 'false'.

2.4 Mood

Up until now we have been discussing sentences as if they were uniformly descriptive: that is, linguistic means of expressing propositions that could potentially be uttered in context to make some particular statement about the world. This is a simplification of the situation, but it's quite a reasonable one to make, at least initially. It helps us to say something about what we want from an account of meaning, and it is in fact a working definition of sentences that has been used by many theorists of meaning. But we don't have to look very far to find examples that indicate that, when it comes to explaining meaning in a natural language, such a definition of sentences is much too restrictive. Not all sentences offer a description that can be compared with reality and judged to be either 'true' or 'false'. So a straightforwardly truth-conditional account of meaning runs into difficulties. Consider the following examples:

18. You do all your food shopping locally.
19. Do you do all your food shopping locally?
20. Do all your food shopping locally!

These three examples are all complete and grammatical sentences of English. What is more, they could all be used to produce acceptable utterances; it's not hard to imagine contexts in which each of them could be used effectively. So it would seem that an account of meaning in language should be able to explain each of these examples. Only in the case of (18) would it be possible to compare the situation described with reality and decide whether it makes a true or false statement. That is, a straightforwardly truth-conditional account of meaning would be effective only in the case of example (18).

Informally, we might want to say that (18)–(20) are closely related to each other in terms of meaning; they are all concerned with the same type of situation or fact. But the three examples would all typically be used to do three different things in relation to this situation. Example (18) would state that it is the case; (19) would ask whether it is the case; (20) would offer an order or instruction that it should be the case. More formally we could say that while (18)–(20) all have a certain semantic element in common they differ in terms of their mood. The linguistic category of mood, then, is concerned with what different sentence types can typically be used to do. That is, it is concerned with the functions to which language can be put. Mood is said to be a constant feature across a diverse range of languages (see Sadock and Zwicky 1985) and although there is a relatively large and somewhat disputed number of different linguistic moods, most commentators working in semantics and pragmatics concentrate on the three 'major' moods illustrated in (18)–(20): declarative, interrogative and imperative.

The evidence of examples (18)–(20), and of course many other sets like this, suggest that mood is a formal element of the language. That is, it is determined by the syntax of the language and as such it should be explained by a compositional linguistic semantics. Yet, as we have seen, it doesn't seem feasible to try to offer a truth-conditional account of the different moods. In response to this challenge, some theorists of meaning have attempted to explain mood within a truth-conditional semantics. Probably the most famous such attempt was by the philosopher of language Donald Davidson. Davidson acknowledged the apparent problem that features of natural language, such as mood, posed for truth-conditional theories of meaning. He proposed to retain a straightforwardly truth-conditional account of meaning for declaratives, such as (18). Non-declaratives such as (19) and (20), he argued, are in fact composed semantically of two separate parts. One part is the element of meaning that is common across all moods: in this case the element connected to the act of doing food shopping locally. The other part is concerned exclusively with mood: it is what Davidson describes as a 'mood-setter' (Davidson 1979). So the semantic form of (19) would be 'my next utterance is a question', 'you do all your food shopping locally' and the semantic form of (20) 'my next utterance is imperative', 'you do all your food shopping locally'. Davidson specifies that both parts of these semantic forms are truth conditional, allowing truth-conditional semantics to be maintained in the face of mood.

Others have argued that, because mood is concerned with how sentences are to be used, and because of the difficulties of accommodating it truth-functionally, the differences between examples in different moods is actually a pragmatic difference. For instance, François Recanati discusses the set of examples (21)–(23), which are of course very similar to our (18)–(20) above, but will be given here for ease of reference:

21. You will go to the store tomorrow at 8.
22. Will you go to the store tomorrow at 8?
23. Go to the store tomorrow at 8.

For Recanati, these 'all have the same descriptive content. The difference between them is pragmatic'. That is, the difference in mood provides a 'non-truth-conditional indication' which gives 'conditions of use for the imperative mood' (Recanati 2004b: 447). Other accounts of mood have attempted to combine both types of explanation. For instance, Robert Harnish (1994) describes mood as partly formal, determined by syntax and explained by semantics, and partly functional, to be explained by pragmatics.

Mood, then, is one of the aspects of linguistic description where there is room for debate over the relative roles of semantic and pragmatic explanation. Or, to put it another way, it is one area in which the semantics/pragmatics borderline is in dispute. But there is a further feature of mood, or more generally of the relationship between form and function, that makes it central to many issues in pragmatics and ensures that it will have a central part to play in this book. Despite intuitively appealing sets of examples such as (18)–(20) and (21)–(23) above, it isn't by any means the case that there is always a straightforward correlation between syntactic form and pragmatic function. Sometimes declaratives are used to make statements, interrogatives to ask questions and imperatives to issue orders, but not always. Consider the following examples:

24. Come and sit down.
25. Would you like to take a seat?
26. We do have chairs here, you know.

Syntactically the differences between these three examples are obvious; in formal terms (24) is an imperative, (25) is an interrogative and (26) is a declarative. But in terms of the functions they would be most likely to be used for, it is by no means clear that there are any such differences. In fact, despite their apparent differences in mood, (24)–(26) could all be used for the same purpose: to order or invite someone to sit down. In the case of (25) we might in fact want to say that, despite its interrogative form, such an example would most usually or most conventionally be used to make an offer rather than to ask a question.

The relationship between mood and function clearly needs further investigation and, because it involves questions of the use of language to do things in contexts, is clearly a prime subject for pragmatic explanation. This is the central concern of an entire branch of pragmatics known as speech act theory, which will be the topic of Chapter 4.1.

2.5 The explicit and the implicit

Even when we concentrate on utterances that are used descriptively, rather than to perform any other of the host of functions that language can be used for, we find problems for an account of meaning that relies entirely on truth conditions. We have already considered a number of examples of this type when we considered possible definitions and terms of reference for pragmatics in the last chapter. Any time that speakers convey more than their words literally mean they are relying on more than truth-conditional meaning. Remember the quotation from the tennis player Roger Federer, the example with which we began:

27. In the end, with the light, it was tough.

We saw that, along with many other aspects of utterance meaning that depend on context, one suggested interpretation of (27) was that the result of the tennis match was unfair. Now even if this was part of what Federer intended to convey by his utterance, we would hardly want to say that this is in any way part of the literal meaning, or the semantics, of the words he used. It is not a necessary condition for the truth of (27) that the match was unfair. The same is true for perhaps the majority of utterances that we encounter in our everyday interactions, where there is a gap between literal and intended meaning. It is certainly true for the various 'figures of speech' that are a feature of communication, such as IRONY and METAPHOR. Consider examples (28) and (29):

28. [*In a context where George has just passed by with a nod and a grunt*]
    George is always so talkative.
29. [*John, who has been working all day, is observed still working late at night*]
    John is a machine.

Informally, we could say that neither of these utterances is intended to be interpreted literally. The context in the case of the ironic (28) and our general knowledge of the nature of people and of machines in the case of the metaphorical (29) lead us to understand that the truth conditions of these two examples do not adequately account for what they are being used in context to convey. In fact, the intended meaning of (28) is something like the opposite of its truth-conditional meaning, while in (29) the intention is to draw attention to some striking similarities, but not an exact identity, between John and a machine.

The notion of 'intention' that we have been using to discuss non-literal meaning is crucial to many of the types of meaning that form the subject matter of pragmatics and to the ways in which they are generally discussed. Pragmaticists are interested in cases where what the speaker intends to convey is different from what the words she chooses literally mean. The former is generally known as the implicit and the latter as the explicit meaning.

The fact that implicit and explicit meaning are so frequently different from each other, together with the fact that communication nevertheless is generally successful, suggests that there must be certain 'pragmatic principles', or assumptions about language use, that are shared by speakers and that guide hearers towards intended interpretations. Pragmaticists are interested in trying to determine the nature and extent of these principles. They have also considered the question of why speakers rely so much on implicit meaning, when the alternative option would seem to be to say exactly and explicitly what you mean all the time. One answer is undoubtedly that implicit meaning makes conversational exchanges more interesting. It would be pretty boring if everyone were constrained to spend their days speaking literally. But there is also the more practical matter of the efficiency of language as a means of conveying thoughts. It takes a long time to say everything explicitly. If we were to try to express fully what is conveyed by (29) we would be hard pressed to be sure to capture all the specific nuances, but would probably produce something like:

30. John works very hard and without apparently tiring, in a way that seems almost non-human. Rather like a machine, in fact.

In nearly all cases where there is a difference between explicit and implicit meaning, the implicit meaning conveys a lot more than is literally expressed; the literal meaning 'underdetermines' the meaning conveyed. So it's simply more efficient to imply part of our meaning than to state everything explicitly, and this enables us to express our ideas at something closer to the speed of our thoughts. Stephen Levinson has suggested that the need to articulate spoken language in order to communicate creates an 'encoding bottleneck'. The solution is to 'find a way to piggyback meaning on top of meaning' (Levinson 2000: 6). That is, to communicate implicitly as well as explicitly.

However, the distinction between the explicit and the implicit is not so clear cut as the examples we have considered so far seem to suggest. The best way to determine which aspects of the total significance of an utterance are explicit and which are implicit is one of the major topics of debate in present-day pragmatics, and it is also one of the areas in which the semantics/pragmatics borderline is in dispute. The examples we have considered so far might suggest that the literal meaning of the words a speaker utters are always sufficient to give a full, truth-conditional proposition (such as 'John is a machine'), which can then be added to by further propositions dependent on pragmatic principles (such as 'John works very hard', 'John is apparently tireless') to give the full intended meaning of the utterance. But note that to reach even that first 'basic' meaning we need to be confident that it is established between speaker and hearer who is being referred to by 'John'. In the context suggested for (29), John was visually present to speaker and hearer, but the bearers of proper names are by no means always before our eyes when we talk about them. In any case, we would hardly want to claim that the presence of a particular individual at the time of speaking (a contextual matter) meant that the name 'John' literally means that particular individual (a linguistic matter). Some pragmaticists have claimed that the identity of individuals mentioned in utterances, whether by proper name or by pronoun, is determined by pragmatic means, and can therefore not be seen as established prior to the application of pragmatic principles.

The situation is even more complicated if we consider utterances that don't include complete sentences. Very often in naturally occurring language use, utterances consist of partial or incomplete sentences. Consider the problems of interpretation posed by the following example:

31. *Q*: Eight years. (Laughter)

Here of course is a classic example of the importance of context to interpretation. Without some knowledge of context, we can't be sure of what information speaker Q was trying to convey, yet alone why the utterance caused laughter. In fact, this is an extract from George W. Bush's final press conference as president, which took place in The White House on Monday 12 January 2009. Here is a little more of the relevant context, in which President Bush invites questions from individual members of the press:

32. *Bush*: Yes, Suzanne. Finally got your name right, after how many years? Six years?
    Q: Eight years. (Laughter)
    Bush: Eight years.

Example (32) illustrates a further important point about the difference between sentences and utterances, as well as a matter of controversy about the relationship between explicit and implicit meaning. Clearly Suzanne conveyed a complete and informative message. There is no sense in which she was interrupted or failed to express herself fully. Everyone understood her. But this is a very different matter from uttering a complete sentence. Suzanne's utterance in (32) doesn't correspond to a complete sentence that expresses a truth-conditional proposition. In fact, her utterance contains only a sentence fragment, or more specifically a single noun phrase. To reach a propositional meaning we have to 'fill in' the rest of the sentence, relying on context. This gives us something like 'You have known me for eight years'. This in turn interacts with aspects of the context to convey implicitly various meanings, such as that she is correcting Bush, that his memory for names is even worse than he realizes, or even that his memory is so poor that he has forgotten how long he himself has been in office for. These implicit meanings explain the general laughter. Note that in analysing this example we have relied on aspects of context to reach a fully propositional meaning for Suzanne's utterance, and then again to reach a range of possible implied meanings and fully to understand the joke. The implications of this for the distinction between explicit and implicit meaning are matters of great interest and controversy in present-day pragmatics, as we will see in Chapters 4 and 5.

2.6 Presupposition

A straightforwardly declarative statement, relating to a complete and grammatical sentence and spoken literally, can be used to communicate propositional meaning in more than one way. This fact has been recognized by philosophers of language and by linguists for more than a century. Let us begin our investigation of this phenomenon by considering example (33):

33. Charlie Farnsbarns was in The Royal Oak pub last night.

Ignoring for the time being the exact status of information such as the time referred to as 'last night', an issue that we will think about in the next section, let us assume that truth-conditional semantics can get us to a propositional meaning for (33). A certain individual was located within a certain public house for some period during the night preceding this statement. But note that (33) communicates other information as well. In particular, it communicates the proposition that Charlie Farnsbarns exists. There is something different about the way in which (33) conveys the proposition that Charlie Farnsbarns exists, compared with how it conveys the proposition that he was in The Royal Oak last night. Informally, we might say that the latter is the point of what is being said in (33), while the proposition that Charlie Farnsbarns exists is one that must be true for the example to make any sense, or to be sayable, at all. Slightly more formally we could say that the proposition that Charlie Farnsbarns was in The Royal Oak last night is an entailment of (33), while the proposition that Charlie Farnsbarns exists is a presupposition of (33).

A common way of distinguishing between entailment and presupposition is the observation that only presupposition is 'preserved under negation':

34. Charlie Farnsbarns was not in The Royal Oak pub last night.

Example (34) certainly has different entailments from (33); in fact it seems to entail the exact opposite. But note that what we identified as the presupposition of (33), the proposition that Charlie Farnsbarns exists, is equally a presupposition of (34). So a presupposition seems to be a necessary precondition for either asserting or denying a particular proposition. What's more, the presupposition survives changes in mood:

35. Was Charlie Farnsbarns in The Royal Oak pub last night?

Example (35) does not share the entailments of (33) – it doesn't entail that Charlie Farnsbarns was in The Royal Oak last night – but it does share the presupposition. You couldn't even legitimately ask the question if it were not in some way safe to assume that Charlie Farnsbarns exists.

Gottlob Frege, a German mathematician who had a major impact on the development of the philosophy of language, and as a result on linguistics, is credited with first recognizing the significance of presupposition, including its property of being preserved under negation. Here is a translation of what he wrote in 1892:

> If anything is asserted there is an obvious presupposition that the simple or proper names used have meaning. If therefore one asserts 'Kepler died in misery', there is a presupposition that the name 'Kepler' designates something. … That the name 'Kepler' designates something is just as much a presupposition for the assertion 'Kepler died in misery' as for the contrary assertion. (Frege 1892: 69)

This observation was picked up and developed further by the British philosopher Peter Strawson. He observed that if someone were to use a statement that has a false entailment we would quickly judge what she had said to be false. If we knew for a fact that Charlie Farnsbarns was not in The Royal Oak last night and someone were to say (33) to us, we would have no hesitation in replying 'You're wrong', or 'That's false'. But if (33) is used in circumstances where we know its presupposition to be false – that is, where we know for sure that Charlie Farnsbarns doesn't exist – we would find it much harder to respond. We would have a clear sense that there was something wrong with what had been said, but it wouldn't be a straightforward matter of the statement being false.

Strawson explains this by saying that when a presupposition is false, the statement in question is itself neither true nor false. It fails to achieve any truth value at all because it fails to say anything meaningful. This situation has been described as 'presupposition failure'. In a book on logic published in the 1950s, Strawson uses example (36), and its presupposition (37), to illustrate his point:

36. All John's children are asleep.
37. John has children.

He uses the abbreviations S for (36) and S' for (37). He observes that an entailment is a necessary condition for the truth of the statement that entails it. By contrast, in the case of presupposition 'S' is a necessary condition for the *truth or falsity* of S' (Strawson 1952: 175).

So Frege and Strawson had developed an account of presupposition based on logic; it made reference to the truth-conditional effects of the phenomenon. And when presupposition first became a focus of attention in linguistics it seemed reasonable enough to stick with this type of account and to see presupposition as a semantic feature concerned with the formal properties of sentences. After all, it is the lexical and grammatical properties of examples such as (33) and (36) that determine what they presuppose, rather than anything to do with the specifics of individual contexts. Linguists noticed that there are many other types of examples that seem to have presuppositions with the same kind of logical properties as those we have been discussing. Examples (33) and (36) have presuppositions concerning the existence of certain individuals, or what are known as 'existential presuppositions'. These are caused by the presence of certain types of lexical expression, such as the proper name 'Charlie Farnsbarns' in (33) or the quantified expression 'All John's children' in (36). Linguists noticed that other types of information can be presupposed by different types of statement and are in turn dependent on the presence of certain types of words or phrases. These particular words or phrases are known as 'presupposition triggers'.

Much has been written about presupposition triggers, and very extensive lists and categories of them have been drawn up. Perhaps the most significant such list is that proposed by Karttunen (n.d.) and summarized in Levinson (1983). Karttunen identified no fewer than 31 kinds of presuppositional triggers. We will consider just a handful here, illustrated with examples from Levinson (1983: 181–2). In each case, the trigger is shown in both positive and negative versions of a statement, to demonstrate that in each case the presupposition is preserved under negation.

(i) So-called 'factive verbs' such as 'regret' in (38) and 'realize' in (39), which introduce the presuppositions (40) and (41) respectively:

38. Martha regrets/doesn't regret drinking John's home brew.
39. John realized/didn't realize that he was in debt.
40. Martha drank John's home brew.
41. John was in debt.

(ii) 'Implicative' verbs, such as 'manage' in (42) and 'forget' in (43), which introduce the presuppositions in (44) and (45):

42. John managed/didn't manage to open the door
43. John forgot/didn't forget to lock the door.
44. John tried to open the door.
45. John ought to have locked, or intended to lock, the door.

(iii) 'Change of state verbs', such as 'stop' in (46) and 'begin' in (47), which introduce the presuppositions in (48) and (49):

46. John stopped/didn't stop beating his wife.
47. Joan began/didn't begin to beat her husband.
48. John had been beating his wife.
49. Joan hadn't been beating her husband.

(iv) 'Temporal clauses', such as those introduced by 'before' in (50) and 'while' in (51), which introduce the presuppositions in (52) and (53):

50. Before Strawson was even born, Frege noticed/didn't notice presuppositions.
51. While Chomsky was revolutionizing linguistics, the rest of social science was/wasn't asleep.
52. Strawson was born.
53. Chomsky revolutionized linguistics.

(v) 'Cleft structures', such as those in (54) and (55), which introduce the presuppositions in (56) and (57):

54. It was/wasn't Henry that kissed Rosie.
55. What John lost/didn't lose was his wallet.
56. Someone kissed Rosie.
57. John lost something.

As even this brief selection demonstrates, 'presupposition triggers' are a pretty diverse bunch of phenomena in terms of the range of vocabulary and structural features they include, but they do collectively seem to point to the idea that it is particular semantic features of sentences that give rise to, and can therefore be used to explain, presupposition.

But problems for a straightforwardly semantic account of presupposition began to emerge once linguists started to consider the behaviour of presuppositions in more varied examples. In particular, they identified the so-called 'projection problem for presupposition', which concerns what happens when presuppositional triggers such as those above appear inside more complex sentences. Presuppositions of simpler sentences are not routinely inherited by, or projected on to, the more complex sentences of which the simple sentences can form a part. It is not that presuppositions never survive when expressions that trigger them are embedded into larger units. Sometimes they do and sometimes they don't. This presents a potentially very complex set of data to be explained by a semantic theory.

As examples of complex sentences that don't inherit the presuppositions of the sentences they contain, consider so-called 'propositional attitude' statements. In fact, we considered these briefly in the last chapter, when we were beginning to think about what types of issues are of concern in theoretical pragmatics. These are statements that concern an attitude that the subject is said to take towards a particular proposition. The proposition is expressed as an embedded declarative sentence. Example (58) below presupposes (60), because of the existential presupposition that attaches to the use of any singular referring expression, a fact noted by Strawson and indeed by Frege. But if (58) is embedded in a propositional attitude statement as in (59) this presupposition does not survive. Example (59) doesn't presuppose (60) because it is quite possible that Tharg is entirely deluded. So (59) could still be true even if (60) is false:

58. The Master of the Universe admires Tharg.
59. Tharg believes that the Master of the Universe admires him.
60. There is a Master of the Universe.

Other complex constructions do seem to inherit presuppositions from their constituent parts. Example (61) presupposes (63). This is because it contains the factive verb 'regret', which acts as a presupposition trigger. And if (61) appears as the consequent of an 'if... then' clause, as in (62), the presupposition is still triggered. That is, (62) presupposes (63); (63) is a necessary precondition for the truth or the falsity of (62):

61. John regrets having invited a famous movie director.
62. If John has invited a film critic to the party, he regrets having invited a famous movie director.
63. John has invited a famous movie director.

The picture that is emerging is one in which some types of complex sentences inherit the presuppositions of their constituent parts while some do not. It might seem that the difference is a fairly easily identifiable property of individual sentence types. And indeed some semantic accounts of presupposition have attempted to include such information. For instance Karttunen (1973) distinguished between 'plugs' – structures in which presuppositions are not projected – and 'holes' – structures in which they are. Arguably, this has the disadvantage of introducing a fairly arbitrary and unexplained element into semantics. But more damagingly it runs into the problem that complex structures don't always fit neatly into one or other category. We have seen that in (62) presuppositions are preserved in a conditional 'if... then' construction. This might seem to suggest that conditionals should be classed as presuppositional 'holes'. But the picture is rather different in the case of an apparently almost identical example. Example (64) is the same as (62), except for the fact that the object of the verb 'invite' is 'a film critic' in (62) and 'Steven Spielberg' in (64). But notice that, unlike (62), (64) does not presuppose (63):

64. If John has invited Steven Spielberg to the party, he will regret having invited a famous movie director.

The issue of John's having invited a famous movie director to the party, far from being a necessary precondition for (64), is in fact the very matter being questioned, or what is being signalled as unknown. The reason, of course, is that we can identify 'a famous movie director' as referring to the same individual as 'Steven Spielberg'. So it is still possible to offer a semantic explanation. Presupposition is not projected in (64) because the antecedent ('John has invited Steven Spielberg to the party') entails the presupposition of the consequent ('John has invited a famous movie director to the party'). In fact, Karttunen (1973) suggests that conditionals should best be described as 'filters' because they sometimes inherit presuppositions from their consequents and sometimes don't, depending on the relationship between antecedent and consequent.

But there is worse in store for semantic theories of presupposition. The different presuppositional behaviour of (62) and (64) could be explained in terms of the difference in the context for the consequent provided by the antecedent. Granted, the difference between the two antecedents was significant only because of our language-external encyclopedic knowledge of the world and of the reference of the name 'Steven Spielberg'. Nevertheless, the clue to the presuppositional difference between (62) and (64) is within the examples themselves. But factors that determine what is presupposed by any particular example need not be present in the example at all. Issues to do with the context for an utterance, including other preceding utterances, can be the deciding factors. Presupposition can depend on contextual, rather than linguistic, factors. What Mary says in (65) presupposes (67) because of the existential presupposition associated with the singular referring expression 'his dog'. Preservation under negation tells us that this presupposition is shared by (66):

65. *Mary*: John will have to take his dog for a walk every day.
66. *Mary*: John won't have to take his dog for a walk every day.
67. John has a dog.

These presuppositional features are familiar to us by now, and might seem to be stable and reliable. But now consider what happens when we put (66) into a specific context:

68. [*Context: John has been talking for a while about the possibility of getting a dog, but has recently told his friends that he has decided against it.*]
   Mary: At least John won't have to take his dog for a walk every day.

In (68), the presupposition that John has a dog seems to disappear, precisely because it conflicts with what Mary and John's other friends already know. Contextual factors and the effects they can have on meaning are, of course, the domain of pragmatics rather than semantics. So it is hardly surprising that some linguists have argued that presupposition should be seen as a pragmatic rather than a semantic phenomenon. After all, attempts to define presupposition semantically were already beset by many apparent complexities and counter-examples. It seemed to some that the evidence that context could be a decisive factor in determining what was presupposed must rule out the possibility that presupposition could be a semantic phenomenon at all. Presupposition must be a feature of utterances in context, or perhaps of speakers and their knowledge, rather than of sentences in isolation. The question that such linguists had then set themselves was that of how to explain the pragmatic mechanisms of presupposition. One intuitively appealing possibility is that what is presupposed in an utterance is what is already known by speaker and audience, or is 'given' in the context. This might seem to be the most straightforward way of re-expressing in pragmatic terms what we have already noticed about presupposition; certain facts need to be established as true to make certain statements sayable. And indeed some pragmaticists have described what is presupposed as usually or generally equivalent to what is given in context, justifying a pragmatic account of presupposition (see for instance Akmajian 1979; Soames 1982; van der Sandt 1988).

But what is presupposed can't always be straightforwardly equated with what is agreed knowledge between speaker and hearer. This fact was noticed by the philosopher Paul Grice, whose work we will be looking at in much more detail in later chapters:

> It is quite natural to say to somebody, when we are discussing some concert, *My aunt's cousin went to that concert*, when we know perfectly well that the person we are talking to is very likely not even to know that we have an aunt, let alone that our aunt has a cousin. So the supposition must be not that it is common knowledge but rather that it is noncontroversial, in the sense that it is something we would expect the hearer to take from us (if he does not already know). (Grice 1981: 274)

The suggestion that what is presupposed is information that is uncontroversial, or easy to take on board, rather than necessarily already known, has been a significant one in pragmatic presupposition. Indeed, it offers a good account of many relevant examples. Gazdar (1979) argued that what was presupposed need not be equivalent to what was assumed in context but must be at least consistent with it. Lewis (1979) outlined an 'accommodation' analysis of presupposition, whereby presuppositions that are prompted by linguistic form will be accepted without challenge, even if they are not already mutually known, as long as they can be easily accommodated with existing knowledge.

There have been a number of other attempts to account for the fact that what is presupposed may introduce new material, but does so in a way that marks it as unsurprising or not particularly worthy of comment (see for instance Stalnaker

1974; Fuchs 1984). Burton-Roberts (1989), although advancing a semantic account of presupposition, acknowledges the importance of pragmatic factors and particularly the notion of what is likely to be easily accepted. In his terms, presuppositions are 'implicit commitments which, because they are implicit are not (presented as) subject to debate. In this they contrast with the explicit commitments one enters into in making assertions, which are (presented as) subject to debate' (ibid.: 137). Saying that something is not presented as liable to be challenged is not of course the same as saying that it might not be challenged, or that it might not be controversial. It is possible to envisage cases where presupposed information communicates something that is new and striking or even shocking in some way. Nevertheless, the speaker has chosen to present it as unremarkable for some communicative purpose.

Various voices have suggested the need for both semantics and pragmatics to play a part in describing and explaining presupposition. Burton-Roberts describes a semantic theory of presupposition as 'only necessarily incompatible with a pragmatic (context-dependent) theory of P[resupposition] if it claims to be an exhaustive theory of P. In and of itself, though, no such theory excludes the possibility of a pragmatics of P, though it does imply some division of labour' (ibid.: 443). In 1983, Levinson concluded his detailed survey of the field by claiming that 'presupposition remains, ninety years after Frege's remarks on the subject, still only partially understood, and an important ground for the study of how semantics and pragmatics interact' (Levinson 1983: 225). Certainly, the logical account suggested by Frege and by Strawson, focussing on preservation under negation, together with the existence of various presuppositional 'triggers', suggest that linguistic form itself has a role to play in the description of presupposition. But the undeniable importance of context, and of the specifics of relationships between speakers, suggests that it can hardly be expected to tell the whole story by itself.

2.7 Deixis

In this chapter we have surveyed some of the types of data that are used most frequently in discussions of the semantics/pragmatics borderline. We began with a tentative suggestion that semantics is concerned with those aspects of meaning that are truth-conditional. We have been looking at some of the problems that natural language throws up for any suggestion that we might be able to explain meaning in purely truth-conditional terms; in other words, we have considered some of the reasons why we need pragmatics. In the course of our investigations we have seen that the division of labour between semantics and pragmatics when it comes to explaining meaning is far from clear-cut. In the case of presupposition, at least, we have seen that it is perhaps not always possible, or desirable, to describe semantic and pragmatic aspects of meaning in entirely separate ways, or even to stipulate which aspects of meaning belong to semantics and which to pragmatics. We have left until last a category of linguistic expressions that forms perhaps the single biggest problem for truth-conditional accounts of meaning, and that also poses some of the most severe difficulties for linguists trying to establish the existence and the location of the semantics/pragmatics borderline. This is a category of expressions whose very purpose is to link uses of language to the context in which they occur. They are so common in language that we have necessarily come across many such examples already, although we have postponed discussion of them until now. Consider the effects of the word in italics in each of the following three examples:

69. *I* am pleased to see *you*.
70. William met Martha *yesterday*.
71. When William met Martha she was standing right *there*.

In each case, we need to fill in some information from the context of utterance in order to understand exactly what is being communicated. Also in each case the italicized word indicates how this extra information can be found or points to some aspect of the context that is relevant to interpretation. Words of this type belong to a large and diverse category of linguistic expressions known as 'deictic' expressions. The linguistic phenomena as a whole is known as 'deixis'.

Example (69) includes two examples of 'person deixis'. The personal pronouns are prime examples of this type of expression. The semantics of the language may specify that *I* refers to the speaker and *you* to the hearer, but we are dependent on the specifics of individual context to establish who those individuals are on any particular occasion. So straightaway it becomes apparent why deixis sits right at the borderline between semantics and pragmatics. Without some semantic knowledge of the language we wouldn't be able to explain the difference in meaning between *I* and *you*, but without some pragmatic knowledge of context we would never be able to know who is being referred to. In fact, many ways of referring to people, other than the most obviously deictic personal pronouns, have deictic elements to them. If you use a definite description to pick out an individual, talking for instance about 'the girl with green eyes', semantics will tell you a lot about what this expression actually means, but you need to know something about context before you can establish who is being referred to.

The word *yesterday* in (70) is an example of 'time deixis'. Again, we know something about the meaning of *yesterday* simply because we are speakers of English, but we need information about the context for any particular use of the word before we can be certain exactly what day it refers to. There are many other words and phrases in English whose primary meaning is a time deictic one, for instance: *tomorrow, next week, in four hours' time, on Tuesday*. There are other ways too of indicating how an event under discussion relates to the moment of speaking, perhaps most strikingly through the use of grammatical tense. The formal properties of English can explain the differences between 'William is meeting Martha', 'William met Martha' and 'William will meet Martha', but only particulars of context can help us to decide what actual times, or what times relative to the moment of speaking, are involved.

We clearly need to know about the context for (71) to know what is meant by *there*. Specifically, we need to know about where the speaker and hearer are located. In other words we are concerned with the third major category of deictic expressions: place deixis. Perhaps the most obvious deictic expressions relating to place are the pair *here* and *there*. The language distinguishes between them, but context gives them specific meaning. Note that we often need to know more than the simple location of speaker and hearer. We might also want to know what gestures if any the speaker was making: *here* and *there* are often accompanied by pointing. If speaker and hearer are in separate locations and are talking perhaps by telephone or over the internet, that would make a difference to our interpretation too, but it would still not be a straightforward matter. Depending on the specifics of what the speaker was talking about, for instance, *here* could be used to refer to 'this room', 'this house', 'this city' or 'this country'.

Place deixis also occurs as part of the meaning of some verbs. For instance *come* and *go* are both verbs describing movement; the difference between them is a difference in direction in relation to the current location of the speaker. That is, they differ in terms of their relationship to the 'deictic centre', a feature which is dependent on context. Defining deictic expressions as ones that depend for at least some of their meaning on a deictic centre, and considering the range of examples we have covered in this brief survey, we can begin to appreciate just how pervasive the phenomenon is. In fact, linguists claim that in some form or other deixis is a universal feature of human language (see Levinson 1983: 63; Huang 2007: 132). So it is clearly something that demands attention from both semantics and pragmatics. The context-dependent nature of deictic meaning might seem to make it a perfect candidate for pragmatic explanation. But this possibility raises some very specific problems. In many cases, including all those we have considered above, it seems that we need to retrieve the relevant information from context in order to know what was communicated: not just to appreciate some extra or non-literal meaning, but to reach any complete proposition at all. That is, contextual information seems to play a central role in establishing truth-conditional meaning, supposedly the domain of semantics. Linguists have responded to this problem in a variety of ways, and we will look at examples of these in later chapters. Some have argued that traditional truth-conditional semantics must simply be an inappropriate model when it comes to explaining such a fluid and subjective thing as meaning in natural language. Others take deixis as an important source of evidence that semantics can't be expected to produce complete propositional meaning in isolation. That is, they argue that semantics and pragmatics can't be autonomous systems, but that pragmatics must intrude on semantic description. Still others have argued that truth-conditional meaning does operate independently of pragmatic factors, but that we must not expect it to deliver too much; in particular, we should expect truth-conditional meaning to be radically underspecified when compared with what is communicated in context.

Some forms of deixis seem to be unproblematically pragmatic. These are less central to the description of the language than deixis of person, place and time, but still important in terms of how the language is used. Consider the implications of the inclusion of the words in italics in the following:

72. I'm pleased to see you *John/Mr Smith.*
73. *By the way*, I'm pleased to see you.

Terms of address are examples of social deixis, which orientate an utterance to the social relationships in its context. There may be no real difference in the propositional meaning conveyed in the two alternatives in (72), but there are substantial differences in terms of what is suggested about social and personal relationships. General terms of address such as 'sir' and 'mate' are also examples of social deixis. The range of such terms available in English is fairly narrow but some languages, such as Japanese, have much more complex systems of terms that denote social standing, known as 'honorifics'. Social deixis is indicated in the grammar of some languages, such as the distinction between the formal *'vous'* and the less formal or more intimate *'tu'* in French.

The expression 'by the way' in (73) is an example of 'discourse deixis'. Such expressions generally do not contribute to truth-conditional meaning, but they serve to anchor an utterance in the discourse in which it occurs. Other such expressions include 'but', 'in conclusion', 'anyway'. As we will see in Chapter 5, discourse deixis has been a recent focus of interest in pragmatics, where it is generally argued to offer a good example of meaning that can't be explained in truth-conditional terms.

Deixis seems to offer a prime example of a linguistic phenomenon where no single or simple label quite accounts for what's going on. As Mira Ariel comments, 'it combines grammatical aspects (there are grammatically specified differences between *I* and *this*) with pragmatic aspects (pinning down who the speaker is, what object this denotes)' (Ariel 2008: 1). Deixis is therefore one important focus for the discussion of different pragmatic theories. It is also an area of interest for those working at the 'margins' of pragmatics, for instance as it relates to language acquisition. For these reasons we will have more to say about deixis, along with the other phenomena introduced in this chapter, throughout the rest of this book.

FURTHER READING

Many textbooks in semantics and in pragmatics look at the relationship between the two fields and there are many more advanced books, collections of essays and individual articles devoted to the same topic. A brief overview of the semantics/pragmatics borderline, and a look ahead to some of the pragmatic theories we will be covering later in this book, can be found in Recanati (2004b). A recent collection of essays entitled *Where Semantics Meets Pragmatics* includes two essays (von Heusinger and Turner 2006a; Horn 2006) concerned with current debates over the borderline between semantics and pragmatics.

Chapter 8 of Chapman (2006) is concerned with the question of whether and to what extent meaning in natural language relates to logic. A very practical introduction to logic and its relationship to linguistic meaning can be found in Chapter 4 of Hurford, Heasley and Smith (2007). Löbner (2002), Chapter 4, and Cruse (2004), Chapter 2, both offer good introductions to the relationship between semantics and logic.

Donald Davidson's discussion of mood is discussed in Martin (1987), Chapter 22, and in Evnine (1991), Chapter 5. For a more recent attempt to explain mood in truth-conditional terms, with specific reference to imperatives, see Han (2000). Harnish (1994) offers an extensive survey of the literature on the subject up until the time of publication.

An overview of the relationship between explicit and implicit meaning, and of some of the approaches to this distinction that we will be considering later in this book, can be found in Horn (2004).

Levinson (1983), Chapter 4, is concerned with semantic and pragmatic theories of presupposition and the types of data typically discussed in relation to them. Semantic and pragmatic theories of presupposition are considered in Atlas (2004). Various presuppositional features and their relationship to pragmatics are discussed in Huang (2007), Chapter 3. Presupposition is discussed in relation to pragmatics in Grundy (2008), Chapter 3.

Levinson (2004) offers an overview of different types of deixis and includes a discussion of the roles of semantics and pragmatics in resolving their reference. A slightly less advanced introduction to the subject can be found in Chapter 2 of Levinson (1983). Chapter 5 of Huang (2007) is dedicated to deixis and its relationship to pragmatics. A collection of papers on the topic can be found in Davis (1991), Section III. For in introduction to deixis in relation to pragmatics see Grundy (2008), Chapter 2.

History of Pragmatics

3

As part of our exploration of what pragmatics is and what it does, in this chapter we will take a brief look at its history, its origins and its development. The history of pragmatics is not a side issue nor an interesting distraction from our current concern with getting an overview of the subject. Thinking about why pragmatics developed – that is, why the need became apparent for a branch of language study specifically concerned with speakers, hearers and contexts – can help us to identify what sets pragmatics apart from other areas of linguistics and what it offers that is unique. Considering how that branch of language study changed and developed in its early days can tell us a lot about the problems and issues faced by those who want to account for language in use, problems still faced in present-day pragmatics. Looking at how it has been received by others in linguistics, and how it has established its own role and subject matter, can help us to understand how it relates to the study of language more generally, and how it might profitably work with other fields in the future.

3.1 Structuralism

Compared to many other fields of academic inquiry, linguistics is a relative newcomer. In fact, what we now recognize as linguistics didn't really exist before the twentieth century. And pragmatics, as a separate and identifiable branch of linguistic study, arrived on the scene even later. As we will see later in this chapter, it only really emerged in the 1970s and became established in the 1980s. Of course, serious interest in language goes back much further than the twentieth century, but it was generally discussed by, and served the interests of, philosophers, classicists and historians, rather than linguists specifically devoted to the study of language as an end in itself. For as long as language has been discussed, it seems that thinkers have acknowledged the importance of situation and context. To take just one example, Aristotle acknowledged that statements or beliefs, in other words what a modern linguist would recognize as propositions, can depend on context to determine their truth or falsity.

'Statements and beliefs themselves remain completely unchangeable in every way; it is because the actual thing changes that the contrary [being false rather than true] comes to belong to them' (Aristotle, quoted in Barnes 1984: 4, 17a, 3).

Modern linguistics is often dated back to the work of Ferdinand de Saussure, a Swiss linguist who was active in the early part of the twentieth century, up until his death in 1913. Saussure made a clear and deliberate statement of the value of language study for its own sake, and carefully distanced himself from some of the ways that language had been discussed by his predecessors. Before Saussure, the study of language had been largely concerned with prescriptivism, that is with establishing rules for how language ought to be used, or with philology, that is with studying the historical stages of individual languages and with comparing these with the development of other related languages. Saussure rejected prescriptivism, arguing that linguists must concern themselves with all forms and uses of language, not just those judged to be 'correct'. He did acknowledge that there was a place in linguistics for the study of the history of individual languages and of language in general, but argued that the study of present day forms of language was just as important. After all, 'in the lives of individuals and societies, speech is more important than anything else' (Saussure 1916: 7).

Saussure set out to establish a new area of scientific inquiry: the systematic study of language and beyond that of systems more generally in which people use signs meaningfully. He labelled this new science 'semiology', and he made a start in it by offering an account of what language is like: that is, he offered not a philological study of the properties of any one particular language, but a general explanation and description of the phenomenon of human language. For Saussure, the words that make up a language are themselves simply arbitrary, in that there is no necessary or natural connection between a word and the idea it stands for. However, these arbitrary words are arranged into a highly complex and structured system. Every word relies for its significance and meaning on its unique place in this system, and hence on its relationship to all the other words in the language. This system of words, existing collectively in the minds of all speakers of a particular language, Saussure labelled using the French term '*langue*', defined as 'a self-contained whole and a principle of classification' (ibid.: 9). He was aware that a language couldn't be entirely summed up in terms of *langue*, because there is also a more practical side to language, when it is implemented, or in Saussure's term 'executed', in speaking. Speaking is an individual matter, dependent on choices and behaviours of specific speakers. Saussure labelled it *parole*, and explained that 'execution is always individual, and the individual is always its master' (ibid.: 13).

Because of his emphasis on language as a structured system, the hugely influential branch of study that Saussure's work established has become known as 'structuralism'. Rather as he had hoped, semiotic study within the structuralist tradition expanded to include not just language but a variety of other sign systems and forms of human behaviour. Within language study, it might be tempting to view Saussure's *parole*, with its emphasis on individual speakers, as the direct ancestor of present day pragmatics, but such an understanding of the term would be far too simplistic. For Saussure, *langue* and *parole* were two necessary and complementary components of the account of language. He didn't distinguish between meaning as a phenomenon determined by the language and meaning as affected in a systematic way by aspects of context. It was left to a later linguist working within the structuralist tradition, Charles Morris, to attempt a more detailed classification of the different areas of language study and to introduce the term 'pragmatics' into linguistics, although the term still had some way to go before it reached its present-day significance.

In 1938, Morris contributed to the ambitious collaborative project of producing an *International Encyclopedia of Unified Science*, by suggesting the 'Foundations of the Theory of Signs'. He acknowledged human beings as the most significant users of signs, and therefore made a case for the principled study of signs in general and language in particular. His motivation may seem surprising to present-day linguists, committed to the idea that language should be studied on its own merits. Morris argued that 'language – including scientific language – is greatly in need of purification, simplification, and systematization' (Morris 1938: 81).

In an important passage that has often been quoted and has been the subject of much discussion, Morris set out what he saw as the three separate areas of the study of signs:

> One may study the relations of signs to the objects to which the signs are applicable. This relation will be called the *semantical dimension of semiosis*, symbolized by the sign 'D_{sem}'; the study of this dimension will be called *semantics*. Or the subject of study may be the relation of signs to interpreters. This relation will be called the *pragmatical dimension of semiosis*, symbolized by 'D_p', and the study of this dimension will be named *pragmatics*... the formal relation of signs to one another ... will be called the *syntactical dimension of semiosis*, symbolized by 'D_{syn}', and the study of this dimension will be named *syntactics*. (ibid.: 84–5)

There is certainly much in this passage that is familiar to the present-day linguist, and so it's not unreasonable to credit Morris with significant foresight as to how the study of language would develop. He is writing here about the dimensions of the study of signs in general, but he goes on to suggest that in the specific case of language these dimensions are separately identifiable. We can recognize descriptions of semantics, pragmatics and syntax in Morris's words. But note that his version of pragmatics is not straightforwardly equivalent to ours. To begin with, he doesn't distinguish pragmatic analysis from narrowly linguistic analysis, as we might distinguish context-dependent pragmatics from formal semantics. For Morris, the relationships between signs and their interpreters is a crucial component of the system of signs, or more specifically the language, itself. He goes on to argue that the study of language simply consists of the sum of the study of these three dimensions, and that 'much confusion will be avoided if it is recognized that the word "language" is often used to designate some aspect of what is language in the full sense' (ibid.: 89).

Secondly, Morris argues that pragmatics is necessary in the study of language because there are certain aspects of a language that can be explained only in terms of their relationship to producers and receivers, and therefore that pragmatic rules are necessary to handle these particular areas: 'Interjections such as "Oh!", commands such as "Come here!", value terms such as "fortunately", expressions such as "Good morning!", and various rhetorical and poetical devices occur only under certain definite conditions in the users of the language' (ibid.: 113). Modern pragmatics at its broadest does of course concern itself with the use of particular conversational terms such as 'oh' and 'good morning', and it is certainly concerned with issues such as how we use and interpret commands. But it is best described as working alongside semantics to explain meaning in context, rather than in being responsible for particular features of a language that are related to producers and interpreters and are therefore not the proper business of semantics. There is no room in Morris's system for pragmatic principles that explain how language and context interact to produce specific interpretations.

3.2 Logical positivism

In the last section we paused briefly over Morris's comment that language was in need of 'purification, simplification, and systematization'. It seemed at odds with Saussure's claim that linguists should describe how language is rather than prescribe how it ought to be. However, it was far from unusual for philosophers of the early to mid-twentieth century who took an interest in language to make rather dismissive comments of this type about natural language. This was particularly the case with philosophers whose primary interests were mathematical, logical or scientific. They had to engage seriously with language, because all these disciplines need a vehicle for expression and discussion, but they generally found ordinary everyday language to be lacking, because of what were perceived as its vagueness, inaccuracy and illogicality. For serious study it was necessary to tidy up language, as Morris suggested, or else to work with an artificial system of symbols which could be logical and precise. Advocates of this approach from early in the twentieth century were Bertrand Russell and Alfred Whitehead, whose complex and highly technical work on mathematical logic, *Principia Mathematica*, was a strong influence on many philosophers working in this area. For Russell and Whitehead, philosophers needed to work with a logically perfect, therefore artificial, language because an artificial language can help the mind in its reasoning while 'ordinary language yields no such help. Its grammatical structure does not represent uniquely the relations between the ideas involved' (Russell and Whitehead 1910: 2).

One school of thought that was influenced by the formal system developed in *Principia Mathematica*, although not one that either Russell or Whitehead endorsed, was logical positivism. This was an approach to philosophy that developed in the 1920s and 1930s, and was associated particularly with a group known as the Vienna Circle. These philosophers came from a variety of scientific backgrounds and were collectively interested in establishing a language in which scientific discussion could proceed. They did deal with natural language, but were wary of its illogical and imprecise nature and, like Russell and Whitehead, were concerned that its grammatical structure could be misleading as to what idea was being expressed. They attempted to tackle these problems by stipulating which types of sentences could and which could not be classified as 'meaningful', defining the term 'meaningful' as the capacity to be either true or false. Science is in the business of judging what is true and what is false, so sentences that aren't capable of being put into either of these categories are of no use in serious discussion, they argued.

Examples (1)–(3) each represent one of the three categories of sentence that the logical positivists allowed as meaningful, and therefore appropriate to serious scientific or philosophical discussion:

1. All bachelors are unmarried.
2. Five plus seven equals twelve.
3. The Earth rotates around the Sun.

Examples such as (1) are meaningful because it is possible to decide about their truth, and in fact to do so simply by looking at the words they contain. That is, the very meaning of the subject and predicate of (1) ensure that it is necessarily true; 'bachelors' are by very definition 'unmarried'. In other words, you don't need to look beyond the properties of the language in which (1) is expressed, to the world around you or to the people in it, in order to establish that (1) is true. Example (1) is a case of an 'analytic' sentence. The logical positivists were not the first to identify analytic sentences as a separate category, but their philosophy depended in part on the special properties of this type of sentence. Example (2) is also true, and known to be true without having to refer to the world. It is not strictly an analytic sentence, because in this case it is the system of mathematics, rather than simply the language, which makes it true. That is, it is not possible for (2) to be anything other than true without the very rules of maths themselves changing. As long as maths stays as it is, (2) is true.

Example (3) is rather different, in that we do need to look beyond the sentence itself to the world in order to establish its truth. There are certain observations and scientific discoveries that have led us to accept (3) as true, but it is perfectly possible to imagine a different set of observations that would have led us to label it 'false'. That is, there is nothing in the meaning of (3) itself that makes it necessarily true; its truth is contingent on outside facts. Example (3) is a case of what is known as a 'synthetic' sentence: a sentence in which different elements are brought together to make a statement about how things are. The logical positivists didn't allow all synthetic sentences into their category of 'meaningful'. In fact, (3) belongs to a particular subset of synthetic sentences which, according to logical positivism, can be said to be meaningful. That is because it is possible for us to state what types of empirical observation have led us to accept (3) as true. Example (3) is the sort of statement that can be tested out against identifiable evidence or, to use the terminology of logical positivism, can be 'verified'. The stipulation that synthetic statements are meaningful only if they are verifiable ruled out many of the things that we can express perfectly easily in natural language as being simply meaningless. Anything that looked like a statement but for which there was no identifiable process of verification was dismissed by the logical positivists as outside of the boundaries of serious discussion. Most controversially, this necessarily included all religious, metaphysical or ethical statements, such as the following:

4. Theft is morally wrong.
5. God is good.

For the logical positivists statements such as these were not false; in fact in order to be defined as false they would need to be capable of being tested against relevant empirical evidence, just as they would in order to be defined as true. Rather, and perhaps in some people's eyes even more damningly for the logical positivists, such statements were simply meaningless. Because there was no way of testing them empirically, such sentences didn't succeed in stating any fact at all; they were pseudo-statements.

Reactions to the logical positivists' account of meaningfulness had profound effects on subsequent developments in philosophy, which in turn had consequences for the beginnings of pragmatics. We will consider these reactions in the next section, and further in the next chapter. In relation to our interest in the emergence of the term 'pragmatics' as a label for a certain area of language study, it is significant that an early usage can be found in the work of one of the leading logical positivists, Rudolf Carnap. In his later work Carnap produced some detailed studies of the structure of language, but because of his concerns about the misleading natural of natural language he chose to concentrate on artificial language. In fact, he was pessimistic about the chances of natural language ever being amenable to systematic analysis, a sentiment that would be at odds with subsequent developments in formal linguistics: 'in consequence of the unsystematic and logically imperfect structure of the natural word-languages (such as German or Latin), the statement of their formal rules of formation and transformation would be so complicated that it would hardly be feasible in practice' (Carnap 1937: 2). Carnap acknowledged that a full account of any language should pay attention to those who used it, and in this connection he used the term 'pragmatics'. Pragmatics for Carnap was concerned with any field where 'explicit reference is made to the speaker, or to put it in more general terms, to the user of the language' (Carnap 1938: 140). However, Carnap himself had little to say about this field of study.

3.3 Ordinary language philosophy

Logical positivism was philosophically fashionable for a fairly brief period. It came to the attention of English-speaking philosophers during the 1930s, to a large extent as a result of the publication of A. J. Ayer's enthusiastic account of it in his book *Language, Truth and Logic* (Ayer 1946). Many of them, particularly younger philosophers, were deeply influenced by this new approach and attempted to impose its tough restrictions on their own philosophical thinking.

They were impressed by the challenge it posed to traditional forms of philosophical speculation. They believed that it was going to overthrow many of the issues traditionally discussed in philosophy by revealing them to be 'pseudo-problems', dependent on unverifiable speculation rather than scientific fact. However, in the course of just a few years the tide of philosophical opinion began to turn. Even some of those who had initially greeted logical positivism most enthusiastically began to worry about the assumptions it made about some crucially important issues, like the nature of language and of meaning, and to be troubled by the rigid limitations on what it allowed to be meaningful, and therefore fit for philosophical inquiry. Historians of the period have suggested that the impact of logical positivism was effectively at an end by as early as 1940 (see for instance Lewey 1976).

One of the new directions in philosophy that was prompted by a reaction against logical positivism, and certainly the most significant one to our interest in the development of pragmatics, was what has become known as 'ordinary language philosophy'. The leading force in this approach was the Oxford philosopher J. L. Austin, and it dominated philosophy as practised at the University of Oxford for a decade or more following the Second World War. Austin's colleagues included P. F. Strawson, Paul Grice, Geoffrey Warnock and J. O. Urmson, all important philosophers in their own right. Austin and Grice, in particular, developed some specific theories of language that were to prove crucially important in the development of pragmatics, and we will look at these in detail in the next chapter. For now, we will briefly consider Austin's motivations in the work that established ordinary language philosophy.

Austin reacted against logical positivism on a number of different counts, but there were perhaps three main reasons for his objections, certainly three reasons that were particularly important to what he did in his own work. Firstly, he objected to the rather dismissive attitude to natural language that underpinned much of the work of the logical positivists: the attitude apparent in the quotation from Carnap about 'word languages' that we considered above. Austin believed that, on the contrary, natural language as it was used in everyday communication was of crucial importance. It wasn't simply that he thought it was an important topic for study in its own right, an underlying assumption of present-day linguistics. Rather, he believed that philosophers would do well to pay attention to ordinary language rather than to artificial logical or technical philosophical language, because it was naturally adapted to explain and describe human beings' experience and understanding of the world. He argued that the picture of the world described by what he called 'our common stock of words' had 'stood up to the long test of the survival of the fittest' (Austin 1956: 130).

Secondly, Austin took issue with the fact that, to the extent that logical positivism dealt with language, it focussed exclusively on language as a tool for making statements of fact. The linguistic examples that the logical positivists used were always declarative statements, and in fact were always declarative sentences which must be understood literally as descriptions of the world. This was in line with their interest in 'truth' or 'falsity' as the defining features of a meaningful use of language. Austin labelled this the 'descriptive fallacy': the mistaken belief that the chief or only philosophically interesting function of language was to make statements of fact that could be judged against appropriate evidence to be either true or false. Austin became interested in the ways in which language could be used to do all sorts of other things besides describing the world; it could be used to ask questions, give orders, make promises, issue threats, as well as a host of other purposes. He also observed the way in which apparent statements of fact are not always intended to be taken at face value; speakers sometimes exaggerate, or speak metaphorically, approximately or sarcastically. These are all valid and interesting uses of ordinary language, but they can't be explained within a theory that restricts meaningfulness to uses of language that fall into the rigid categories of 'true' or 'false'.

Thirdly, Austin wasn't convinced about the category of 'analytic' sentences, which was a crucial component of logical positivism. The definition of meaningfulness depended on being able to distinguish between analytic sentences, true simply by virtue of the words they contain, and synthetic sentences, dependent on external facts to make them true or false. Analytic sentences couldn't be verified, because their truth had nothing to do with anything outside of the language itself, but nevertheless they counted as meaningful, along with those synthetic sentences that could be verified. Austin was troubled by the distinction because it rested on an unquestioned assumption that words have fixed, settled meanings that could be depended on never to change and always to be understood in the same way by all speakers of a language. If words were not stable, fixed and uncontroversial in their meanings, then analytic sentences as a class simply couldn't exist, because there could be no guarantee that the meanings of the words they contained would always make them true. Austin considered the ways in which the meanings of words appeared to change depending on what context they occurred in, including the question of what other words they appeared next to or near. He argued that a consideration of these issues, entirely neglected by the logical positivist, would reveal that 'there is *no* simple and handy appendage of a word called "the meaning of (the word) 'x'"' (Austin 1940: 30).

Austin was not the only philosopher to be worrying about these aspects of logical positivism. As we have seen, there was a general trend at the time to take issue with its assumptions and the limitations these imposed on what philosophers could do with language. The American philosopher W. V. O. Quine, for instance, took issue with the analytic/synthetic distinction because of the unjustified assumption on which it rested that words have fixed, independent, universally recognized meanings (Quine 1951). In Cambridge, Ludwig Wittgenstein famously objected to any attempt rigidly to pin down linguistic meaning, and became associated with the slogan 'meaning is use' (Wittgenstein 1953). Even closer to home for Austin, his senior colleague at Oxford, Gilbert Ryle, argued that in discussing the significance of a word it was not appropriate to describe its 'meaning', but rather 'the role it is employed to perform' (Ryle 1957: 144). But Austin was different in that he actually tried to devise a method for studying ordinary language and the fluidity of meaning. However flawed and even amateurish it may now seem, especially in the light of developments over the last few decades in the storage and analysis of massive amounts of linguistic data, it was a genuine attempt to focus philosophers' attention on ordinary language and its use, and Austin claimed that it could be extremely revealing and informative.

Austin's method of study ideally involved collaborative work. A group of philosophers would gather together and select a particular topic or area of inquiry for investigation. Then they would draw up a list of vocabulary and phrases relevant to that topic, using the resources of their own knowledge of the language, backed up as necessary by consulting dictionaries and other technical books. Next they would consider the connections, similarities and differences between the words they had identified, thinking about what contexts they most naturally could and could not be applied in, and how their meanings might change depending on situation of usage. They would do this by considering imaginary scenarios or invented dialogues in which the words might appropriately be used. Finally, Austin and his colleagues would be in a position to say something systematic about an area of vocabulary, and therefore the aspects of human experience it was used to describe.

Austin was a controversial figure among his philosophical contemporaries. To his detractors (most notably Gellner 1959) he was an uncreative pedant: more like a lexicographer than a real philosopher. But he also had his admirers, some of whom saw ordinary language philosophy as an important new development that would do away with many of the problems that had traditionally beset philosophers, by revealing the mistakes made by those who assumed rather than studied what words mean. His work was to find its real home, however, in the field of linguistic pragmatics.

3.4   The beginnings of pragmatics

Austin studied meaning in natural language, particularly in terms of its dependence on changeable factors of context and situations of use. But he didn't describe his own work, or his subject matter, as being 'pragmatic'. Theories of ordinary language philosophy, particularly those developed by Austin and Grice, are nowadays seen as fundamental to pragmatics, but as far as the theorists themselves were concerned they were contributing to philosophy, not linguistics. The term 'pragmatics' was in use during the heyday of ordinary language philosophy and immediately afterwards, in connection with a very technical branch of the philosophy of language, along the lines envisaged by Morris and Carnap. In 1954 Yehoshua Bar-Hillel, who was later to coin the phrase 'the pragmatic wastebasket', drew attention to the prevalence of linguistic expressions that depend 'on the pragmatic context of their production' (Bar-Hillel 1954: 3459). He singled out expressions such as tensed verbs and personal pronouns, linguistic features of the type that pragmaticists now discuss as instances of deixis, and suggested a very formal account. Over a decade later, the mathematician Richard Montague, who had established a reputation for his formal and logical analysis of language, proposed a 'precise technical structure' (Montague 1968: 103) for pragmatics as it had been outlined by Morris.

By this time, linguistics was becoming established as an academic subject in its own right. It was dominated by interest in the formal structural properties of natural languages and the search for so-called 'linguistic universals'. In this it was heavily influenced by the still relatively new force of Chomskyan linguistics, with its emphasis on syntax as the primary focus of linguistic study and the key to the nature of natural human language. Chomsky argued that syntactic rules produced or generated a series of 'deep structures' that were subsequently formed into recognizable 'surface structures' by various 'transformational rules'. Interpretation was assigned subsequent to the production of deep structures by separate semantic rules. But some linguists, initially at least followers of Chomsky, became convinced that meaning should be much more central to linguistic theory. Under the heading 'generative semantics' they proposed a programme in which the rules of the grammar themselves were responsible for generating interpretations at the level of deep structure. As a result the deep structures of generative semantics, and the transformational rules that subsequently produced syntactic surface structures, were much more complex than in Chomsky's account. The generative semanticists quickly established that it would be desirable to find a principled way of explaining and modelling the relationships between language and the contexts in which it is used, or the effects of context on meaning. They found terminologies and theories that had been developed independently by the philosophers of ordinary language fitted their purposes well. These philosophical accounts therefore crossed over into linguistics, where they have subsequently received most attention.

Generative semantics itself eventually lost out to the more exclusively syntactic concerns of Chomskyan linguistics and it didn't really continue beyond the 1970s. But interest among linguists in how the relationships between context and meaning could be described and explained continued, now in the form of the branch of linguistics that became known as pragmatics. Within pragmatics, unlike in generative semantics, pragmatic principles were generally described as external to the formal structures of language itself, but acting in conjunction with linguistic rules to explain how speakers created and hearers interpreted meaning in context. To Chomsky and many of his followers this in fact seemed to be a more satisfactory situation; generative linguistics could again be as it were 'freed' from issues relating to speakers, hearers and contexts, topics which could be left to pragmatics. Speaking at a conference in 1969, Chomsky argued that if certain features of meaning 'can be explained in terms of general "maxims of discourse" ... they need not be made explicit in the grammar of a particular language' (Chomsky 1972: 113).

When the *Journal of Pragmatics* was established in 1977, its editors defined a place for their discipline that set it apart from the approach of formalists such as Montague. They argued that the pragmatics that was to be the subject of the journal was concerned with natural, not artificial, language. Montague had argued that there was no real distinction between the two, but for them '"natural languages" are a universal means of organising man's processing of nature, his structuring of experience, and his interaction with others. Artificial languages, on the other hand, cover only one aspect of man's activities at a time, and their reconstruction ("modelling") of natural language will therefore always be limited to this particular aspect' (Haberland and Mey 1977: 5).

Looking back on this time on the occasion of the twenty-fifth anniversary of the founding of the *Journal of Pragmatics* the same editors commented that:

> For us, it was obvious that the growing interest in linguistics and language perspectives in the 1970s was deeply rooted in society's need for language studies. The use of computer applications – computational linguistics, the re-awakened interest in machine translation, and the boom in artificial intelligence – the relevance of language studies for the social crisis management of linguistic, ethnic, and migrant minorities, and the emphasis on language in education planning and qualification design seemed to prove to us that the study of language was at the very core of important dynamics of modern society. Political relevance did not have to be constructed, it was 'always-already' *there*. (ibid. 2002: 1672)

Pragmatics continued to grow in stature as an academic discipline. By the 1980s text books on general linguistics frequently made reference to at least some work from pragmatics, and university departments of linguistics began to teach pragmatics as a subject in its own right. The discipline became wider in focus, including the study of many different aspects of language, context and communication. The International Pragmatics Association was established in 1986, with the aim of representing 'the field of pragmatics in its widest interdisciplinary sense as a functional (i.e. cognitive, social, and cultural) perspective on language and communication'. In 1989 Jacob Mey argued that pragmatics had now outgrown Bar-Hillel's 'wastebasket' analogy or, as he paraphrased it, 'pragmatics today is more than a rag-bag collection of ill-clad youngsters, claiming parentage in the higher ranks of linguistic society' (Mey 1989: 826).

The next chapter will begin back in the time before pragmatics had emerged as a field of linguistics, because it will be concerned with the theories of meaning and context developed by the philosophers of ordinary language. In Chapter 5 we will move forward to consider some of the subsequent developments, refinements and revisions of these in more recent pragmatics. Later chapters will take up the theme of the expansion and pervasive influence of pragmatics, looking at its impact on a variety of areas of linguistic inquiry and beyond.

FURTHER READING

Levinson (1983), Chapter 1, offers a brief but useful account of some of the different ways in which the term 'pragmatics' has been used since Morris.

The first book to introduce logical positivism in English, and still one of the best introductions to and overviews of this type of philosophy is Ayer (1946). For an argument from a philosophical point of view as to why the analytic/synthetic distinction is unempirical, see Quine (1951).

The impact of ordinary language philosophy on generative linguistics and from there to the emergence of pragmatics is discussed in Kasher (1982), Mey (1989) and Mey (1993). Lakoff (1989) concentrates in particular on attempts to incorporate the theories of ordinary language philosophy into linguistic description, undertaken by the generative semanticists.

The development and expansion of pragmatics over the last 30 years or so, particularly in relation to the *Journal of Pragmatics*, is documented in a series of editorials in that journal (Haberland and Mey 1977, 1989, 2002). Some articles published in the journal also engage with aspects of the history of pragmatics (see for instance Biletzki 1996; Korta 2008).

'Classical'
Pragmatics

4

In the last chapter we considered how ordinary language philosophy developed in the middle part of the twentieth century against a backdrop of philosophical approaches to language that were primarily concerned with logic and truth. J. L. Austin argued that philosophers should pay attention to how people actually used and understood language in their everyday lives. The descriptions of language and the theories about how it works in communication that were developed by Austin, and by others working broadly within the framework of ordinary language philosophy, were based on careful consideration of the significance of factors such as context, speakers' intentions and hearers' reactions. As we have seen, the philosophers of ordinary language didn't spend much time collecting and analysing actual instances of spontaneous language use – they weren't very empirical by the standards of present day linguistics – but they did base what they said about language on the premise that these factors, which didn't feature much if at all in the work of their philosophical contemporaries, were of central importance.

The descriptions of language that emerged from ordinary language philosophy have been of immense significance in the development of pragmatics. They are certainly not universally accepted without question by pragmaticists. But they have set the tone for how work in pragmatics, at least in theoretical pragmatics, has been conducted. As we will see in the next chapter, the development of pragmatics has in general been a story of responding to, revising and trying to solve the problems of the work of the ordinary language philosophers.

This chapter will be concerned with two related but separate theories, arguably the two most significant ideas to emerge from ordinary language philosophy, and certainly the two that have had the most impact on pragmatics. They can be viewed as the 'classical' theories of pragmatics – for two reasons. Firstly they are classical in the sense of being original or founding; whether supportive or critical, most of what has happened subsequently in pragmatics has been to some extent motivated by them. Secondly they are classical in the sense that they represent the establishment within the discipline: setting the standard for the types of explanation, the frameworks for analysis and in many cases the actual terminology used in pragmatics. We will consider first Austin's own account of language use, which has become known as 'speech act theory'. Then we will turn our attention to the ideas of Austin's Oxford colleague Paul Grice, and in particular to his work on what he called 'implicature'. In the next chapter we will consider some more recent responses to and refinements of these theories. After that we will look at how classical pragmatics, together with subsequent developments, has been used to study various different aspects of language and its use, and the impact it has had on other branches of linguistics and even on other academic disciplines.

4.1   Speech act theory

Austin's description of language use as a series of speech acts developed out of his dissatisfaction with what he described as the 'descriptive fallacy' among many philosophers of his day who wrote about language. As we saw in the last chapter, Austin became convinced that they placed too much emphasis on language as a vehicle for describing, or making statements about, how things are in the world. For Austin, this notion of the function of language was much too limited. The title of the book in which most of his ideas about speech acts were eventually published is *How to Do Things with Words*; Austin was interested in the host of different things that we do using language, not just in language as a vehicle for description.

Austin's opposition to the descriptive fallacy, and his ambitions for a different way of describing language, seem plausible and intuitively appealing. But reading about speech act theory, both in *How to Do Things with Words* itself and in later developments by those who worked in this area after Austin, involves dealing with a large, technical and potentially rather confusing array of terminology. This situation is not helped by the fact that Austin developed and changed his ideas and the particular words that he used to express them as he went along; even within *How to Do Things with Words* itself, the version of speech act theory presented by the end of the book is strikingly different from that found at the beginning. Of course this is evidence of speech act theory as a dynamic and fruitful area of study. Austin was constantly trying to find new and better ways to explain his insights. But it can prove rather confusing for those first trying to get to grips with speech act theory. We will work through the development of the theory, starting with Austin's account of 'PERFORMATIVES'. Although Austin became less convinced of the value of this term in his later work it makes an excellent starting point for understanding his aims and motivations. It is also an important term to understand in its own right, because it is still used by many writers in different fields of inquiry who want to make use of the basic premises of speech act theory.

Performatives

In identifying the 'descriptive fallacy' in philosophy, Austin was objecting to the assumption that the prime, or the only interesting, function of language was to make statements of fact. He wasn't denying that language can be used to make statements, but he was claiming that this should be recognized as just one of the many different things that we can do with words. Austin adopted the term 'CONSTATIVES' to identify this one specific type of use of language. Examples (1) and (2) below are constatives, both taken from *The Sun* newspaper on 30 June 2009. We can understand their specific features by comparing them with (3) and (4), which are both Austin's own examples:

1. Desperate Michael Jackson was spending £30,000 a month on prescription drugs.
2. The Met Office last night predicted the heatwave could hit a new high of 33°C (91°F) on Thursday.
3. I name this ship the *Queen Elizabeth* .
4. I give and bequeath my watch to my brother.

The constatives in (1) and (2) both report on some aspect of the world. They can both appropriately be said to offer a piece of information 'about' something. In the case of (1) this is a piece of information about the habits of a particular individual, the singer Michael Jackson, at the time of his death. Example (2) describes the issuing of a particular statement, a prediction of high temperatures, by a particular institution, the Meteorological Office. One way, perhaps the most obvious way, to assess these examples would be to ask whether or not they are true. Even if we can't immediately give a definite answer to this question, we can identify ways in which we could go about establishing the truth or otherwise of (1) and (2). We can assume that there would be documentation or personal testimonies available that would lead us to accept (1) as true or alternatively to reject it as false. And we can imagine the sort of printed or online written evidence that would satisfy us of the truth of (2).

The features of (1) and (2) that we have just identified are simply not shared by (3) and (4). They too are declarative sentences, but it doesn't really seem to make sense to say that they report on how the world is or that they are 'about' anything. We couldn't really offer a paraphrase of an event of situation described by (3) or (4), as we could for (1) and (2). Most strikingly of all, it simply doesn't seem appropriate to look into the question of whether (3) and (4) are 'true' or 'false'.

Austin introduced the new term 'performative sentence', or simply 'performative', to describe uses of language such as his examples (3) and (4). The term sums up his insight that rather than describing some situation or event in the world such examples actually perform an action. They bring about some sort of change in how the world is: typically a change in social or institutional relationships or facts. Performatives operate in individual contexts, and their effects are tied to the particular circumstances of their use. So someone uttering (3) or (4) is not actually describing an action in which they are engaged. They are there and then performing that action: the act of naming a ship in (3) and the action of giving and bequeathing a watch in (4). It would be odd to question whether such performatives were true or false, because actions are not the sort of thing that can be said to be either true or false. There are of course other sorts of judgements that can be applied to actions. In particular, they can be either appropriate or inappropriate in the context in which they occur, and this can determine whether they are successful or not. Significantly, Austin provided a short sketch of context for his examples. Example (3) is to be understood 'as uttered when smashing the bottle against the stern' and (4) 'as occurring in a will' (Austin 1962: 5). During the course of his work on speech acts, Austin adopted the term 'FELICITY CONDITIONS' to describe the particular conditions, or the set of circumstances, that have to be in place for a performative to count as successful.

The felicity conditions for examples such as (3) and (4) are very specific in nature and dependent on particular social situations and hierarchies. Even if you were smashing a bottle against a ship, (3) would completely fail to perform the act of naming a ship unless you were an invited dignitary taking part in an officially arranged ceremony. Similarly, you could write down (4) but you would succeed in leaving your watch to your brother only if the document you were producing were correctly worded, dated, witnessed and so on. Austin proposed that there were three distinct types of felicity conditions. The first type specified the need for the existence of certain conventional procedures and forms of words to perform a particular act, and further the need for the people involved in an individual act to be appropriate to that procedure. This explains why an example like (3) would not be successful if, for instance, uttered by an unruly member of the crowd rather than by the appointed VIP.

Austin's second type of felicity conditions state that 'The procedure must be executed by all participants both correctly and completely' (ibid.: 15). An interesting example of what can happen when there are doubts over whether this felicity condition has been met is provided by the controversy over the swearing in of Barack Obama as US president in January 2009. The inauguration of a president is, of course, exactly the sort of occasion on which there is a certain conventional procedure for performing an act using words. The presidential oath is set out in the US Constitution, and includes the promise 'to faithfully execute the office of president of the United States'. Between them the Chief Justice of the US Supreme Court and the new president stumbled over the words, so that Barack Obama actually promised 'to execute the office of the president of the United States faithfully'. A huge controversy followed as to whether the oath had in fact been taken successfully, and it could be seen as a testimony to the importance of felicity conditions that the decision was taken for the president to repeat the oath, this time using the correct form of words, two days later.

Austin's first two types of felicity conditions apply most obviously to very formal situations, such as naming a ship or swearing in a president. Indeed, many of the examples that Austin discusses early in *How to Do Things with Words* are of a very specific and formal or ritualized nature. They include words spoken during a marriage ceremony, during a baptism, during sentencing in a court of law, or when declaring war on another country. But Austin was aware that performatives play an important part in everyday lives as well as in the more formal or institutional settings. Examples (5), (6) and (7) below, adapted from Austin, are just some of the many types of performative that we might use without any particular institutional or ritualized framework:

5. I apologize for what I did.
6. I bet you five pounds that it will rain tomorrow.
7. I promise to be there on time.

Austin's third type of felicity condition is more obviously relevant to examples of this sort, because it has more to do with the personal psychological state of those taking part, than with the formal performance of the speech act. If someone undertakes to perform a speech act that is related to having certain thoughts, feelings or intentions then it's imperative that the person really has these. Acts such as promising or apologizing are examples of this sort; they don't really work unless the speaker actually intends either to do what is promised or to avoid the mistaken course of action in the future. Austin pointed out that performing a speech act in breech of this third type of felicity condition results in a different type of problem from the first two. If you try to perform a speech act when there is no established procedure in place, or alternatively when you don't follow the procedure correctly, as was arguably the case with Barack Obama, then you simply fail to achieve the intended act. However, if you perform an act such as promising, but do it insincerely, without the necessary intentions, then the act really is achieved – you really have promised – but you have misused, or abused, the procedure for promising.

The performatives we have considered so far, like the ones that Austin considered early in his work on speech acts, all have particular grammatical properties in common. They are all declarative sentences in the present tense. More specifically, they all have 'I' as the grammatical subject of an indicative verb ('name', 'give and bequeath', 'apologize', 'bet' and 'promise'). Austin suggested that performatives of this form were distinguished by the fact that it would be possible coherently to insert the adverb 'hereby' in-between the subject and the verb. So 'I hereby apologize for what I did' is acceptable because 'I apologize for what I did' is performative, but 'I hereby love Marmite' is distinctly odd, because 'I love Marmite' is descriptive or constative.

However, Austin was insistent that the class of performative utterances was defined functionally, not in terms of any specific grammatical properties. None of the grammatical properties of the examples we have considered so far were necessary for a sentence to count as a performative. In fact, the form of expression of a performative could vary more or less without limit; what was essential to the definition of a performative was that it performed some sort of action, not that it conformed to any particular grammatical pattern. In this way Austin introduced the importance of distinguishing between the 'form' of a sentence, which can be said more or less to correspond to its lexical and grammatical make-up, and the 'function' that the utterance fills in context. Austin proposed the term 'explicit performative' for the types of examples we have been considering so far, in which the speaker makes explicit what action is being performed. He draws attention to the many types of 'primary performatives' that can operate in the same way. In the pair below, (8) is a primary performative and (9) an explicit performative that does the same thing:

8. I shall be there.
9. I promise that I shall be there.

As Austin points out, in the case of the primary performative it is possible that we might remain uncertain as to exactly what act had been performed. We might therefore have to ask 'Is that a promise?'. We could receive answers such as 'Yes', or 'No, but I intend to be', or 'No, but I predict that I shall be'. Primary performatives, just like explicit performatives, require certain felicity conditions to be in place for their success. For instance, for either (8) or (9) to succeed as an act of promising, it is necessary that the speaker believes that she will be capable of being where she says she will be, and that she sincerely intends to act so as to ensure that she is there. Austin's central distinction, then, was that between constatives, dependent on conditions for truth, and performatives that might come in various different grammatical forms but were all dependent on conditions for felicity.

Illocutionary acts

In drawing attention to a distinction between constatives and performatives, Austin had established his reasons for objecting to the descriptive fallacy and for claiming that people routinely did many more things with words than simply making statements of fact. He had drawn attention to the fact that whereas some uses of language could be judged in relation to the labels 'true' and 'false', many others simply didn't fit these descriptions and should instead be described as being more or less successful, in relation to relevant felicity conditions. And he had demonstrated why in the study of language it's important to be able to distinguish between the 'form' of a particular expression and its 'function'. All these remained important features of speech act theory, and indeed have been founding assumptions of pragmatics. But Austin became dissatisfied with the actual terms 'constatives' and 'performatives'. He began to doubt that it was possible to draw such a clear and firm distinction as he had been suggesting, or that the terms were particularly useful in saying what he wanted to about language. So during the course of *How to Do Things with Words* he began to look for alternative ways of describing speech acts.

Austin distanced himself from his own distinction between constatives and performatives because he realized that, although he still wanted to maintain that both conditions for truth and conditions for felicity were important in explaining how we do things with words, it was far from clear that the former were restricted to constatives and the latter to performatives. He noted, for instance, that if an utterance of the performative 'I apologize' meets the relevant felicity conditions for it to succeed as an apology, then it follows that 'I apologize' is true as a descriptive statement, in other words as a constative. 'I warn you that the bull is about to charge' might appear to be straightforwardly performative. However, its success, or felicity, seems to depend on something that looks very like a truth condition: on the fact that the bull is about to charge. If the bull is not about to charge, Austin suggests, we would be likely to say not that the warning was void or unsuccessful, but that it was false.

In place of attempting to distinguish between constative and performative statements, Austin proposed a rethink of what it is that we do, or rather what collection of things we do, any time we say something. So Austin's attention switched from trying to classify speech acts into different types, to trying to define the common properties of all speech acts. He claimed that any time someone says something it is possible to identify three different acts that take place. Introducing some new terminology into speech act theory, Austin labelled these the 'LOCUTIONARY ACT', the 'ILLOCUTIONARY ACT' and the 'PERLOCUTIONARY ACT'. It is important to be clear from the outset that according to Austin all three acts are constituent parts of what happens when we speak. In analysing a speech act in relation to these terms, we aren't concerned with deciding which type of act we are dealing with; we will be dealing with all of them. The locutionary act, the illocutionary act and the perlocutionary act are different features of a single speech act. Which one we focus on will depend on what aspect of the speech act interests us most, although as we will see Austin makes it clear that he sees one of these aspects as the most significant.

In order to determine what locutionary act has been performed when someone has said something, we need to consider what the words spoken meant in the language she was speaking. So an account of a locutionary act basically goes no further than a report of what was said, filling out matters of disambiguation and reference assignment as required. Imagine that you are witness to a speaker, let's call her Lizzie, uttering (10) to a hearer, let's call him Freddie:

10. I wish you would stop shouting.

If you subsequently decided to tell someone what locutionary act had taken place, you would report that Lizzie uttered the words 'I wish you would stop shouting', and that on this occasion 'I' referred to Lizzie and 'you' referred to Freddie. In describing the locutionary act you wouldn't say anything about why Lizzie said this or what she was hoping to achieve. Information such as this is part of the illocutionary act. Austin pointed out that the illocutionary act is derived from the locutionary act, but it is determined by other factors as well as simply what was said. In particular, you can't be sure what illocutionary act was performed without knowing something about what was going on in the mind of the speaker. It might well be that Lizzie uttered (10) because she wanted to get Freddie to stop shouting. In reporting the illocutionary act you might say 'Lizzie asked Freddie to stop shouting', 'Lizzie begged Freddie to stop shouting' or 'Lizzie ordered Freddie to stop shouting', and so on. Which particular report is most accurate will depend on factors to do with Lizzie's state of mind, her relationship to Freddie, and so on.

The illocutionary act is distinct from the literal meaning of (10) – all Lizzie actually said was that she wished Freddie would stop shouting – but it is quite strongly associated with it for most speakers of English. This is so in the case of many different speech acts, perhaps most noticeably those when we are trying to get someone else to do something. We tend to be rather reluctant to issue direct orders to other people, so instead we say things that begin 'I wish you would ... ', 'please could you ... ', 'would you mind ... ', and so on. Austin pointed out that both locutionary and illocutionary acts are dependent on conventions. Locutionary acts are dependent on the basic conventions of the language; the meanings of the words chosen and the significance of the way they are put together grammatically. Illocutionary acts are determined by the conventions of language use within a society: for instance that when we say 'I wish you would ... ' we are very often trying to get someone else to do something. But unlike locutionary acts, illocutionary acts are not defined entirely in relation to conventions; they depend also on the intention of the speaker.

In describing an illocutionary act we confine ourselves to this combination of convention and intention. That is, we go no further than why the speaker used the locutionary act she did, or what she was hoping to achieve. Something else also happens when a speech act is performed; what is said has, or fails to have, a particular effect on the hearer, whether that be in terms of the hearer's subsequent actions or in terms of his emotions or thought processes. The effects or consequences of a speech act make up the perlocutionary act. As Austin points out, this may correspond to what the speaker was hoping for, but it may be very different from this, since it is not governed by convention. In reporting on the perlocutionary act in (10), we might say 'Lizzie persuaded Freddie to stop shouting', but we might equally well have to say 'Lizzie tried to persuade Freddie to stop shouting, but she only succeeded in annoying him further'.

Austin made it clear that for him the illocutionary act was by far the most interesting. It was the one most centrally concerned with why and how people use language. Describing an illocutionary act meant describing the 'performance of an act *in* saying something' (Austin 1962: 99). He argued that its significance had generally been overlooked by philosophers of language, because they tended not properly to distinguish it from the 'performance of an act *of* saying something' – the locutionary act. Austin was proposing a philosophy of language in which it was not possible to talk simply about 'the meaning' of a sentence or of a particular utterance of a sentence. Rather, for every occasion of speech, it was necessary to account for no fewer than three acts, or types of significance. Most importantly, Austin's account of speech acts was based on the premise that the literal meaning of words, determined by the rules of the language, might often be distinct from what the speaker meant by those words in a particular context. This idea was certainly present in his earlier account of the difference between the 'form' and the 'function' of performatives, but it was brought into even sharper focus by his account of locution and illocution as two separate acts. He proposed distinguishing between 'meaning', determined at the level of the locutionary act, and 'force', which was accounted for by the illocutionary act.

Perhaps not surprisingly, given Austin's observation about philosophers' tendency to overlook the importance of the distinction between the act in saying and the act of saying, he was criticized by some of his contemporaries for producing an account of meaning that was unjustifiably and unnecessarily complicated. These philosophers argued that the meaning of an expression was best explained in terms of how speakers of the language most readily interpret it. In the case of our example (10) above, the meaning of Lizzie's utterance simply is that she is trying to get Freddie to stop shouting. To separate off this aspect of meaning, label it 'illocutionary' and to insist that it was distinct from some basic but intuitively less accessible notion of literal meaning was to indulge in unnecessary abstraction. For Austin, the complication and abstraction involved was clearly worth it, in terms of being able to get to grips with the complex question of how language operates in context. And many of those working in present day pragmatics would agree with him. But the full power of his ideas perhaps emerged only after speech act theory had been developed further by others, and indeed only after a different account of language, developed within ordinary language philosophy, had found it worth while to make a similar distinction.

Classification of illocutionary force

Austin's final thoughts in *How to Do Things with Words* are about the desirability, and the problems, of classifying speech acts into a finite number of different types, dependent on their illocutionary force. He proposes a possible list, which he admits is little more than a first try or an intuitive guess, as to how speech acts might be arranged. He proposes five categories, which he names 'verdictives', 'exercitives', 'commissives', 'behabitives' and 'expositives'. These categories are distinguished for Austin in terms of types of verbs which appear in utterances with particular illocutionary forces. Verdicitives include examples such as 'acquit', 'convict' and 'rule'. They are concerned with delivering a finding based on evidence. Exercitives involve exercising power or influence in some way, in the form of making a decision about a particular course of action; examples include 'appoint', 'dismiss', 'order' and 'veto'. Commissives are those speech acts that commit the speaker to some future course of action. A typical commissive is 'promise'; other examples include 'undertake', 'intend' and 'guarantee'. Behabitives are orientated towards social interaction, concerned primarily with expressing reactions and attitudes to others' behaviour. Examples include 'apologize', 'thank', 'congratulate' and 'welcome'. Expositives are concerned with making clear how what is being said fits into its context, such as a particular conversation or argument. 'Deny', 'swear', 'concede' and 'testify' are some of Austin's examples of expositives.

   The brief and tentative nature of Austin's account of these categories can be read as a challenge to come up with something better, and there have been many attempts to formulate alternative classifications of speech acts. Perhaps the most influential of these is that developed by John Searle during the 1970s. Searle was a pupil of Austin's at Oxford who went on to become a distinguished philosopher of language in his own right. He disagreed with his former tutor in many ways, but he remained impressed by the power and importance of describing the use of language in terms of speech acts. Indeed, for Searle speech act theory was the key to understanding language as a whole, since 'speaking a language is performing speech acts' (Searle 1969: 16). Searle also retained the notion of 'illocutionary force'. Any speech act, he argued, consisted of a propositional content, or a description of some actual or possible situation, and an illocutionary force, or an intention or attitude of the speaker towards that content. Felicity conditions were important for Searle, as they had been for Austin, but he offered a more formal and systematized account of these, and used them as defining properties of different speech acts. Searle's felicity conditions included preparatory conditions (facts that needed to be in place before the speech act could successfully be performed), sincerity conditions (beliefs or attitudes that it was necessary for the speaker to hold) and essential conditions (what the speaker intended the speech act to be or to achieve). So, for example, Searle is able to distinguish formally between a request and an assertion as follows (where 'H' stands for hearer, 'S' for speaker, 'A' for some future act by H and 'p' for some proposition):

Request
Preparatory conditions: H is able to do A. S believes H is able to do A.
It is not obvious to both S and H that H will do A in the normal course of events of his own accord.
Sincerity condition: S wants H to do A.
Essential condition: Counts as an attempt to get H to do A.

Assertion
Preparatory conditions: S has evidence (reasons, etc.) for the truth of p.
It is not obvious to both S and H that H knows (does not need to be reminded of, etc.) p.
Sincerity condition: S believes p.
Essential condition: Counts as an undertaking to the effect that p represents an actual state of affairs. (ibid.: 66)

When he turned his attention to the business of classifying illocutionary forces into distinct groups or types, Searle argued that Austin had based his tentative list of types on different potentially performative verbs, rather than different speech acts, and that this had introduced various problems. For one thing, it was possible in different contexts for the same verb to occur with different illocutionary forces. Austin's own examples had demonstrated this. He had listed, for example, 'describe' as both a verdictive and an expositive, calling into question the rigidity of the distinction. More generally, there seemed to Searle to be no clear principle for classifying the different verbs that Austin considered. Searle's proposed classification of speech acts was in terms of illocutionary force, as opposed to choice of verb. His different categories of speech acts were to be defined in terms of what he calls 'illocutionary point', together with the related notions of 'direction of fit' and 'sincerity conditions'. This new notion of direction of fit is a way of accounting for how the words relate to the world; basically, the words used may be intended to fit the facts of the world, or the intention may be for the facts of the world in some way to change so as to fit the words used. There are two possible directions of fit: 'words-to-world', in which the intention is for the words to correspond accurately to the world, and 'world-to-words' in which the intention is to affect the world in such a way that it comes to fit the words.

Like Austin, Searle arrived at a classification of speech acts into five categories. The method by which he reached this classification, however, were rather different, as were the formality with which he defined the types and the nature of the types themselves. Searle's categories are: 'assertives', 'directives', 'commissives', 'expressives' and 'declarations'. These are broad accounts of the types of things that speakers typically do, rather than individual definitions of illocutionary acts. So, for instance, 'directives' include such individual acts as commanding, requesting, begging, asking, inviting, advising and challenging. Searle's five separate categories are each illustrated in examples (11)–(15) below:

11. The Earth is surrounded by a gravitational field.
12. Please come to my party.
13. I'm sorry for standing on your toe.
14. Well done on winning that race!
15. You're fired.

Assertives commit the speaker to something being the case. Directives are attempts by the speaker to get the hearer to do something. Commissives for Searle, as for Austin, commit the speaker to some future course of action. Expressives express a psychological state of the speaker towards some state of affairs. Declarations bring about some change in the world. In terms of direction of fit, we can distinguish between assertives and directives, for instance, by saying that in (11) the direction of fit is words-to-world (the words are intended to fit how the world is) but in (12) it is world-to-words (the words are intended to bring about a change in the world so that it fits the words).

Note that these examples don't contain explicit performative verbs, although they could of course be paraphrased so that they did ('you're fired' could be expressed as 'I fire you', for instance). They represent the different classes because of their illocutionary point. As Searle reminds his readers, individual verbs don't always relate to particular illocutionary forces. The verb 'advise', for instance, can be associated with a directive in (16) and an assertive in (17):

16. I advise you to leave. (directive)
17. Passengers are hereby advised that the train will be late. (assertive)

Searle drew an interesting moral from his five-way classification of speech acts, concerning the number of different things that people actually do with words: 'if we adopt illocutionary point as the basic notion on which to classify uses of language, then there are a rather limited number of basic things we do with language: we tell people how things are, we try to get them to do things, we commit ourselves to doing things, we express our feelings and attitudes and we bring about changes through our utterances. Often we do more than one of these at once in the same statement' (Searle 1975b: 29).

This idea that people are capable of doing more than one thing within the same statement underlies one of Searle's most important contributions to speech act theory: his account of 'indirect speech acts'. Searle developed and discussed his notion of indirect speech acts particularly in relation to directives. We will concentrate on directives here, although in theory it can be used to describe speech acts in any one of Searle's categories. It is no coincidence that directives are most frequently performed indirectly. Getting someone else to do something is a socially tricky act to perform. If you want to get someone to pass you the jam, for instance, you could use an explicit performative as in (18) or an imperative as in (19), but you would be much more likely to use one of the forms of words in (20)–(23), and would probably be more successful if you did:

18. I order you to pass me the jam.
19. Pass me the jam!
20. I wonder if I could trouble you for the jam?
21. Can you reach the jam?
22. I would like you to pass the jam.
23. You could pass the jam.

Certainly these examples are all directives and all have the same illocutionary point, but that is not at all the same thing as saying that they all have the same meaning. According to Searle, examples such as (20)–(23), unlike (18)–(19), have the function of performing directives in addition to performing some other illocutionary act; 'the speaker issues a directive *by way of* asking a question [in (20) and (21)] or making a statement [in (22) and (23)]' (Searle 1975a: 43). The primary illocutionary act in all these cases is to issue a directive, but in (20)–(23) there is also another secondary, or literal, act. The form of expression may be highly conventionalized – asking a question such as (21), for instance, is a very common way to try to get someone to do something for you – but that is not the same as saying that it has the directive force as part of its literal meaning, or even that it is linguistically ambiguous between a question and a request.

In support of this claim that directive force is not part of the literal meaning of an example such as (21), we need only recognize the fact that in some contexts it can occur without any such force. Imagine that the speaker is the host at a tea party and the hearer is her guest. The hearer, but not the speaker, currently has some bread and butter on her plate. In such circumstances, (21) is highly unlikely to be interpreted as a request; it is more likely to be a genuine question about the hearer's ability or even a polite offer to pass him the jam. Furthermore, even when such a speech act can be interpreted as a directive, it still retains its more core meaning of a question. The person addressed can reply in terms of his ability, as in (24Bi), or can respond to both the literal question and the indirect directive, as in (24Bii):

24. A: Can you reach the jam?
    Bi: No, sorry, it's too far from me.
    Bii: Yes I can [passes the jam over].

Searle's suggested explanation as to why such forms of words are so frequently used indirectly to make requests, and of how they are so easily interpreted as they are intended, relates to his own definitions of different illocutionary forces in terms of their felicity conditions. Remember some of the felicity conditions for directives: a preparatory condition was that the hearer (H) was able to perform the act (A) in question. A sincerity condition was that the speaker (S) wants H to do A. If we look at the indirect speech acts above, we can see that (21) is literally a question about whether the preparatory condition is met, and (23) is literally a statement that it is. Similarly, (22) is literally a statement that the sincerity condition holds. Searle proposes that, among other common devices, a speech act can be performed indirectly by stating that a preparatory condition for it holds, by questioning whether a preparatory condition for it holds or alternatively by stating that a sincerity condition for it holds.

With Searle's work on indirect speech acts the commitment to different levels or types of meaning within a single utterance became even more deeply ingrained in speech act theory. This commitment was already apparent in Austin's work, with his controversial division of speech acts into the locutionary, the illocutionary and the perlocutionary, and more generally with his insistence that surface form doesn't always relate to intended function. Searle was now arguing that a single utterance could have a force close to its linguistic meaning and another further force that relied, not on the language itself, but the conventions by which the language was used in a particular society, as well perhaps as the individual's specific intentions. We will be returning to ideas developed in speech act theory in later chapters. In Chapter 6 we will see that they have been important in the development of theories of linguistic politeness and in frameworks for describing children's acquisition of language; and in Chapter 7 we will consider how they have been used in relation to recent studies of spoken language in corpus linguistics. For now, however, we will turn our attention to another theory of language use initially developed within the framework of ordinary language philosophy. The issue of the nature, and the viability, of different levels of meaning remains with us.

4.2 Implicature

Speech act theory has a lot to say about various differences between the literal meaning of the words we use and the force of what we can do with them. When it was first developed it was one of the earliest attempts to offer a systematic account of these differences, and as a result it became an important factor in the establishment of pragmatics. However, there are many aspects of the distinction between literal and intended meaning that speech act theory can't really explain.

Classifying language uses in terms of types of illocutionary force can ultimately go no further than proposing a list of the different functions that language can perform. As we have seen, Searle claimed that the basic list was actually strikingly short, and that there were principled ways of determining which function or functions were intended by a speaker on any particular occasion. But there are many ways in which what we literally say differs from what we patently mean – we might informally say many ways in which we get our message across indirectly – which can't be explained in terms of a list of illocutionary forces. Consider examples (25)–(26):

25. Pietersen's performance felt subdued at times as England looked to dig their way out of a small hole at 90 for three shortly before lunch.
   [*Report on the first day of the Ashes cricket tournament in* The Guardian, *Wednesday 8 July 2009*]
26. *Anne*: My ex-husband has just told me he can't look after our daughter tomorrow after all.
   Bess: He's such a considerate man!

There is an obvious way in which literal and intended meaning differs in each of these examples. If we tried interpreting (25) literally we would come up with something that was patently false, in fact absurd: the proposition that an entire cricket team were trapped in a little hollow, perhaps in the middle of the cricket pitch, and that they were attempting to move the soil away so that they could get out, perhaps using their hands or small spades. We recognize instead that (25) includes a metaphorical use of language. What the sports journalist meant was that the team were in slight difficulty and had to act in a way most likely to resolve this. We also have a clear sense that the literal meaning of Bess's words in (26) can't tell us everything about what she meant, although without further knowledge we might be a bit unsure as to exactly what she did mean. It is perhaps most likely that she is speaking sarcastically; that she is saying the opposite of what she really means, in order to convey in a humorous way her opinion that the ex-husband in question is extremely inconsiderate. If Bess does genuinely believe that he is considerate, however, it's possible that she means to convey something else by what she says; that his behaviour is surprising and out of character, for instance, or that there must be some explanation for it. Note that we are not tempted to say that the comment about the hole in (25) simply means that the team were in trouble, or that Bess's remark in (26) simply means that the ex-husband is inconsiderate. It is perfectly possible for these same forms of words to be used in different contexts to describe people really trying to get out of a hole or a man who is really considerate. What we need is a way of describing how we know when words are being used literally and when they are being used non-literally, and hopefully also a way of explaining how we know what that non-literal meaning is.

The fact that what we literally say and what we clearly mean often differ is intuitively obvious but difficult to describe or explain systematically. This was one of the driving forces behind the work of Paul Grice, another philosopher of ordinary language. Like Austin, Grice was convinced that any account of meaning that focussed on the conditions that make propositions true or false would be inadequate to explain the use of natural language. We might want to say that both the comment about digging out of a hole in (25) and the praise for the ex-husband in (26) are literally false. But that doesn't of course prevent them from making significant, interesting and possibly true contributions in the particular contexts in which they occur. However, unlike Austin, Grice was interested in developing a systematic explanation of how and why literal and intended meaning differ. What he was looking for was an account of the particular features of how language is used in communication that would be able to explain the full, diverse and potentially baffling array of ways in which people use language non-literally. It is worth bearing in mind that, although Grice was a near contemporary of Austin's, working on similar problems and in some ways going beyond what Austin was able to do by way of explanation, he was not straightforwardly responding to speech act theory or attempting to improve on it. In fact, the two philosophers appear to have been developing their theories at much the same time as each other and with little reference to each other's work. Austin's and Grice's theories do rather different things from each other so they are not necessarily incompatible. Austin was attempting to show how literal meaning is not always the best guide to the host of functions that language can be used to perform. Grice was attempting to show how the differences between literal meaning and what speakers can convey in context were not random and unpredictable, but rather can be explained in relation to some general principles of language use.

Whereas Austin had distinguished between three different types of acts – the locutionary, illocutionary and perlocutionary – performed any time someone spoke, Grice focussed on two different versions, or levels, of meaning. These he labelled 'WHAT IS SAID' and 'what is implicated'. Grice's account of 'what is said' was never very fully elaborated, but we can take it as being more or less equivalent to literal meaning. He acknowledged that as well as the conventional meaning of the words used it must include information about reference assignment (the identity of 'he' in (26), for instance) and, if necessary, the disambiguation of any ambiguous words or phrases. He points out that 'what is said' is that aspect of overall meaning contributed straightforwardly by linguistic knowledge: 'given a knowledge of the English language, but no knowledge of the circumstances of the utterance, one would know something about what the speaker had said' (Grice 1975: 25). We can relate 'what is said' to the truth-conditional meaning of the sentence uttered. If we know the language used we know what conditions would have to be in place for the sentence to be true. This is of course not at all the same thing as knowing what conditions would have to be in place for what the speaker intended to convey to be true. 'What is said' is very important in explaining meaning in general – even in cases where what a speaker intends seems to differ markedly from literal meaning we need to understand what was said as a necessary starting point – but it can't tell us everything. We need to add to it information about what is implicated, or about any implicatures that are conveyed by the saying of 'what is said'. The word 'implicature' is specific to this area of pragmatics; Grice coined it himself because he couldn't find a word already in existence that covered the very specific type of meaning that he was interested in describing. Much of Grice's work on language was concerned with the different ways in which what is implicated can be derived from 'what is said'.

Conventional implicature

According to Grice's classification of types of meaning there is one form of implicature which, although distinct from 'what is said', seems to be dependent on the actual meaning of the words used. It is a property of certain words that when they are used, as well as contributing to 'what is said', they also give rise to this form of implicature, which Grice labelled 'CONVENTIONAL IMPLICATURE'. The example with which Grice introduced conventional implicature is (27), which we can contrast with (28):

27. He is an Englishman; he is, therefore, brave.
28. He is an Englishman; he is brave.

The only difference between (27) and (28), of course, is the presence of the adverb 'therefore'. Grice's contention is that this introduces into (27) the implicature that the referent of 'he' is brave as a consequence or result of the fact that he is English. No such relationship between the two parts of the statement is implicated in (28). Grice argues that the 'as a consequence' meaning of 'therefore' is an implicature rather than an element of 'what is said' because it is not part of the truth-conditional meaning of (27). That is, if you didn't agree with either the statement 'He is an Englishman' or with the statement 'he is brave', you would say that (27) was false. But if you agreed that both these statements were true but not with the idea that there was any connection between these two facts, you would be unlikely to say that (27) was strictly false. Grice doesn't make clear what (27) would in fact be in such circumstances, but it seems feasible to suggest that it would be in some way misleading or inappropriate.

Another canonical example of conventional implicature is (29) below, which Grice originally drew attention to, and which has been discussed in a similar way to (27) by many of his commentators:

29. She is poor but she is honest.
30. She is poor and she is honest.

In truth-conditional terms, or with regard only to 'what is said', there is no difference between (29) and (30). If it is true that she is poor and true that she is honest, then both (29) and (30) are equally true. The meaning of contrast, or of something unexpected, that is introduced into (29), is a conventional implicature introduced by the presence of the word 'but'. It relies entirely on the presence of this particular word, as is apparent when 'and' is substituted in (30) and no such meaning occurs. But it is not part of what is literally said when 'but' is used. If you were to disagree that she was poor or that she was honest, then you would be inclined to say that (29) was false. But if you objected to the suggestion that it is surprising that someone could be both poor and honest, your objection to (29) would be of a different, non-truth-conditional kind.

Grice said little more about conventional implicature, although he did acknowledge that more work was needed on this topic. Its status, and indeed its very existence, has remained a very controversial issue in pragmatics. Karttunen and Peters (1979) took Grice's notion of conventional implicature very seriously, because they saw it as one way of dissolving the problematic category of semantic presupposition; many apparent examples of presupposition could simply be reanalysed as conventional implicatures, while others could be explained in terms either of conversational implicatures or of preparatory conditions for speech acts. They proposed a formal treatment of conventional implicature within the framework of Montague grammar. In doing so they expanded considerably on Grice's original examples, including in the category both particles like 'too', 'either', 'also', 'even', 'only' and also the apparently presuppositional meanings of verbs such as 'forget', 'realize', 'take into account', 'manage' and 'fail'. Of Karttunen and Peters's proposed additions to the list, examples such as 'even' have gained the most currency in subsequent discussions of conventional implicature. They argue that (31) and (32) are truth-conditionally equivalent. The suggestion that it is in some way surprising that Bill likes Mary, present in (31) but not in (32), is the result of the conventional meaning of 'even', but this is implicated rather than literally said. As they put it, 'the truth of what [31] actually SAYS depends solely on whether Bill likes Mary' (ibid.: 12):

    31. Even Bill likes Mary.
    32. Bill likes Mary.

Many of Karttunen and Peters's proposed expansions of the category of conventional implicature have not been generally accepted, however. Gazdar (1979) criticizes their inclusion of verbs like 'fail' and 'try' on the grounds that they were going against the original definition of conventional implicature, according to which the meaning in question must arise solely from the conventional meaning of the word in question, and not from any contextual factors.

Levinson (1983) argues that the phenomena that Karttunen and Peters discuss have entirely different properties from conventional implicature. He does propose extensions to the concept of his own, however, which he sees as being more within the original spirit of conventional implicature. Levinson suggests that what he terms 'discourse-deictic' items – such as 'however', 'moreover', 'besides', 'anyway', 'well', 'still', 'furthermore', 'although', 'oh' and 'so' – and 'social-deictic' items – such as 'sir', 'madam', 'mate', 'your', 'honour', 'sonny', 'hey' and 'oi' – have just the same properties as Grice identified for conventional implicature. They don't make any difference to the truth conditions of the expressions they occur in when they are used, but as part of their conventional meaning they do convey information about social relations or the status of some piece of information.

Both Gazdar and Levinson acknowledge that, since conventional implicatures are defined as aspects of conventional meaning that are not part of what is literally said when an expression is used, the category itself implies that there must be room for pragmatic aspects of meaning within the description of a language, not just in discussions of its use. As Gazdar put it, 'the dictionary entry for "but" would have to have some pragmatic component that would specify its implicature potential' (Gazdar 1979: 38). For Levinson, 'a lexicon for a natural language will contain reference to pragmatic components of meaning' (Levinson 1983: 129–30).

Karttunen and Peters may have used conventional implicature as a means of obviating the need for a separate category of presupposition, but others have argued that conventional implicature itself is an unnecessary category that pointlessly complicates discussions of meaning. Bach (1999) argued that conventional implicature was a misguided notion, based on some not fully inspected intuitions about meaning. For Bach, many supposed examples of conventional implicature were in fact part of 'what is said' on any occasion of use, but because they contributed to a secondary or less important proposition, they didn't readily introduce intuitions of falsity.

A recent defence and reassessment of conventional implicature is proposed by Potts (2005). Although he seeks to base his account on Grice's original definition, he distances himself from many of the early discussions of the topic by choosing not to focus on words such as 'but', 'therefore' and 'even'. In fact, one of his claims is that words introducing conventional implicatures don't also introduce what he calls 'at-issue' meanings. This is Potts's term for asserted content or for Grice's 'what is said'. Terms that introduce conventional implicatures, he claims, are not concerned with contributing to at-issue meaning, but to guiding the discourse or to signposting what is important. As he acknowledges, this stipulation in fact has the controversial consequence of ruling out 'but' itself from the category; 'but' includes the meaning of 'and', which is part of the at-issue content, as well as the supposed conventional implicature of contrast (Potts 2005: 8).

In place of the traditional markers of conventional implicature, Potts proposes that the category is most centrally illustrated by supplements and expressives. Both add some comment to the main or at-issue content. Supplements include relative clauses and utterance modifying adverbials. Expressives include markers of emotional attitude, such as 'damn', as well as honorifics. Potts describes them as adding 'discourse-new, speaker-orientated entailments' (ibid.: 13). Contrary to the assumptions of linguists such as Gazdar and Levinson, Potts argues that conventional implicature as a category does not suggest that linguistic descriptions of meaning need to take account of pragmatic as well as semantic factors. Rather, conventional implicature is itself a semantic feature, part of the core linguistic description of individual words or phrases. Potts suggest that, because Grice coined the term in his lectures on 'Logic and Conversation', conventional implicatures are generally taken to be pragmatic phenomena, 'but none of their main properties follows from pragmatic principles. They are narrowly grammatical entailments' (ibid.: 38).

Note that we'll be returning to some of the types of expressions that have been claimed to belong to the category of conventional implicature in the next chapter, when we look at the rather different type of analysis and explanation advanced within relevance theory.

Conversational implicature

After his brief outline of conventional implicature, Grice moved on to the much more complicated task of describing and explaining the types of implicature that depend not on the conventional meaning of the words used but on principles or regularities concerning how people use language in general. That is, while knowledge of the language is enough to understand 'what is said' and what is conventionally implicated, this needs to be supplemented by knowledge about language use before a full understanding of what has been conveyed by a particular utterance can be reached. 'What is said' feeds into a hearer's understanding of what is implicated in this way but is not sufficient on its own. The hearer needs also to assume that the speaker is adhering to general principles of language use and to take into account various aspects of the context of utterance. Grice labelled this type of implicature 'conversational implicature', a name that demonstrates that, unlike conventional implicature, it is dependent on aspects of the context in which it occurs. Grice didn't in fact have much to say about the specific properties of conversation; for him the term was a convenient way of summing up what people typically do when they use language to communicate with each other.

Grice's central claim was that an overarching principle of human interaction, not limited to conversation but perhaps most interestingly apparent there, was an impulse towards cooperative behaviour. He summed this up in relation to language use in what he labelled the 'cooperative principle': 'make your conversational contribution such as is required, at the stage at which it occurs, by the accepted purpose or direction of the talk exchange in which you are engaged' (Grice 1975: 26). The cooperative principle is expressed as an imperative and this, together with certain associations of the word 'cooperation', can make it sound rather like a rule of etiquette or a guide to good social behaviour. But rather than telling people how they ought to behave, Grice was in fact interested in trying to pin down the general norms by which people actually operate. In effect, whether we realize it or not we tend to act in accordance with this principle and to assume, sometimes in the face of apparently strong evidence to the contrary, that other people are acting in this way too. Cooperation in Grice's use of the word doesn't really have anything to do with being nice to each other or with trying to be helpful. In fact, as we will see, it is often when people are being less than nice, or apparently behaving in a particularly unhelpful way, that the cooperative principle can really start to explain how we understand that what they mean is rather different from what they are saying.

The cooperative principle may be a general norm, but it doesn't say anything very specific about how people actually behave or what being cooperative in this specialized sense would involve. To do this, Grice suggested some specific ways in which behaviour, including conversational behaviour, can adhere to the cooperative principle. He suggested that there are various maxims for behaviour that together constitute the way in which we follow the cooperative principle, and that can be divided into four different categories. Grice was somewhat hesitant about the precise phrasing of the maxims, and indeed about how many there should actually be, but it's worth seeing them all together in his original formulation, because they underpin what he said about conversational implicature and are the basis of many of the subsequent responses to and proposed revisions of his work:

Category of Quantity

1. Make your contribution as informative as is required (for the current purposes of the exchange).
2. Do not make your contribution more informative than is required.

Category of Quality
1. Do not say what you believe to be false.
2. Do not say that for which you lack adequate evidence.

Category of Relation
1. Be relevant.

Category of Manner
1. Avoid obscurity of expression.
2. Avoid ambiguity.
3. Be brief.
4. Be orderly.

The Category of Quantity is concerned with the amount of information that it is appropriate to give in a conversational contribution. It consists of two maxims that in effect require that speakers give enough but not too much information. The Category of Quality is concerned with the truthfulness of a contribution. The two maxims of Quality together require that speakers make their contributions true. The Category of Relation contains just one maxim and this also relates to the information that the speaker provides. The maxims in the Category of Manner, however, relate more to how the information is conveyed, rather that to the information itself. They are, as Grice acknowledges, a rather various and possibly incomplete list.

The cooperative principle, as detailed in the maxims of conversation, explains how 'what is said' can lead to what is implicated. The key to understanding this is to remember that, according to Grice, a hearer will interpret what is said to him on the assumption that the speaker is adhering to the cooperative principle and will cling to this assumption even when faced with an utterance that might look less than cooperative or even downright uncooperative. The hearer interprets what he hears in a way that will make it consistent with observation of the cooperative principle; anything that the hearer has to add to 'what is said' in order to do so is a conversational implicature.

Perhaps most straightforwardly, many conversational implicatures arise as a simple and generally unnoticed consequence of the speaker straightforwardly observing the maxims and the hearer assuming that this is the case. Consider the exchange in (33):

33. *Visitor*: I'd like to read today's newspaper.
    Local: There's a shop round the corner.

The local has certainly led the visitor to believe that the shop is one that sells newspapers. But notice that this is not part of the literal content of her utterance or 'what is said'; all she has actually said is that there is a shop round the corner. The visitor would probably be rather annoyed if he walked round the corner and found that there was indeed a shop there, but that it was a clothes shop or a greengrocers. He would be forced to concede, however, that what the local had said to him was not actually false; she said that there was a shop and here was the shop. But it was certainly misleading or unhelpful in the context because she led him to believe that what she was saying was relevant to his wish. So the proposition that the shop was one that sold newspapers was a conversational implicature of the local's utterance, based on the assumption that she was adhering to the maxim of Relation.

On some occasions, however, what a speaker literally says may not just need something added to it in order to understand how it conforms to the cooperative principle. Rather, 'what is said' may appear to go quite blatantly and deliberately against what is expected, such that a completely new interpretation is needed if the assumption of cooperation is to be maintained. Grice describes this process as one in which a speaker 'flouts' a maxim for communicative effect. Examples of this sort are central to understanding conversational implicature and how it works. They are also perhaps the single biggest source of potential misunderstandings of Grice's theory; they look like examples of speakers doing exactly what Grice says they don't do and being uncooperative, whereas in fact they are examples of people being entirely cooperative. That is, utterances that are indeed extremely uncooperative in terms of 'what is said' can turn out to be extremely cooperative once we take account of what is implicated. Let's consider some examples, which are adapted or updated from Grice:

34. *Guest A*: What a boring party this is.
    Guest B: We've had such lovely weather this month.

On the face of it, that is considering only 'what is said', Guest B would appear to be being very uncooperative by saying something which is completely unrelated to what Guest A has said. However, Guest A will be reluctant simply to give up on the person he is talking to as bizarrely uncooperative. Rather, sticking with an assumption that she is adhering to the cooperative principle, and noticing that what she has said seems to be blatantly in breach of the maxim of Relation, he will seek an alternative, implicated interpretation. Guest B certainly seems to be implicating that what Guest A has said is not an appropriate topic of conversation. Depending on the context it may simply be that she doesn't want to be drawn into this sort of negative talk; it may be that she is a friend of the host and finds the remark offensive; or it may be that she knows that the host is within earshot so they had better change the subject at once. In any case, her remark was not randomly irrelevant but was motivated:

35. Boys will be boys.

This is an example of a statement that is literally completely uninformative but that is nevertheless used, and used meaningfully. On the face of it, in terms of 'what is said', it seems to offer so little information as to be simply trivial; it seems to be in breach of the first maxim of Quantity. However, imagine that (35) is uttered by someone watching a group of boys behaving in an exuberant and rowdy manner. The person she was talking to would be unlikely to dismiss what she was saying as a pointless tautology. Rather, he would understand her as having implicated things that were neither tautologous or pointless: perhaps that every group of boys behaves in much the same way, that the children shouldn't be scolded for their behaviour, or that the way in which boys play is strikingly different from the way in which girls do. The speaker has flouted the first maxim of Quantity in order to communicate a conversational implicature:

36. You are the sunshine of my life.

If spoken to a fellow human being (36) is literally, clearly and absurdly false. It is simply not possible for a person to be sunshine. But it's false only at the level of 'what is said'. When addressed to a particular person, its obvious falsity will prompt a further non-literal interpretation: that the person in question has certain, but only certain, qualities in common with sunshine, such as the ability to bring pleasure and happiness. That is, the speaker has flouted the first maxim of Quality in order to convey a conversational implicature. This, in fact, is Grice's explanation of how metaphors in general work.

Grice describes all cases where a maxim is flouted in order to convey a conversational implicature, which include what we might describe as 'figures of speech' such as metaphor, as examples that involve exploitation of the expectations of cooperation. In some particular instances the apparent disregard of a maxim may lead to a conversational implicature not because the speaker is blatantly flouting the maxim, but because she is not in a position to observe the maxim without going against a different maxim. That is, she is faced with a clash of two maxims. Here is Grice's example:

37. *A*: Where does C live?
    B: Somewhere in the South of France.

B might appear to be going against the demands of the first maxim of Quantity, by not giving as much information as is required by A's question. However, she isn't doing so in order to flout the maxim. She is doing so because she couldn't give any more information without disregarding the second maxim of Quality, which requires that she doesn't say anything for which she has no adequate evidence. She is faced with a clash between the first maxim of Quantity and the second maxim of Quality. She conversationally implicates that she doesn't know precisely where C lives.

There are two further ways in which speakers go against the requirements of the maxims. Unlike in cases of flouting which leads to exploitation, neither of these generate implicatures. Firstly, a speaker may simple violate one or more of the maxims: she may simply choose to disregard them. The maxims, after all, are not rules that we are bound by but are conversational norms. Perhaps the most obvious example of violating a maxim is lying. If someone tells a lie she is simply choosing to disregard the maxims of Quality. This is different from flouting the maxims of Quality, as in (36) above, because there is no intention that the breach of the maxim be recognized so as to lead to a different implicated meaning. The purpose of flouting is to disregard the maxim at the level of 'what is said' so blatantly that the hearer arrives at a different interpretation at the level of what is implicated. The purpose of lying is to disregard the maxim in a way that is not detected, so as to deceive.

Secondly, a speaker might choose explicitly to opt out of the cooperative principle. Unlike in the case of violating, there is no intention to deceive or to conceal the non-fulfilment of a maxim, but unlike in flouting there is no intention that the deliberate disregard for a maxim should give rise to a conversational implicature. Rather, the speaker is straightforwardly pointing out that she will not be acting in accordance with one or more of the maxims, usually because some more pressing concern overrides cooperation. A classic case is that of a politician asked about a recent allegation or scandal. Any of the following would be familiar possible replies:

38. No comment.
39. I have nothing to say on this matter.
40. I'm afraid I can't go into that for legal reasons.

In each case, the politician's utterance indicates that she will not be following the demands of a maxim, in this case the first maxim of Quantity. Cases where speakers opt out can be interesting in relation to the cooperative principle because, although the speakers are not interested in communicating anything by means of the cooperative principle, they do still demonstrate an awareness of the usual expectations of cooperation. They feel the need explicitly to state that they will not be observing a maxim, as in (39), and perhaps also to offer some explanation or excuse for this, as in (40).

In the course of his lectures on 'Logic and Conversation', Grice introduced a number of defining properties of conversational implicatures. These can be used as tests for conversational implicature: ways of determining whether a particular aspect of utterance meaning is a conversational implicature, rather than a conventional implicature or part of 'what is said'. They also together build up a picture of how and why conversational implicature is different from these two forms of conventional meaning: that is, why it is necessary to distinguish it as a separate type of meaning. There are five distinct identifying properties of conversational implicatures; they are cancellable, reinforceable, non-detachable, calculable and non-conventional.

These properties can be illustrated in relation to a single relatively straightforward conversational implicature, such as that in (41) below:

41. *She*: Have you put out the lights and locked the doors?
    He: I've put out the lights.

In this case, all he actually says is that he has put out the lights, but he implicates that he has not locked the doors. It would have been both relevant and appropriately informative for him to tell her that he had locked the doors. On the assumption that he is observing the cooperative principle, she is likely to assume that the reason he has not said anything about the doors is not that he is ignoring the maxims, and particularly the first maxim of Quantity, but rather that he is not in a position truthfully to say that he has locked them.

The first defining property of conversational implicature is that it is cancellable. Because it isn't part of the literal content of an utterance, it's possible to add something that is logically incompatible with it, without thereby committing yourself to something that is simply contradictory. You can't cancel 'what is said', at least not without producing an utterance that is self-contradictory and therefore sounds very odd:

42: *He*: !I have put out the lights, but I haven't put out the lights.

However, it is possible explicitly to cancel an aspect of meaning that is conversationally implicated, as in (43):

43. *He*: I have put out the lights; in fact, I've also locked the doors.

In such cases the conversational implicature is simply cancelled or disappears. Grice suggests that conversational implicatures can be cancelled if they are inconsistent with some aspect of the context as well as by the addition of a specific clause such as this.

A related feature of conversational implicature is reinforceability. Just as the meaning conveyed as a conversational implicature can be cancelled without contradiction, so too it can be reinforced without redundancy, or without a sense that the speaker is simply repeating herself. Reinforcing what has been said generally leads to a sense of rather pointless repetition, as in (44):

44. *He*: !I have put out the lights; I have put out the lights.

However, it is perfectly possible to reinforce what has been conversationally implicated without any such sense of redundancy:

45. *He*: I have put out the lights; I haven't locked the doors.

Conversational implicature is also non-detachable. It isn't possible to re-express 'what is said' in different words that convey the same literal meaning but which don't share the conversational implicature. Conversational implicatures are brought about by what Grice describes as 'the conventional commitment of the utterance' (Grice 1975: 39), what we might call the proposition it literally conveys, not by the actual choice of words used to express it. So the conversational implicature is still present when our speaker says the same thing as in (41), but in different words, as in (46):

46. *He*: I have dealt with the lights.

Grice insists that the presence of a conversational implicature must be something that can be worked out by a hearer interpreting an utterance. A conversational implicature must be calculable; reached by an identifiable process of calculation and reasoning. This may at first seem like a rather odd claim. Surely the hearer in (41) will simply recognize right away that the speaker is implicating that he hasn't locked the doors. She will hardly have to take much time to work this out. But Grice's claim is not that hearers always go through a conscious and laborious process of calculation. Rather, it must be in principle possible to explain a process of reasoning that gets us from 'what is said' to what is implicated. No such process can be described in relation to understanding the meaning of 'what is said' or of what is conventionally implicated; we know these simply because we know the language being spoken. We need to add this knowledge to various aspects of the context and the assumption that the speaker is abiding by the cooperative principle and the maxims in order to reach an understanding of what is conversationally implicated. Following Grice's template, the process of calculation that the hearer goes through in order to understand the conversational implicature in (41) might be along the following lines:

47.   i. He has said that he has put out the lights but not that he has locked the doors.

    ii. There is no reason to suppose that he is not observing the maxims.

    iii. If he had been in a position to say that he had locked the doors this would have been cooperative (following the first maxim of Quantity).

    iv. He must not be in a position truthfully to say that he has locked the doors.

    v. He knows (and knows that I know that he knows) that I can see that the supposition that he has not locked the doors is required.

    vi. He has done nothing to stop me thinking that he has not locked the doors.

    vii. He intends me to think, or is at least willing to allow me to think, that he has not locked the doors.

    viii. And so he has implicated that he has not locked the doors.

(Adapted from Grice 1975: 31)

These specific properties of conversational implicature all build up a picture of an aspect of meaning that is 'non-conventional'. Grice explains this in terms of priority. In effect, you need to know what an expression conventionally means before you can calculate what it conversationally implicates in context. Hence, what is conversationally implicated can't be part of the conventional meaning of 'what is said'.

Generalized conversational implicature

All the examples of conversational implicature that we have considered so far have in fact been of one type. They are all examples of PARTICULARIZED CONVERSATIONAL IMPLICATURES. That is, they are all particular to the specific context in which they occur. If someone said 'I have put out the lights' in a different context from the one we have been considering, in which there had been no mention of locking doors, the implicature that the speaker hadn't locked the doors wouldn't arise. Similarly, if someone says 'we're having lovely weather this month', but unlike in (34) there had been no preceding remark about a boring party, there would have been no implicature concerning the need to change the subject. Particularized conversational implicatures are often the most striking and apparently most interesting examples. But in his original formulation of them Grice distinguished them from another type, which he describes as 'GENERALIZED CONVERSATIONAL IMPLICATURES'. Although in some ways less intuitively obvious, generalized conversational implicatures (often abbreviated in the literature of pragmatics to GCIs) were central to how Grice used his cooperative principle to explain meaning in context. They have also been a major focus of debate in subsequent discussions of Grice's work, as we will see in the next chapter.

Like all conversational implicatures, GCIs are dependent on context. However, unlike particularized conversational implicatures, which can be explained only in relation to individual contexts, GCIs are default implicatures. That is, they will occur when certain forms of words are used unless they are cancelled, or blocked, by some aspect of the context. They are entirely separate from conventional implicatures, because they share all the general characteristics of conversational implicatures that we have just been considering; they are cancellable, reinforceable, non-detachable, calculable and non-conventional. Unlike conventional implicatures, they can be explained in relation to the cooperative principle and the maxims. Grice developed the notion of GCIs in order to explain various ways in which natural language appears to differ from logic. In fact, explaining the relationship between language and logic was one of his motivating purposes in developing his theory of conversation.

We considered some of the problems that logic seems to pose for natural language in Chapter 2. Remember that there were problems with natural language expressions that might appear to correspond closely to terms in logic, but in fact behaved rather differently from them. Natural language 'and', for instance, might appear to have much in common with logical conjunction. Logical conjunction operates to determine the truth condition of a complex proposition from the truth conditions of the propositions that it joins together. So if we take two true propositions and join them using logical conjunction we get a further true proposition. This works well enough in examples such as (48). But in many cases when 'and' is used there seems to be some additional meaning conveyed too:

48. Camels are herbivores and lions are carnivores.
49. Herbert passed his exams and went to college.
50. Herbert went to college and passed his exams.

If we take the truth-conditional meaning of 'and' as ensuring that when two true propositions are joined together a further true proposition is produced, it might seem that (49) and (50) must be both equally true and therefore equivalent in meaning. The same two simple propositions are joined in each case. But in interpreting (49) and (50) we understand them rather differently. We understand that in (49) Herbert passed his exams first and then went to college; maybe he passed exams while at school that enabled him to get into college. In (50) we understand that Herbert passed his exams after getting to college; maybe he passed the exams that he took while he was there. If we were to suggest that the meaning of 'and then', perhaps of 'and as a result', is part of the actual linguistic meaning of 'and', or is part of 'what is said' when it is used, we start to run into all sorts of problems. It's simply not the case that 'and' always means 'and then'. It doesn't have that meaning in (48), and nor does it have it in (51):

51. Hubert hasn't been offered a place at college, and he passed all his exams last year.

Here, 'and' doesn't seem to introduce the meaning 'and then'; in fact the two conjoined propositions appear in the reverse of the order in which the events described happened. The speaker seems to be registering some sort of surprise or outrage that the event described first could take place despite the event described second. If aspects of the meaning of 'and' beyond that of basic conjunction are to be included in its linguistic meaning, we seem to have a word here that is multiply and bafflingly ambiguous. Sometimes it means just that two facts are both the case. Sometimes when two events are described it means that they took place in the sequence in which they are described, but sometimes it doesn't.

Grice argued against allowing multiple ambiguities of this type into our account of the language; to him, this made for an unnecessarily complicated linguistic system. It was unnecessary because there was a mechanism already in place that could explain the different interpretations, leaving 'and' with the simple and unitary literal meaning of logical conjunction. This mechanism was conversational implicature. The meaning 'and then' in (49) and (50) shows all the properties of being a conversational implicature. It is non-detachable, for instance, because the implicature of sequence can arise when two propositions are stated one after the other, whether or not they are joined by 'and'. It is cancellable, as is demonstrated by (51), where the implicature of sequence is cancelled by the fact that the second event is explicitly said to have taken place 'last year'. It is also dependent on a conversational maxim. In this case, the final maxim of Manner, 'be orderly', determines that we assume, unless we have reason to believe otherwise, that the order in which information is presented to us is helpfully chronological.

GCIs, then, share many properties with particularized conversational implicatures, but they differ in that they don't depend for their very existence on the peculiarities of context. They transfer across contexts; when two events are described we will generally assume that they occurred in the order in which they have been narrated, unless this assumption is cancelled by some particular piece of information, such as that given in (51). This is why GCIs are described as 'default' implicatures. They will occur in the absence of any particular indications to the contrary, but if particular aspects of context prevent them, they will be blocked.

The notion of default implicatures became significant and also controversial in subsequent developments in pragmatics, and we will think about these issues further in the next chapter. For now, as one other example of a GCI, consider the different properties of the use of 'a' in the following examples:

52. I went into a house yesterday and found that all the downstairs rooms were flooded.
53. I have been sitting in a car all morning.
54. I broke a finger yesterday.

The indefinite article 'a' seems to be doing more than just introducing a particular object in these examples. In (52) we get the impression that the house mentioned was not the speaker's own. In (54) we get the impression, however, that the broken finger was one of the speaker's. In (53) we perhaps don't form a very clear impression of whether the car mentioned was the speaker's car or someone else's. Again, Grice argues against saying that 'a' is ambiguous between meanings that we could informally paraphrase as, 'not mine', 'just any one' and 'mine'. Rather the basic meaning of identifying a particular object is added to differently in different contexts by a process of implicature. In (52) the default GCI arises that the house in question is not the speaker's own. If it was her own house this would be potentially interesting information, so by failing to give this information she has implicated by the first maxim of Quantity that she is not in a position to give it: that it is not her house. Grice admits that it is difficult to explain precisely why, if the implicature is default, it doesn't arise, or doesn't necessarily arise, in examples such as (53) and (54). He suggests that this may come down to the matter of whether or not the more specific 'my car' or 'my finger' would be considered likely to allow the hearer to access significant other pieces of information about the situation. If the more specific version would do so 'then there is a presumption that the speaker should include it in his remark; if not, then there is no such presumption' (Grice 1975: 38).

Responses to Gricean implicature

Grice developed his theory of conversation while working as a professional philosopher and trying to address some specific philosophical problems, such as the nature of meaning and the similarities and differences between language and logic. But linguists were quick to pick up on the significance of his ideas in relation to their own interests in how people communicate using language and where best to draw the line between meaning that is specified by the language and meaning that is dependent on specific features of context. Grice's work has had an influence on the study of language use that would be difficult to exaggerate. The phrase 'Gricean implicature' quickly became recognized within linguistics as the description of a certain kind of non-literal meaning. More generally, 'Gricean pragmatics' is used as a general cover term for attempts to explain meaning as a two-stage process in which what is contributed by the language can be distinguished in a principled way from what is added by the context or by general features of language use. Much of the work that has been produced in formal pragmatics since Grice's ideas first became widely known, and indeed much of what is going on in formal pragmatics today, has its origins in his theory of conversation.

That is not to say that Grice's ideas have been accepted without question. Indeed, most pragmaticists recognize a variety of problems with his specific version of pragmatic theory. But nevertheless much of present day pragmatics is defined by how it departs from classic Gricean implicature. We will consider a range of such work in the next chapter. Outside of theoretical Gricean pragmatics, the theory of conversation has been influential in the analysis of many different features of language and its uses. We will consider some of these in Chapters 6 and 7. To conclude this chapter we will consider briefly two types of criticism of Grice's theory of conversation that have not been concerned so much with addressing details of its formulation, or of developing new pragmatic principles within his general framework, but with challenging what critics saw as some of the very assumptions underlying it, and the implications of these. We will look first at an accusation that the theory of conversation is based on an unjustified assumption of universality. Then we will consider complaints that it idealizes the ways in which speakers actually behave.

Grice himself didn't have much to say about the universality or otherwise of his cooperative principle and maxims, but they are certainly open to interpretation as making general claims about human behaviour rather than specific claims about what goes on in one country or culture. If Grice was really describing general features of cooperative behaviour, independent of the specifics of any particular language and its semantics, then it might be reasonable to assume that these features should hold across different languages and the societies that use them. In an article published in the 1970s, Elinor Ochs Keenan criticized this implicit assumption within the theory of conversation and accused Grice of concentrating on just one society and then attempting to extrapolate human universals from his observations.

In support of her charges against Grice, Keenan offers some examples from the indigenous people of the plateaus area of Madagascar where, she argues, the maxims of Quantity, particularly the first one, which concerns giving as much information as is appropriate, simply don't operate. If someone in this society is asked 'Where is your mother?' she might reply 'She is either in the house or at the market', even if she knows precisely where her mother is (Keenan 1976: 70). According to the first maxim of Quantity, this is not apparently a very cooperative response, because it would be more informative for the speaker to say precisely where her mother is. Yet, Keenan claims, in saying something that is clearly not as informative as it might be, the speaker is not introducing any conversational implicature, as we would expect in cases where a maxim is flouted. She is simply giving a response that is less informative than it might be. Keenan claims that this is to do with culture-specific values, such as the scarcity of new information and the related prestige of knowing something that your interlocutor doesn't, together with a reluctance to take on responsibility for the truth of what you say.

Keenan was not suggesting that Gricean implicature should be abandoned altogether, but rather that any precise formulation of it should take more account of actual ways in which language is used and be more sensitive to differences between cultures. She suggested that the maxims might hold in different areas of life and to different degrees in different cultures. In the Malagasy society, for instance, the maxims of Quantity operated rather differently from Grice's model and were affected by factors such as importance of the information, the relationship between the speaker and hearer, and even the sex of the speaker. However, a number of linguists have defended Grice against Keenan's proposed reform of his theory of conversation, generally on the grounds that there is no need for his formulation of the maxims to be seen as universally applicable for it to be valuable. For instance, Georgia Green argued that it was the principle of cooperation that was to be seen as a universal. The individual maxims were just specific ways in which this manifested itself, so there was no need for any particular maxim to hold in every society (Green 1989: 95 n.). Robert Harnish claims that in many types of conversation, including Keenan's examples but including also many others from different societies, one or more of the maxims may be mutually known not to be in operation without this endangering the more general assumption of cooperation (Harnish 1976: 340n.). Geoffrey Leech simply drew attention to the fact that Grice never claimed that the cooperative principle must apply in the same way in every society (Leech 1983: 80).

A more widespread criticism has been that even for the culture he was most obviously describing, roughly the English-speaking society of Britain and the USA, Grice was presenting an idealized, under-researched and therefore unrealistic picture of how people behave in conversation. That is, he was taking a model of a particularly polite, helpful, informative way of behaving in conversation and trying to impose this on every type of interaction. People often simply don't behave, the claim goes, in the neat and orderly way stipulated in the maxims. Uses of language, including those in arguments, negotiations and hierarchically loaded situations, are often just not cooperative. Such criticisms have generally been coupled with a complaint that Grice didn't spend any time trying to find out what conversation is really like, but simply dreamt up an account of what he thought it should be like. As examples of linguists making this sort of criticism, see McHoul, quoted in Mey (1998: 227–8), Hymes (1986: 49), Pope (1995: 129) and Sampson (1982: 203). Sandra Harris has even gone so far as to suggest that Grice's theory of conversation has 'prescriptive and moral overtones' (Harris 1995: 118).

This view of Grice as trying to lay down the law as to how people ought to behave in conversation has presumably arisen in part because of his choice of imperative forms in which to phrase the cooperative principle and all the maxims. This choice was perhaps unfortunate; as we saw above Grice was actually interested in accounting for how people generally behave and for the assumptions they make about other people, not in telling them how they ought to behave. More generally, he has perhaps been criticized for idealizing conversation because of his choice of the term 'cooperative' which has positive social and perhaps even ethical associations. Grice was not in fact particularly interested in examining specific social factors such as people's motivations and attitudes. He wasn't really even that interested in conversation as a socially occurring phenomenon with specific properties and regularities. Rather, he was looking for as coherent an account as possible of the apparently disparate ways in which meaning in context might depart from meaning specified by the language. An assumption of cooperation offered a good way of explaining the various different principles that appeared to be at play, without necessarily have anything to say about what people were individually doing or what their motivations or intentions were. A number of linguists have defended Grice against the accusation of idealism and pointed out that such criticisms have missed the point of what he was doing (see, for instance, Brown and Levinson 1987: 95; Lakoff 1995: 191). Nevertheless, accusations that Grice was idealizing human behaviour still sometimes resurface.

EXERCISES

1. Look at these examples and decide which ones could be performative and which constative. Give your reasons. What felicity conditions might need to be in place for the success of the performatives?
   1. I pronounce this building open.
   2. I forbid you to go.
   3. I declare. [*Spoken by the captain of one side in a cricket match*]
   4. I declare that I am innocent.
   5. I declare that I have never seen a room as untidy as this one.
   6. I will be there on time.

2. In the following examples, determine a locutionary, illocutionary and perlocutionary act.
   1. Is this your paper? [*Said by a passenger on a train to a fellow passenger sitting next to a folded newspaper*]
   2. I wouldn't go around staring at people like that if I were you.
   3. I hope to see you at 9 o'clock.
   4. Do you know what time it is?

3. Distinguish between the assertives (act of making an assertion) and the directives (act of issuing a request) in the following examples, according to Searle's classification of illocutionary forces.
   1. Pass me that spoon!
   2. John has been offered that job he applied for.
   3. Could you just come here a moment?
   4. You are to be declared the winner.
   5. You are to report to my office tomorrow morning.
   6. I wish you could keep quiet.
   7. You should be more careful.

   Which of these examples might be described as indirect speech acts, and why?

4. In this chapter we have considered various examples of how a speaker deliberately flouting a maxim can lead to a conversational implicature. Take a short excerpt from a play, a film or a novel and analyse what the characters say. Can you find examples of flouting leading to implicature? What conversational implicatures are produced?

5. Grice proposes several different types of meaning that may occur whenever an utterance is produced. Of course it's perfectly possible for several or even all of these different types of meaning to occur in relation to a single utterance. Consider the following example:

Alice: Did your brother make a good impression on his first day at work?
Beth: I knew he was a little accident-prone, but this time he tripped coming through the door and spilled coffee all down his new boss's dress.

Beth could be said to have conveyed the following pieces of information, beyond what she has literally said:

   i) There is some sort of contrast between her knowing that her brother was a little accident-prone and what happened on his first day at work.
   ii) Her brother spilled the coffee after and as a result of tripping in the doorway.
   iii) Her brother did not make a good impression on his first day at work.

According to Grice's classification, what sort of implicature is involved in each case?

Consider how Grice's five properties of conversational implicature might be used to establish which of (i)–(iii) are conversational implicatures. What alternatives are there to analysing (ii) as an implicature? Does the implicature analysis have any advantages over such alternatives?

6. In *How to Do Things with Words*, Austin claimed that 'the total speech act in the total speech situation is the *only actual* phenomenon which, in the last resort, we are engaged in elucidating' (Austin 1962: 147). But one of his contemporary critics complained that 'the only proper unit for investigation seems to be what Austin has called an illocutionary act and the supposed locutionary act is at best a dubious abstraction' (Black 1963: 410).

How do you respond to Austin's claim, in the light of his theories about speech acts? Do you find Black's criticism convincing? More generally, is there any justification for positing different levels or types of meaning, or does this necessarily result in 'dubious abstraction'?

FURTHER READING

Most textbooks on pragmatics cover at least some aspects of classical pragmatics. Useful sources include: Levinson (1983) Chapter 5 for speech acts and Chapter 3 for implicature; Huang (2007) Chapter 4 for speech acts and Chapter 2 for implicature; Christie (2000) Chapter 5 for a feminist perspective on implicature; Grundy (2008) Chapter 4 for speech acts and Chapter 5 for implicature; Thomas (1995) Chapter 2 for speech acts, Chapter 3 for implicature and Chapter 4 for a detailed critique of Searle's classification of illocutionary forces.

More detailed discussion of classical pragmatics can be found in Bach (2006a), which also discusses some of the developments we will be considering in the next chapter. The essays in Tsohatzidis (1994) offer some useful and detailed treatments of the implications of speech act theory and some discussion of its relationship to implicature.

The main primary source for Austin's own account of speech act theory, the ideas discussed in section 4.1 of this chapter, is Austin (1962), although Austin (1961a) is another significant source. Searle's work is presented particularly in Searle (1969, 1975a, 1975b). Examples of contemporary philosophers who took issue with Austin's distinction between locution and illocution include Black (1963), Strawson (1964) and Cohen (1964).

Subsequent developments of or alternatives to speech act theory that have not been discussed here include Katz (1977), who attempted to incorporate speech act theory into grammar in the 'performative hypothesis'. Sadock (1974) proposed an 'idiom model' as an alternative to indirect speech acts. Sadock (2004) provides a useful overview of different attempts since Austin to produce a classification of speech acts.

The main primary source for Grice's theory of implicature is the collection of essays in Grice (1989). Of these, Grice (1975) introduces the concept of implicature and Grice (1978) develops it further; Grice (1967) includes most of what he does in terms of explaining the relationship between language and logic; Grice (1981) suggests that so-called presupposition can in fact be explained in terms of conversational implicature. Horn (2004) offers an overview of Gricean implicature and of some of the more recent reactions to it that we will be considering in the next chapter.

Contributions to the debate over the nature of conventional implicature include Bach (1994), Francescotti (1995), Rieber (1997), Barker (2003) and Vallée (2008).

A broadly Gricean approach to figures of speech such as metaphor is adopted by Martinich (1984), but is challenged by Harnish (1976) and Davis (1998).

Implications of Grice's theory for the relationship between logic and language are developed further by Horn (1989), Levinson (1983), Allwood, Andersson and Dahl (1979) and McCawley (1993).

Modern Pragmatics

5

Pragmatics as it was conducted in the last decades of the twentieth century, and as it continues today, takes its cue from Austin and Grice's basic insight. That is, it is based on the premise that a full description of how people communicate needs to take account of both what they literally say and what they mean in context. There were problems, as we have seen, with Austin's explanation of the differences between the 'meaning' and the 'force' of an utterance. Meanwhile, Grice's 'what is said' was never explained in very much detail so the exact starting point for the maxims to produce 'what is implicated' was not particularly clear. Nevertheless, their shared goal of distinguishing between different types or levels of meaning, and of detailing specific and motivated principles that explain how speakers and hearers get from one to the other, has remained central to subsequent developments in the discipline. As we saw in Chapter 2, the distinction between types of meaning is nowadays generally discussed in terms of the relationship between semantics and pragmatics, terms that Austin and Grice did not themselves use. It is important to avoid the mistake of assuming that Grice's 'what is said' must correspond more or less with semantic meaning and his 'what is implicated' with pragmatic meaning. As we will see in this chapter, the picture is far more complicated than that. We will consider some widely different ideas about where the dividing line between types of meaning should be drawn, and indeed about how many different types or levels of meaning there actually are. But all the pragmaticists whose work we will discuss share the assumption that meaning can't be explained all in one go: that different types of rules and principles, both linguistic and non-linguistic, are at work.

This chapter is divided into three main sections, which correspond to the main types or branches of theoretical pragmatics that have developed since Grice. The types are not always very clear cut, and there are points of disagreement between individual pragmaticists whose ideas are given the same general label. But nevertheless it's helpful to think of modern pragmatics in terms of broad categories of theories that share certain starting points and assumptions about what is required in a theory of meaning in context. In this chapter we will consider the group of pragmatic theories that have become known as 'neo-Gricean', then the work which has been conducted within 'relevance theory', and finally the work of some of those concerned with the plausibility of 'semantic autonomy' and the extent of 'pragmatic intrusion'. None of these is a straightforward update of or replacement for either speech act theory or Gricean implicature. Modern pragmaticists agree that the distinction between semantics and pragmatics involves far more than a few specific and fairly easily identifiable types of 'non-literal' meaning. Rather, what people mean is almost always underdetermined by the language they use. As Kent Bach has explained, 'what a speaker *normally* means in uttering a sentence, even without speaking figuratively or obliquely, is an enriched version of what could be predicted from the meaning of the sentence alone. This can be because the sentence expresses a "minimal" (or "skeletal") proposition or even because it fails to express a complete proposition at all' (Bach 2005: 15). The question that Bach raises about what type of proposition, if any, a normal sentence may express is central to modern pragmatics.

5.1   Neo-Gricean pragmatics

The term 'neo-Gricean' has become associated with those pragmaticists who have continued to develop an account of meaning broadly along the lines suggested by Grice. In effect, they are attempting to refine, improve and develop Grice's original programme. They don't necessarily adopt his specific terminology or agree with him in detail, but their work can be recognized as belonging within a broadly Gricean framework. They retain some notion of 'implicatures' and an interest in determining the non-linguistic principles by which these are derived from what is specified by the language itself.

In comparison to Grice's theory of conversation, neo-Gricean accounts are reductionist in nature. That is, they are interested in developing pragmatic theories that can do the work of Grice's theory of conversation, and hopefully more besides, but with a less complex pragmatic framework: with individual pragmatic principles that are as few in number and as well motivated as possible. This reductionist tendency is prevalent in much of modern pragmatics, in response to a general feeling that Grice's complicated and possibly open-ended list of categories and maxims is more complex and less coherent than would be ideal. Some early proposed revisions to Gricean implicature retained the categories and maxims. For instance, Kasher (1976) suggested that the cooperative principle needed to be replaced by a principle of rationality, from which Grice's maxims followed much more naturally. But most commentators on Grice have tried to tackle the number of maxims and reduce them to a few general principles.

Horn's Q- and R-Principles

Laurence Horn has developed a pragmatic theory in which implicatures are central to explaining many aspects of speakers' meanings, but are generated by just two pragmatic principles. Horn saw various overlaps and redundancies within

Grice's complex set of maxims and proposed that the job of the various maxims of Quantity, Relation and Manner could be performed by what he termed the Q-Principle and the R-Principle. 'Q' is an abbreviation for 'Quantity' and 'R' for 'Relation', although as we will see they are not straightforwardly equivalent to Grice's categories with the same names. The maxims of Quality can't be fitted into this two part system; the onus on speakers to make their contributions truthful is of primary importance and remains outside of Horn's system, which is concerned with conveying information in the most economical way possible. In effect, Horn's principles mean that speakers can convey information that they don't need to spell out in so many words, because certain types of implicature are licensed by two fundamental assumptions about language use shared by speakers and hearers.

The Q-Principle does the job of Grice's first maxim of Quantity ('make your contribution as informative as is required') together with his first two maxims of Manner ('avoid obscurity of expression' and 'avoid ambiguity'). The Q-Principle can be summed up as an injunction on the speaker to 'make your contribution sufficient', that is to 'say as much as you can'. The requirement is of course limited by the primary requirement of truthfulness; speakers should say as much as they can, but only within the bounds of what is truthful. The Q-Principle is 'hearer-oriented'; its function is to serve the needs of the hearer by ensuring that he receives as much information as possible. It can be described as a lower-bounding principle that induces upper-bounding implicatures. That is, the principle itself sets limits on how little information the speaker can offer (she must give as much as she can); and, on the assumption that the speaker is adhering to the principle, the hearer can infer the extent of the information available (if there's something more informative that the speaker might have said but hasn't, this is because, as far as the speaker knows, it isn't the case).

The R-Principle covers the same ground as Grice's maxim of Relation ('be relevant'), but it also accounts for the work done by Grice's second maxim of Quantity ('do not make your contribution more informative than is required') and the last two maxims of Manner ('be brief' and 'be orderly'). It requires the speaker to 'make your contribution necessary', that is to 'say no more than you must'. It is 'speaker-oriented', serving the needs of the speaker by ensuring that she doesn't need to go to the effort of saying more than the minimum required. It is an upper-bounding principle that induces lower-bounding implicatures. It sets limits on how much information the speaker should offer (only as much as is necessary) and licenses the inference of more information than was actually given. From what the speaker has said, and on the assumption that she is giving the smallest amount of information necessary, the hearer is able to infer more precise or more informative meanings.

Now, it may sound from the descriptions of the Q- and R-Principles above that Horn's two principles are working in opposite directions: almost that their operations make them incompatible with each other. The Q-Principle is urging the speaker to do as much work as she possibly can, while the R-Principle urges her to do as little work as she can get away with. The Q-Principle requires the hearer to assume that if he hasn't been told something it isn't the case, while the R-Principle allows him to understand more than was actually said. And indeed this sense of opposition between the two principles is central to how they work. Their incompatibility doesn't mean that they simply cancel each other out, but it does mean that they limit each other's effect. The full and unrestricted operation of the Q-Principle is incompatible with the full and unrestricted operation of the R-Principle, so what happens in practice is that each sets a limit on the influence of the other. Left to its own devices, the Q-Principle would require a speaker to talk and talk, giving every detail in case it might be useful to the hearer; the R-Principle puts a check on this. In its turn, the R-Principle would leave the hearer without sufficient information by requiring the speaker to be taciturn or even silent; the Q-Principle prevents this from happening. The constant tension between the two principles ensures that the needs of both the speaker and the hearer are addressed and that, generally speaking, language use precedes in a balanced and regulated manner. Horn has claimed that 'the functional tension between these two fundamental pragmatic principles motivates and governs a wide range of linguistic phenomena', including pronoun interpretation, lexical change and the workings of conversations (Horn 1989: 194). In the rest of this section we will focus on the types of implicatures most commonly generated by the Q-Principle and the R-Principle.

The Q-Principle makes it the speaker's responsibility to give the most informative account of a situation that she can truthfully give and encourages the hearer to assume that if the speaker doesn't offer some piece of information it is because she is not in a position to do so. As Horn points out, this means that an implicature based on the Q-Principle 'is typically negative in that its calculation refers crucially to what could have been said but wasn't' (Horn 2004: 13). Q-based implicatures can generally be described as implicatures that something is not the case. One typical and very productive type of Q-based implicature is what has become known as 'SCALAR IMPLICATURE'. The explanation of scalar implicatures relies on Horn's insight that the language contains many sets of words or phrases that are closely related to each other in meaning, but differ in terms of the degree of intensity of what they describe or in terms of their 'semantic strength'. The pair 'warm' and 'hot' is an example of such a set of words. They are closely linked semantically, both being used to describe a judgement of temperature, but they differ in that 'hot' describes a greater amount, or a stronger intensity, of temperature. Now let's consider what happens when words such as these are used:

1. The bath water is warm.
2. The bath water is not cold.
3. The bath water is not hot.

When we hear someone say (1) we understand her as conveying both (2) and (3). But according to Horn's account those two aspects of the meaning of (1) have different explanations. In effect, (2) is part of the semantic meaning of (1), whereas (3) is dependent on pragmatic principles of interpretation, specifically the Q-Principle. The literal, semantic meaning of 'warm' specifies that it describes something with a higher temperature than would be described as 'cold', but there is nothing in the semantics of the word that

makes it incompatible with 'hot'. To explain how we get from (1) to the interpretation in (3) we need to make reference to the Q-Principle. The hearer
assumes that the speaker has made the strongest, most informative statement
she is in a position to make. If she could have used it truthfully, 'hot' would
have been a semantically stronger option than 'warm'. The fact that she has
not used it implies that it is not the case. In effect, semantics tells us that the
water is 'at least warm', and pragmatics tells us that it is 'at most warm' or 'no
more than warm; not hot'.

The difference in status between (2) as part of the semantic meaning and
(3) as an implicature of (1) can be illustrated using Grice's original properties of implicature. Example (3) but not (2) is both cancellable and reinforceable. An attempt to cancel (2), as in (4) below, leads to semantic inconsistency.
Cancelling (3), as in (5), is perfectly acceptable. Similarly, (3) can be explicitly added to an utterance of (1), as in (6), without a sense of redundancy or
pointless repetition:

4. !The bath water is warm; in fact it's cold.
5. The bath water is warm; in fact it's hot.
6. The bath water is warm; it isn't (actually) hot.

The semantic scales of the language, which are sometimes described as
'Q-scales' or 'Horn-scales', can be expressed by means of ordered lists which
progress from semantically stronger to semantically weaker items. So the scale
we have been considering so far is: <hot, warm>. The operation of the
Q-Principle ensures that, in the absence of particular reasons to prevent it, the
use of an item on a Q-scale will introduce the implicature that any item to its
left is not appropriate. The reasons that might prevent it are generally to do
with the moderating operation of the R-Principle, and we will consider some
of these below. There are many other Q-scales, which all operate in this same
way. In comparing 'hot' and 'warm' we have been considering two adjectives
with different degrees of intensity, but Q-scales are by no means limited to
adjectives. Verbs, articles, adverbs, nouns, conjunctions and quantifiers can all
form such scales, as the following examples illustrate:

<love, like>
<the, a>
<always, usually, often, sometimes>
<thumb, finger>
<and, or>
<all, some>

In his early work (for instance 1972: 41, 43) Horn also proposed that the car-
dinal numbers could be arranged on a Q-scale, as follows: < ... five, four, three,
two, one>, but in more recent work (e.g. Horn 2006: 23) he has abandoned
this idea, conceding that the relationship between the use of a number and
the negation of larger numbers must have some semantic, rather than a purely
pragmatic, basis.

As mentioned above, for items to appear on the same Q-scale they must be semantically related; that is, they must be concerned with the same semantic property or relation. There is a further restriction on the formation of Q-scales; the items involved must be lexicalized to an equal degree. That is, a concept that is expressed by a single word can't appear on a scale with a related concept that is expressed using a longer form of words. The list of Q-scales above includes <thumb, finger>, because 'thumb' is more specific and therefore a more informative word than 'finger', and is therefore one that the speaker should use if she is in a position to do so. And as predicted by the Q-Principle, uses of 'finger' generally seem to implicate 'not thumb'; (7) would generally implicate (8):

 7. I cut my finger.
 8. I didn't cut my thumb.

Now, 'thumb' and 'finger' might appear to be in very much the same semantic relation to each other as 'big toe' and 'toe'. But note that 'big toe' and 'toe' aren't equally lexicalized; we have no single word to describe the big toe. And 'big toe' and 'toe' don't belong on a Q-scale together. Example (9) wouldn't generally introduce (10) as an implicature:

 9. I stubbed my toe.
 10. I didn't stub my big toe.

Horn's account of scalar implicature explains the way in which we generally understand a wide range of different words and phrases by means of two separate systems: the semantic and the pragmatic. That is, the lower limit for any item on a scale is set by the semantics of the language ('usually' means 'at least usually' or 'not just sometimes'), while the upper limit is set by the operation of the Q-Principle ('usually' implicates 'not always'). This might appear to be a rather cumbersome way of explaining the meaning of the expressions that are said to belong to Q-scales. As we will see, Horn has been criticized by other pragmaticists for confusing encoded with implicated content. But on the other side of the argument, there is a case to be made for the simplicity and the explanatorily successful nature of Horn's system. The systematic nature of Q-scales, and the fact that a single principle and a single explanation can be applied to our usual interpretation of so many different features of the language, offer a neat way of avoiding what would otherwise have to be explained as multiple and widespread linguistic ambiguity. We saw above that the supposed implicatures generated by the Q-Principle are cancellable without contradiction. If these types of meaning were instead given a semantic explanation, we would be left with a series of semantic ambiguities, whereby the 'upper bounded' meaning was sometimes present and sometimes not. As further evidence of this, consider the following examples:

 11. Some of the children were good all day.
 12. Not all of the children were good all day.

13. Some of the children were good all day; in fact they all were.
14. !Some of the children were good all day; in fact none of them were.

The use of the quantifier 'some' very often seems to bring with it the meaning 'not all'. So for instance if you hear (11) you are quite likely to understand it as meaning (12). We could opt for a purely semantic explanation of this, that is we could say that 'not all' is simply part of the meaning of 'some'. But then we would be at a loss to explain why (13), where (11) is conjoined with the negation of (12), is perfectly acceptable. We would be forced to admit that 'some' is simply ambiguous; sometimes it means 'not all' and sometimes it doesn't. If however we adopt a scalar account of the relationship between 'some' and 'all' we can explain the acceptability of (13) simply by pointing out that the implicature from the use of 'some' to the meaning 'not all' is cancellable in context. And note that there does seem to be an asymmetry between the relationships of 'some' to its upper-bounded and to its lower-bounded meaning. The upper-bounded meaning can be cancelled, as in (13). Attempts to cancel the lower-bounded meaning, as in (14), lead to contradiction. This asymmetry is captured by the explanation in terms of implicature.

Positing a pragmatic explanation for part of the meaning of scalars also offers a solution to the problem of the apparent ambiguity of 'or'. In different contexts 'or' seems to demonstrate two significantly different meanings. Sometimes it has an exclusive meaning: in effect, it indicates that either one or other of the alternatives described is or can be the case but not both. For example, (15) would usually be taken to mean (16):

15. You can have wine or beer with your meal.
16. You can't have both wine and beer with your meal.

However, sometimes 'or' is interpreted inclusively, meaning that it is perfectly possible for both of the alternatives to be the case. The 'not both' meaning we noticed in (15) seems to disappear without any sense of contradiction in (17). And 'or' is also interpreted inclusively in an example like (18). Someone who was both over 60 and on a low wage could reasonably be expected to receive the discount described:

17. You can have wine or beer with your meal – in fact you can have both.
18. You get a 20 per cent discount if you are over 60 or on a low wage.

If we tried to explain all this within the semantics of 'or', we would be forced to describe it as simply ambiguous between an exclusive and an inclusive reading. Placing 'or' on a Q-scale with 'and', however, and letting it retain a single, inclusive, semantic meaning, gives us a unitary explanation of these examples. The use of 'or' generally implicates the negation of the semantically stronger 'and' (if a speaker is in a position to use the more informative 'and' she should do so) but this implicature can be cancelled either explicitly, as in (17), or by features of the context, as in (18). Semantic ambiguity is not a very satisfactory way of explaining differences in interpretation because it leads to a very complicated linguistic system. Pragmaticists tend to view it as an option of last resort and to provide pragmatic explanations for such phenomena if they can.

Horn's account of scalar implicature might seem to meet a serious challenge in examples such as the following, which appear to go against all his predictions:

19. This bath water isn't warm – it's hot!
20. Freddie didn't have cream or ice cream with his pudding – he had both!

Now according to Horn, the meanings of scalar expressions such as 'warm' and 'or' are lower bound by their actual semantics. 'Warm' literally means 'at least warm' and 'or' is literally inclusive in its meaning. The upper-bound meanings of 'not hot' and 'not and; not both' are implicatures. Yet in (19) and (20) we seem to have negation operating to deny not the semantic meaning (on Horn's account 'not warm' should mean 'cold' and 'not or' should mean 'neither') but the pragmatically implicated meaning. Suddenly we seem to have a supposed implicature that actually comes under the scope of negation. It looks as if the supposed implicature might in fact be part of semantic meaning after all.

Horn has responded to the challenge posed by examples such as (19) and (20) by drawing attention to what he sees as the rather special nature of the use of negation in these examples. It simply isn't the usual straightforward use of 'not' to deny some propositional content. Rather it is a use of 'not' to register objection to a possible way of expressing a state of affairs and to replace it with a different and more suitable form of expression. Horn has termed this 'METALINGUISTIC NEGATION': a form of negation that is concerned with some aspect of the use of language, rather than with the literal meaning of the language used. Certainly, such examples often occur in response to some previous utterance or choice of expression:

21. *Tai Lung*: You're just a big fat panda.
     Po: I'm not a big fat panda; I'm THE big fat panda.
         [*From the film* Kung Fu Panda, *2008*]
22. *Linguini*: You're thin for someone who likes food.
     Ego: I don't like food; I LOVE it.
         [*From the film* Ratatouille, *2007*]

For Horn, the second speaker in these examples isn't denying what the first speaker has literally said, but is objecting to the form of words chosen: specifically to the use of 'a' in (21), because it implicates 'not any specific one', and the use of 'like' in (22), because it implicates 'not love'. In support of his answer to this apparent challenge to scalar implicatures, Horn draws attention to the fact that in metalinguistic negation 'the negative particle is used to object to any aspect of an alternate (actual or envisaged) utterance, including its conventional and conversational implicata, register, morphosyntactic form or pronunciation' (Horn 2004: 10). That is, metalinguistic negation isn't exclusive to scalar implicatures but can be used to reject a wide range of aspects of how a message is expressed. As examples of the other types of objection that

Horn mentions, consider the following. In each case, we could say that what is being objected to is not what has just been said, but the way in which it has been expressed: the choice of a colloquial rather than a more formal phrase in (23), an Anglicized rather than a Latinate form of the plural in (24) and an American rather than a British pronunciation of 'tomatoes' in (25):

23. Gemma isn't up the duff; she's expecting a baby.
24. There aren't three hippopotamuses in that pool; there are three hippopotami.
25. We didn't eat [tʰəmeidəz]; we ate [tʰəmɑːtəʊz].

Horn has claimed that scalar implicatures play a central role in natural language (ibid.). We'll be returning to this topic in the next chapter in relation to experimental pragmatics, where scalar implicatures have become a major focus of study. However, as we'll see straight away in the remaining sections of this chapter, their existence is a matter of controversy; in fact it is one of the focusses for the distinctions and disagreements between modern pragmatic theories.

Horn's R-Principle has not received nearly as much scrutiny as his Q-Principle, either from Horn himself or from his commentators and critics. Nevertheless, a number of significant types of pragmatic meaning are explained in Horn's system as R-based implicatures. The R-Principle enjoins the speaker to say as little as is necessary and therefore encourages the hearer to fill in material that may have been left out from what the speaker said. That is, R-based implicatures are generally examples where the hearer is licensed to understand a statement that is stronger than what has actually been said:

26. John finished writing his book and went on holiday.
27. I have had breakfast.
28. Mary was well enough to go to school today.

We saw in our discussion of Gricean implicature that the temporal and causal meanings often but not always associated with 'and' threaten to make 'and' semantically ambiguous, and that one of Grice's motivations in introducing the notion of implicature was to avoid this. Grice didn't make his own account of 'and' very clear, but it is usually understood that it can be explained in relation to the maxims of Manner, and specifically the obligation they impose on the speaker to 'be orderly'. In Horn's system there are no separate maxims of Manner, but the general operation of the R-Principle allows the hearer to fill in information that is not literally stated, such as that to do with sequence and possibly causality in (26). Similarly in (27) the hearer will generally understand something rather stronger than what was literally said: that the speaker has had breakfast within a relevantly interesting time scale, for instance that day, rather than simply that she has at some time in her life had breakfast. All that is literally said in (28) is that Mary was able to go to school, but the R-Principle licenses the strengthening of a statement of ability to an implicature that Mary actually did go to school.

The R-Principle can also explain a range of ways in which we leave certain things unsaid in the interests of politeness or discretion but can be confident that the speaker will fill in what is missing. These include examples of deliberate understatement (we can well imagine (29) being used to describe someone who is obviously very drunk), euphemism (the person described in (30) may be violently sick) and even indirect speech acts (the hearer in (31) is left to fill in the important facts that the speaker would like him to pass the salt, and is in fact asking him to do so):

29. He's had a little too much to drink.
30. The scheduled speaker is indisposed.
31. I wonder if you could pass me the salt.

The R-Principle also encourages interpretations of an utterance that are in line with normal expectations about likely scenarios. That is, if some specific detail is not made clear, the hearer is licensed to assume that this is because there is nothing remarkable or noteworthy about that detail. In some cases this can apparently push the hearer in the opposite direction to the Q-Principle in reaching an interpretation. Consider the following, which we considered in relation to Gricean implicature in the last chapter:

32. I broke a finger yesterday.

On hearing (32), if there were no particular reasons to think otherwise, we would probably assume that the finger in question belonged to the speaker: that she broke one of her own fingers rather than someone else's. However, according to the theory of scalar implicatures, the use of 'a' will generally implicate that a semantically more specific and stronger term such as 'the' or 'my' doesn't apply. In this case the R-Principle seems to overrule the Q-Principle because of a set of expectations about how the world is and what normally happens in it. Remember that the Q-Principle operates with other things being equal; the R-Principle is one of these other things. Arguably, this offers a clearer account of the differences between the various interpretations of 'a' than that offered by Grice in terms of generalized conversational implicatures based on the maxims of Quantity. Grice acknowledged that 'a' seemed sometimes to implicate 'not mine' and sometimes to implicate 'mine', but didn't delineate very clearly between the different pragmatic forces in operation in arriving at these two different implicatures.

The fact that in cases such as this the Q-Principle and the R-Principle come into conflict, a situation that has to be resolved by outside forces should not come as any great surprise; we saw when we first considered the nature of these two principles that they were inherently in contradiction with each other. Horn has suggested that one consequence of this contradiction is that in some cases the principles actually end up operating together to determine some significant aspects of implicated meaning. As we have seen, as a result of the R-Principle what is communicated by the use of certain expressions tends towards the most stereotypical or most normal interpretation. If an unmarked expression is used it tends to implicate an unmarked situation. Something is unmarked if there is nothing unusual or striking about it. In the case of expressions, an unmarked form is one that is as brief, or at least as simple in terms of the number of words needed to express it, as possible. In the following pairs of examples, all taken from Horn (2007: 172), the utterance in (b) contains the unmarked expression:

33. a. Her blouse was pale red.
    b. Her blouse was pink.
34. a. It's not impossible that the Sox will win.
    b. It's possible that the Sox will win.
35. a. That's my father's wife.
    b. That's my mother.

The Q-Principle explains what happens when a marked expression is used, as in the (a) examples above. The hearer is licensed to infer that since the speaker has used a more complex expression, despite a general tendency dictated by the R-Principle to speak as economically as possible, she must have done so for a reason. The Q-Principle prompts the implicature that this reason is because the unmarked expression is in some way not applicable. If we were to hear any of the (a) utterances, which contain marked expressions, we would be likely to assume that there was something unusual or striking about the situation. We might assume that the blouse described in (33) was not exactly pink, that the Sox winning in (34) was not really very likely, and that the woman described in (35), despite being married to the speaker's father, was not her mother. In this way, the Q- and R-Principles actually end up operating together to explain a wide range of implicated meanings; they are joined in what Horn describes as the 'division of pragmatic labour'. General pragmatic principles can explain why expression such as 'pale red' and 'pink' or 'not impossible' and 'impossible' are not in fact straightforwardly interchangeable, without having to complicate their lexical meaning by trying to describe all these separate facts in the semantics. Note that the exact reason why the unmarked expression is not applicable remains, as Horn puts it, 'indeterminate'. The division of pragmatic labour can't necessarily explain exactly what reason the speaker has for withholding the unmarked form. Other factors to do with the wider context may be necessary to explain this.

Levinson's Q-, I- and M-Principles

The other main branch of neo-Gricean pragmatics to have emerged over the last few decades is that associated most closely with Stephen Levinson. Levinson's pragmatics has much in common with Horn's, including its basically Gricean approach and its focus on the importance of implicature as a means of explaining many types of non-literal meaning, but it differs from it in a number of important ways. Like Horn's pragmatics, it is reductive in relation to Grice, but whereas Horn proposes to reduce Grice's various maxims to two fundamental principles, Levinson's system consists of three such principles: the Q-Principle, the I-Principle and the M-Principle. Like Horn, he sees the requirements of Quality to be primary and distinct from the operation of the fundamental pragmatic principles. His Q-Principle is concerned with Quantity, his I-Principle with Informativeness and his M-Principle with Manner. Each principle can be summarized in terms of a speaker's maxim, concerned with the restrictions that it imposes on what the speaker says, and a recipient's corollary, concerned with what it allows a hearer to understand from what the speaker has said, on the assumption that she is following the speaker's maxim. Levinson's presentation of each maxim is very long – see Levinson (2000) for the full versions – but he has also provided summaries as follows:

Q-Principle
Speaker's maxim: do not say less than is required (bearing the I-principle in mind).
Recipient's corollary: what is not said is not the case.

I-Principle
Speaker's maxim: do not say more than is required (bearing the Q-principle in mind).
Recipient's corollary: what is generally said is stereotypically and specifically exemplified.

M-Principle
Speaker's maxim: do not use a marked expression without reason.
Recipient's corollary: what is said in a marked way is not unmarked.

There are obvious similarities between Levinson's principles and Horn's, and as you might expect they do very similar work in terms of explaining pragmatic meaning. In particular, the balance between saying enough and not saying too much, necessitated by the combination of Levinson's Q- and I-Principles, has much in common with the relationship between Horn's Q- and R-Principles. The presence of the 'extra' principle concerned with Manner in Levinson's system is motivated by the fact that he believes it is necessary to distinguish maxims concerned with propositional content from ones concerned with the form of an utterance, something he claims that Horn fails to do.

The most fundamental differences between Horn's system and Levinson's are in terms of how the relationship between literal meaning and speaker meaning in context is understood. In this, Horn is closer to Grice. Although as we have seen Grice was never very clear about what it is that forms the input into pragmatic interpretation, his 'what is said' is clearly intended to be pretty close to literal, linguistically specified content, once you allow for the disambiguation of any ambiguous terms and the settling of references. Early in the development of Levinson's pragmatic theory, in an article he coauthored with Jay David Atlas, he admits the attraction of, but also challenges, this version. The result of the Gricean approach is 'theoretical simplicity in our theory of language', in that the logical form or the literal proposition expressed by any example can be explained by pointing to the semantics of the terms used; everything else can be left to pragmatic principles. 'Simplicity is indeed a virtue of theories', Atlas and Levinson acknowledge, but it needs to be tempered by the nature of the subject matter, in this case the complexity of communicated meaning. They argue that on the contrary 'even the pragmatic features of the sentence, its use in the language, can in principle bear on the assignment of logical form, especially if the resulting form increases the overall coherence and explanatory power of the theory' (Atlas and Levinson 1981: 50–1). Here, then, is the crux of the difference between the system that Levinson went on to develop and the original Gricean conception of how utterance meaning was to be explained. Far from being an autonomous system, specifying the literal content of sentences before any pragmatic principles might begin to operate on them in context, logical form must be open to input from systems other than semantics, including pragmatics.

The notion of generalized conversational implicature is central to Levinson's pragmatics, where it is seen as a productive force in linguistic communication. The amount of information we want to convey might threaten to overwhelm the time and energy we have available to express it if it all had to be spelled out fully and literally. For Levinson, the solution to this potential problem is expressed in the following general principle: 'let not only the content but also the metalinguistic properties of the utterance (i.e. its form) carry the message' (Levinson 2000: 6). Levinson has developed the theory of GCIs into an account of 'presumptive meanings' or preferred interpretations. These will accompany the use of certain expressions by default, because of the general pragmatic principles he has outlined, rather than because of either linguistically encoded meaning on the one hand or context-specific inferences on the other. GCIs follow just from the assumption that the general pragmatic principles are being observed, rather than from any information drawn from context or from knowledge shared between speaker and hearer. They 'constitute our third level of utterance-type meaning, sitting between the coded meanings of linguistic expressions on the one hand, and nonce-inferences to speaker-meaning on the other' (ibid.: 367).

Levinson argues that it is not possible to maintain a theory of meaning in which semantics is autonomous from pragmatics, because 'generalized conversational implicatures seems to play a role in the establishment of truth-conditional content' (ibid.: 166). He gives many examples of this process, including the following that involve the resolution of deictic expressions in context. He suggests that the values of deictics are uncontroversially determined pragmatically but are also input to semantic interpretation. His case is that general pragmatic principles, resulting in GCIs, are required to explain this process:

36. a. This sofa is comfortable; come over here.
    b. California is beautiful; come over here.
37. Some of you know the news; I'm not talking to you; I'm talking to the rest of you.
38. The meeting is on Thursday. (ibid.: 178)

The exact interpretation of the place deictic expression 'here' in the examples in (36), Levinson argues, depends on the I-Principle. The hearer can assume that what the speaker is describing is stereotypical; that the speaker is using the most economical means to describe a particular place. Thus 'here' is given the very specific interpretation 'to where I am sitting' in (36a) but the much freer reference to 'to the State in which I live' in (36b). The interpretation of the person deictic expression 'you' throughout (37) depends on the Q-Principle. By assuming that the speaker is saying as much as she can, the hearer understands 'some of you' to convey the meaning 'some but not all of you', which then allows the specific references of the other pronouns to be determined. Imagine that example (38) is uttered on a Wednesday. The hearer will most probably interpret 'Thursday' as meaning 'not tomorrow but Thursday next week'. But this interpretation depends on the assumption of the Q-Principle. It would have been much more informative for the speaker to have said 'tomorrow' if that is what she meant; the hearer can infer that since she didn't say 'tomorrow' she didn't mean it.

Levinson has developed his theory of presumptive meanings in a number of directions to explain a variety of linguistic phenomena. A particular focus of his attention has been the resolution of anaphora. The task of explaining anaphora, he notes, has previously been attributed to the grammar, whereas in fact it is perhaps better handled by pragmatic principles of preferred interpretation. As just one illustration of this, consider Levinson's account of the following examples:

39. a. John came in. He sat down.
    b. John came in. The man sat down.
40. a. John likes his father.
    b. John likes the man's father.

Levinson argues that 'I-implicatures predominate in the absence of countervailing Q or M implicatures' (ibid.: 272). In the (a) examples above there will be a general tendency to interpret the pronouns as referring locally (that is, 'he' and 'his' refer back to 'John'), because they are unmarked forms. However, in the (b) examples, 'a marked, more prolix expression has been used' and 'we obtain an M-implicature that is complementary to that which would have arisen by I-implicature from the use of the simple expression'. That is, we assume that 'the man' in each case must refer to someone other than John.

Levinson's pragmatics remains essentially Gricean in spirit, especially in relation to his commitment to GCIs. However, Levinson's Q-, I- and M-Principles do a lot more work that Grice's maxims of conversation. For Grice, literal meaning is filled out in relation to reference assignment and disambiguation to give 'what is said'. This may then be added to further by conventional implicature. Only at this stage do the maxims become relevant in establishing what is communicated. For Levinson conventional meaning is much less powerful and coherent than Grice's 'what is said', needing help from pragmatic principles before it can even provide a basis for interpretation.

5.2 Relevance theory

Beside the neo-Gricean theories the other most significant trend in modern post-Gricean pragmatics has been the development of relevance theory. This can rightly be described as a pragmatic theory, because of its focus on the use of language in communication, and specifically on the relationship between meaning and context. But it is also a cognitive theory, in that it is concerned with the relationship between language and mind. Unlike the neo-Griceans, and certainly unlike Grice himself, relevance theorists are interested in describing the cognitive processes that speakers and hearers go through when they produce and interpret language, in saying something about what the human mind is like, and in explaining communication in these terms.

Relevance theory (RT) emerged during the 1980s in the collaborative work of linguist Deirdre Wilson and anthropologist Dan Sperber and it is still most closely associated with these two names, although many others have contributed to its development. It retains some elements and theoretical commitments that can be traced back to Grice, most notably the understanding that what is communicated in context must be explained with reference to more than one type or level of meaning, and that both linguistic and non-linguistic factors play a part in determining it. It is, however, much less close to Grice than neo-Gricean pragmatics is, not least because it is the most reductive of post-Gricean pragmatic theories, proposing that the work of all of Grice's various maxims can be done by a principle of relevance: a principle that has both a communicative and a cognitive aspect. Moreover, the principle of relevance is not a conversational norm that speakers follow and hearers assume they are following. It is a general principle, or a fact, of human cognition. As such, it's not possible for speakers to violate or exploit it. So while, as we will see, there are implicatures in RT, there is no place for the type of Gricean implicature that typically arises when a maxim is blatantly flouted.

The principles of relevance

Deirdre Wilson and Dan Sperber published an article in 1981 in which they set out both where they agreed with Grice and also where their disagreements with him prompted them to suggest modifications or changes to his theory. The real value in Grice's work, they explained, is the insight that with an appropriately defined set of pragmatic principles, 'a wide range of what at first seem to be arbitrary semantic facts can be seen as consequences of quite general pragmatic constraints' (Wilson and Sperber 1981: 155). They differed from him over the nature of the relevant pragmatic principles and the ways in which they operated in the process of interpretation. They identified three main differences from Grice, and we will look at each of these briefly in turn, because they have remained central to RT.

Firstly, Wilson and Sperber picked up on some of the issues raised by Grice's distinction between 'what is said' and what is implicated. In itself, this isn't particularly surprising; there were some well-established problems with the lack of precision in Grice's definition of 'what is said' and in how he envisaged its relationship to literal, semantic meaning. But Wilson and Sperber took issue not just with the formulation of 'what is said', but with its very viability as a distinct level of meaning on which pragmatic principles such as the maxims could operate to produce implicatures. They argued that pragmatic principles themselves had to apply before even this basic level of meaning, the apparent starting point of interpretation, could be reached. The consequences of this would be very serious for a traditional Gricean picture of meaning. It would no longer be possible to relate 'what is said' closely to linguistic semantic meaning and to distinguish what is implicated as the result of the operation of pragmatic principles. If Wilson and Sperber were right, pragmatic principles would have to operate much earlier in the process of interpretation than previously believed, and would in fact often have to assist linguistic semantics in producing any complete meaning at all. That is, in RT, pragmatic inference was to be just as important in determining what is explicitly communicated as in determining what is implicitly communicated.

An initial account of why for Wilson and Sperber pragmatic principles have a role to play in determining Grice's 'what is said' can be made with reference to the allowances that Grice himself makes for content additional to linguistic semantic meaning. Remember that Grice suggested that in order to reach 'what is said' it is necessary to add to literal meaning the reference of any referring expressions and the disambiguation of any ambiguous ones. Wilson and Sperber's argument is that pragmatic principles play a necessary role in both these processes. Consider their example, reproduced here as (41):

41. Refuse to admit them.

Without any indication of context, we are at a loss to give a precise interpretation to (41). Our problem here can be explained, at least in part, by the fact that 'admit' has at least two distinct meanings in English (roughly, 'let in' and 'confess to') and the fact that 'them' could potentially be used to refer to any of an infinite range of possible groupings of people or objects. Now consider (42) and (43), as two possible contexts for an utterance of (41):

42. What should I do when I make mistakes?
43. What should I do with people whose tickets have expired?

If (41) is produced in response to (42), it seems clear that 'admit' will be interpreted in its 'confess to' sense and 'them' will be seen as referring to the mistakes. If it is produced in response to (43), 'admit' will be understood as meaning 'let in' and 'them' as referring to the people with invalid tickets. For Wilson and Sperber, the different interpretations reached in these two contexts must be dependent on the assumption that the speaker is being cooperative in response to the question: that is, 'the hearer's ability to select the appropriate interpretation for [41] in the context of [42] or [43] must depend on his tacit assumption that the speaker has observed Grice's maxims, and in particular the maxim of relevance' (Wilson and Sperber 1981: 157). Grice's 'what is said', or for Wilson and Sperber the proposition expressed when (41) is uttered, appears to draw on both semantic and pragmatic phenomena.

Their second issue with Grice concerns figures of speech such as irony and metaphor. For Grice these could be explained as particularized conversational implicatures, usually dependent on the maxims of Quality. What is literally said in either (44) or (45) is blatantly false, and therefore apparently simply uncooperative. But on the understanding that the speaker does intend to make a cooperative contribution the hearer will interpret these examples as implicating something else; probably the opposite of what was literally said in (44) and the related proposition that the mother-in-law is like an angel in possessing various positive qualities in (45):

44. That was a really useful way to spend an afternoon.
    [*Said at the end of a long and obviously unproductive meeting*]
45. My mother-in-law is an angel.

Wilson and Sperber claimed that the operation of the maxims is simply not adequate as an account of how we get from literal to intended meaning in such examples. In most other cases of implicature, the operation of Grice's maxims adds some extra meaning to what has been said in order to produce a fully cooperative contribution. In these cases, however, the supposed implicature is incompatible with what was said and seems to be able to overrule or replace literal meaning; for Wilson and Sperber, this was an unacceptable exception to the usual operation of implicature. Further, there seemed to be no principled way of explaining why some but not all false statements could be interpreted as figurative or why one blatantly false statement leads to an ironic interpretation, while another leads to a metaphorical one.

Finally, Wilson and Sperber argued that Grice's various maxims are not all independently necessary. A single principle of relevance, which leads the hearer to believe that the speaker has done her best to be maximally relevant in the particular context of utterance, can replace them all. Furthermore this principle doesn't follow from any general commitment to cooperation on the part of speakers and hearers.

Sperber and Wilson elaborated a more detailed account of their concept of relevance, and explored its operation, in the book *Relevance*. This was first published in 1986 and has remained the central text in RT. The book's subtitle is *Communication and Cognition*; it is concerned with explaining communication in terms of the general properties of human cognition, rather than of specific norms of human social behaviour. The authors note that coded communication, where a particular message is put into a coded form such as into words of a language so that it can be decoded by a receiver, is only one minor type of human communication. Where coded communication is used, it is one part of a larger process that they call 'ostensive-inferential communication' and which they define as follows:

> The communicator produces a stimulus which makes it mutually manifest to communicator and audience that the communicator intends, by means of this stimulus, to make manifest or more manifest to the audience a set of assumptions $\{I\}$. (Sperber and Wilson 1995: 63)

Ostensive communication draws attention to itself as communicative behaviour. To put it in terms of language use, the speaker attracts the hearer's attention to the fact that she intends to behave informatively, leading him to believe that it will be worth his while to pay attention. The promised benefits are that something potentially useful, interesting or relevant will be communicated. This promise is conveyed not because of some shared understanding between speaker and hearer, or some general norm of human behaviour, but in the very act of communication itself, because of underlying human cognitive principles. That is: 'every act of ostensive communication communicates a presumption of its own optimal relevance' (ibid.: 158). In early presentations of their theory Sperber and Wilson termed this 'the principle of relevance', and you will find it described as such in discussions of RT published up until the mid-1990s. In later revisions, they suggested that in fact two ontologically different principles of relevance were required, one to do with the nature of human communication and a complementary one concerning the nature of human cognition. From then on, the original principle of relevance is often referred to as the second, or communicative, principle of relevance. The first, cognitive principle of relevance is: 'human cognition tends to be geared to the maximisation of relevance' (ibid.: 260).

One further definition is needed to complete the scheme: the definition of 'optimal relevance', which is central to the principle of relevance itself. As we have seen, for Sperber and Wilson every act of ostensive communication communicates a presumption of its own optimal relevance. An act of ostensive communication can also be described as an 'ostensive stimulus'. They define the presumption of optimal relevance as follows:

(a) The ostensive stimulus is relevant enough for it to be worth the address-ee's effort to process it.
(b) The ostensive stimulus is the most relevant one compatible with the communicator's abilities and preferences. (ibid.: 270)

Assumptions communicated by the ostensive stimulus are relevant to the extent that they are capable of producing so-called 'contextual effects' or 'cognitive effects' for the hearer. Hence the notion of relevance that Sperber and Wilson are concerned with is one that is always dependent on the specifics of context, and that concerns the cognitive state of the hearer. What is optimally relevant in one context, or to one hearer in one context, may not be optimally relevant to a different hearer in a different context. The assumptions communicated may have any one of three different types of contextual effect. Firstly, they may add to the hearer's existing knowledge by producing in context a new piece of information or contextual implication. This is something that the hearer knows because of the combination of communicated assumptions and his existing knowledge. Imagine that Martha's friend Jane is aware that Martha usually goes to her salsa class on a Tuesday evening but that sometimes, if she has had a hard day at work, she gives it a miss and stays home. We could express an assumption that Jane holds on some particular Tuesday evening as follows:

46. Martha is either at her salsa class or at home.

Now imagine that a mutual friend, Samantha, talks to Jane during the Tuesday evening and says:

47. I have just been past Martha's house and seen that her car is not there; she must be out.

Combining Jane's existing assumption (46) and the new assumptions communicated to her by Samantha (47) she can arrive at the new contextual implication (48):

48. Martha is at her salsa class.

The second type of cognitive effect that a communicated assumption may have is that it may contradict an existing assumption. If the strength of the communicated assumption, the hearer's reason to believe it, is stronger than the strength of the existing assumption, then the effect will be that the existing assumption is cancelled. If Jane is assuming that Martha has gone to her salsa class because it is a Tuesday evening and that is what she normally does, and if Samantha then says to her:

49. I have just called Martha at home and got a reply.

Then Jane will have reason to give up on her tentative assumption that Martha was at her salsa class. Jane's set of assumptions has been altered, making Samantha's remark cognitively significant and therefore relevant to her. Finally, a communicated assumption may have cognitive effects by strengthening an existing assumption. As before, Jane assumes that Martha has gone to her salsa class because it is a Tuesday evening. This time, Samantha says:

50. I have just seen Martha going into her salsa class.

Samantha's utterance has contextual effects and is therefore relevant to Jane not because it introduces a brand new piece of information, but because it makes into a firm belief something that was previously only an educated guess. This last possibility explains why the assumptions being communicated can be intended to be made 'manifest or more manifest'; if an assumption that is already manifest, or apparent, to a hearer is strengthened, then something relevant has been achieved.

Notice that not just any number of contextual effects are sufficient to make an act of communication optimally relevant. The degree of relevance, that is the number of contextual effects, must be balanced by the question of whether they are 'worth the addressee's effort': that is, whether the amount of cognitive work required is the least possible to achieve those effects. The effort expended by the hearer is generally referred to as 'processing effort': the work he has to go through in analysing a speaker's utterance in order to get contextual effects from it. To illustrate this point, the following examples are modified versions of those discussed by Sperber and Wilson:

51. People who work with poultry should have a flu jab.
52. Bill works with poultry.
53. Bill works with poultry and 1967 was a great year for French wines.

In the context provided by (51) an utterance of (52) would be of clear relevance because it would produce the new contextual implication (54):

54. Bill should have a flu jab.

An utterance of (53) will produce exactly this same contextual implication. However, it also conveys extra information, and this information requires processing effort, but has no contextual effects in the context provided by (52). Therefore, despite producing the same contextual implication as (53), (54) is less relevant because this implication is achieved using greater processing effort.

This balance between contextual effect and processing effort is what stops an interpreter from going on and on, attempting to derive more and more contextual effects. The process of interpretation will stop when a sufficient number of contextual effects have been achieved, because to carry on would be to expend effort that wouldn't be sufficiently rewarded by effects. Optimal relevance is not the same as maximum relevance, because it is balanced against effort. Sperber and Wilson ask their readers to consider the example presented in (55):

55. George has a big cat.

The first interpretation that a hearer is likely to reach is that George has a large domestic cat. Of course (55) is also compatible with George having a pet such as a lion or a tiger. It is perfectly possible for the hearer to go on processing and looking for possible contextual effects of (55) and to entertain the idea that maybe George is keeping one of these wild animals. However, if this is what the speaker had meant then either (56) or (57) would have been a more relevant way to express it, since it would allow the hearer to reach this understanding without the extra processing effort involved:

56. George has a tiger.
57. George has a tiger or a lion, I'm not sure which.

Remember that the second part of the definition of optimal relevance states that the stimulus (here, the utterance) was the most relevant that could have been produced. The hearer was quite justified in stopping when he reached the 'large domestic cat' interpretation.

Sperber and Wilson defend themselves against what might appear to be unrealistic optimism about how relevant people actually are in their everyday interactions. The principle of relevance shouldn't be taken as suggesting that every act of ostensive communication is in fact optimally relevant, but that in every case the communicator intends the addressee to believe that it is; 'even bores manifestly intend their audience to believe that they are worth listening to' (Sperber and Wilson 1995: 158).

Explicatures and implicatures

In their initial discussion of where they differed from Grice, Wilson and Sperber argued that pragmatic principles must come into play much earlier than he had assumed. Rather than waiting for literal meaning to be filled out into a recognizable 'what is said' and then acting on this to produce various types of implicated meaning, pragmatic principles were needed to assign even an initial level of meaning to an utterance, or in relevance theoretic terms to determine the propositional form of what has been expressed. We now know that in RT the 'pragmatic principles' are constituted by the second, communicative principle of relevance. This principle may be used to derive various types of contextual inferences. But before that this same principle contributes, along with linguistic factors, to producing a propositional meaning.

Recall that Sperber and Wilson argued that even reference assignment and disambiguation, the processes that Grice allowed must add to decoded meaning to form 'what is said', were reliant on the pragmatic principle of relevance. Decoding without pragmatic enrichment can't produce a full propositional meaning. In fact Sperber and Wilson go further than that. Even once reference assignment and disambiguation have taken place, and Grice would have been satisfied that a unique 'what is said' had been reached, it is generally the case that further enrichment is required before there is a truly propositional meaning:

58. Peter's bat is grey.

Sperber and Wilson argue that even after the identity of 'Peter', the specific meaning of 'bat' (in this instance, its zoological sense) and the time referred to by the present tense 'is' have been established, the meaning of (58) is still not complete enough to be truth-evaluable. The exact nature of the relationship between 'Peter' and 'bat' is unclear; it could be the bat owned by Peter, but it could also be the bat chosen, mentioned, killed and so on by Peter. Sperber and Wilson reject the possibility that the genitive form might simply be multiply semantically ambiguous. They also reject the idea that there might be a single definition of the genitive which is broad enough to cover all these possible meanings. Rather, they suggest, that (58) remains less than propositional even after reference assignment and disambiguation have taken place. 'Contextual information is needed to resolve what should be seen as the semantic incompleteness, rather than the ambiguity, of the genitive' (Sperber and Wilson 1995: 188). The semantic incompleteness of the genitive results in a sentence that is itself semantically incomplete. Here is a further example:

59. It will take some time to repair your watch.

As Sperber and Wilson explain it: 'the interpretation recoverable from this utterance by decoding and reference assignment is a truism and thus irrelevant. It goes without saying that watch-repairing is a process with temporal duration, and a speaker aiming at optimal relevance must have intended to express something more than goes without saying' (1995: 189). Hearers will generally understand (59) as conveying that the watch repair will take an amount of time that it is relevant to remark on; someone who has just taken his watch to a watchmaker who usually takes about a week to repair a watch will understand the speaker of (59) as conveying that the watch repair on this occasion will take more than a week.

Sperber and Wilson argue, then, that linguistic decoding, even aided by reference assignment and disambiguation, is rarely sufficient to give a full proposition. The incomplete linguistic semantic form needs to be filled out to give a truth-conditional meaning. A meaning that is reached by a process of developing the incomplete linguistic semantic form is known in RT as an 'EXPLICATURE'. The details of the relationship between Peter and the bat in (58) and the information that the watch repair will take longer than expected in (59) are explicatures. They are derived from decoded meaning in accordance with the principle of relevance. The type of meaning represented by the relevance theorist's explicature has no exact equivalent in Gricean pragmatics. It is derived from linguistically encoded meaning but, unlike Grice's 'what is said', it will vary from one context to the next. Establishing an explicature depends on the principle of relevance, which itself always applies in context. The explicature derived from an utterance, of say (58), in one context will be different from the explicature derived from a different utterance of (58) in a different context. Further, and again unlike Grice's 'what is said', explicature is a matter of degree. A single utterance may in fact convey a number of different explicatures in context. These will differ in degree of explicitness depending on how far pragmatic processing has removed them from the literal content. But they will be explicatures so long as they are still developments of what is present in linguistic form.

The explicatures of an utterance don't of course tell us everything about what can be communicated in context. There are all sorts of further pieces of information that a hearer might understand from (58) or (59) that can't be explained as deriving from the linguistic form used. Suppose that (58) was in fact uttered in the context suggested in (60):

60. Is Peter's bat eligible to be judged in the brown bats category at the bat show?

Here, (58) conveys the information that Peter's bat isn't eligible to be judged in the brown bats category at the bat show, although that can't be seen as a development of anything in logical form. Suppose that (59) was uttered in the following context:

61. Will I have my watch back in time for my exam tomorrow?

The hearer of (59) will understand that he won't have his watch back in time for the exam, again not something that can be seen as a development of logical form. These further pieces of information are known in RT as 'implicatures', although they aren't exactly the same class of meanings as Gricean implicatures. As relevance theorist Robyn Carston explains it, linguistic semantic representation 'consists of an incomplete conceptual representation which functions as a schema or template for the pragmatic construction of propositional forms'. Some propositions derived in context are developments of the linguistic template, others not; 'the former are called explicatures, the latter implicatures' Carston (2004: 633). As Carston points out, the relevance theoretic distinction between explicature and implicature isn't the same as the traditional distinction between decoded and inferred. No proposition is, typically, entirely decoded; inferential pragmatic processing is needed from the start as layers of meanings are established.

Recall from their initial presentation of their disagreements with Grice that Sperber and Wilson identified his account of figurative uses of language such as metaphor and irony as problematic; there was no principled way of explaining how the hearer reached a meaning that was the opposite of literal content in the case of irony, and one that was different from but in some way related to literal content in the case of metaphor. In RT, such figurative meanings can be explained as implicatures. Because all implicatures are triggered by the principle of relevance, metaphorical and ironic meanings are themselves explained in terms of relevance rather than in terms of truthfulness, as they are for Grice. Here is a metaphorical example from Sperber and Wilson:

62. Robert is a bulldozer.

On a Gricean interpretation, of course, the hearer would recognize the blatant falsity of 'what is said' in (62), seek an interpretation of it that remained consistent with the assumption that the speaker was being cooperative, and arrive at an implicature such as that Robert is persistent, unstoppable, etc. In RT there is no potential for flouting of conversational expectations. Rather, the hearer will process (62) in order to arrive at a maximally relevant interpretation without unnecessary effort. Many of the contextual implications of (62) are contradictory and can be disregarded. 'The relevance of [62] will be established by finding a range of contextual effects which can be retained'; in effect this will be a 'range having to do with Robert's persistence, obstinacy, insensitivity and refusal to be deflected' (Sperber and Wilson 1995: 236).

Sperber and Wilson go on to suggest that 'the same is true of irony as is true of metaphor; whatever abilities and procedures are needed to understand it are independently needed for the interpretation of quite ordinary non-figurative utterances' (ibid.: 238). Ironic utterances in fact occur in very particular types of contexts; they generally pick up on or in some way 'echo' a previous utterance or at least a previous thought on the part of someone other than the current speaker. In instances of irony there is an implicit expression of an attitude on the part of the current speaker towards someone else's thought; the relevance of such examples depends on the information they convey about that attitude:

> 63. *Peter*: It's a lovely day for a picnic.
> [*They go for a picnic and it rains*]
> *Mary*: (*sarcastically*) It's a lovely day for a picnic, indeed.

The context for Mary's utterance in (63), together perhaps with her particular tone of voice, mean that her utterance will be interpreted as expressing an attitude of scornful rejection of what Peter previously said. This account, Sperber and Wilson argue, explains not just what is communicated on such occasions but why an ironic rather than literal form of expression was chosen. If Mary had just meant the opposite of what Peter said, namely 'it's not a lovely day for a picnic', it would have been much more relevant for her simply to say so. What she meant to convey was an attitude to what Peter said earlier. This explanation can be applied in cases such as (63) where an actual previous utterance is echoed, and in other cases where what is echoed is a thought that someone is attributed with. So on Sperber and Wilson's account, metaphor and irony turn out to be the results of very different forms of interpretation, rather than, as had traditionally been assumed, co-occurring in a class of 'trope' or figure of speech in which language is used figuratively rather than literally (ibid.: 243).

Relevance theorists, most notably Robyn Carston, have elaborated how the notion of explicature can incorporate many aspects of utterance interpretation which on a Gricean account would be explained as GCIs. The fact that the filling out of incomplete linguistic semantic representations to fully propositional explicatures always follows the demands of relevance and therefore always takes place in context, explains why in RT there is no place for default implicatures. Recall from our discussion of GCIs in Chapter 4 that the word 'and' appears to be interpreted differently in different contexts. Carston illustrates this in relation to the following examples. Example (64) would generally be interpreted as meaning that the two events described occurred in the sequence in which they are presented, whereas in (65) there is an understanding of situations occurring simultaneously. In (66) the meaning seems to include not simply sequence but causality; he mistook her for a hat stand because he was short-sighted. Examples such as (67) demonstrate that it's possible for an interpretation of a conjunction to give the understanding that the two conjuncts occurred in the reverse order to that in which they are presented:

> 64. He took off his boots and got into bed.
> 65. It's summer in England and it's winter in New Zealand.
> 66. He was short-sighted and mistook her for a hat stand.
> 67. She lives now in Crouch End and she lived in Muswell Hill three years ago.

Like Grice and the neo-Griceans such as Levinson, Carston rejects analyses of these differences based on semantics: the claim that 'and' is simply semantically ambiguous. However, unlike Grice and his successors she also rejects the idea that these examples can be explained in terms of a core meaning of 'and' that is equivalent to logical conjunction, together with GCIs to the more specific meanings. Carston argues rather that, although the specific meanings in context of 'and' are indeed pragmatically inferred, they contribute to the actual proposition expressed, or the basic explicature, of the utterance in each case. The question becomes no longer just one of trying to explain the semantic and pragmatic factors that account for the meaning of 'and'; it is an issue to do with the interpretation of the entire linguistic expression in which it occurs. 'And' itself provides merely a framework to be augmented pragmatically; it ensures, in effect, that the two conjuncts are taken together as a single pragmatic processing unit. 'Once we drop the untenable assumption that a pragmatic inference inevitably results in an implicature, it becomes pretty clear that these 'and'-enriching inferences have to be taken as contributions to the explicit content of an utterance' (Carston 2002: 258).

Carston offers a similar explanation of that specific type of GCI that Horn describes as 'scalar implicatures'. Recall that for Horn linguistic expressions that can be placed on scales of semantic strength are lower bounded by semantic content and upper bounded by implicature, as a result of the operation of the Q-Principle:

68. Some of the children were sick.
69. Some but not all of the children were sick.

Carston explains that, on the contrary, for relevance theorists the more precise or enriched meaning of (69) is an explicature of (68). It is not a matter of the presence of the word 'some' generating a default implicature of 'not all'. Rather, (68) as a whole fails to express a complete propositional meaning and must be filled out in accordance with the principle of relevance, always specific to its context of utterances.

As Carston explains, many aspects of utterance interpretation – which in a broadly Gricean framework must be added to 'what is said' by implicatures generated by the operation of the cooperative principle – are in a relevance theoretic framework explained as explicatures. 'There is a wide range of cases where it appears that pragmatics contributes to the proposition explicitly communicated by an utterance although there is no linguistic element indicating that a contextual value is required. That is, there is no overt indexical, and there is no compelling reason to suppose there is a covert element in the logical form of the utterance, and yet a contextually supplied constituent appears in the explicature' (Carston 2004: 639). Pairs of examples such as the following are particularly widely discussed in the pro- and anti-RT literature:

70. I've had breakfast.
71. I've been to Tibet.

Despite the apparent similarities between (70) and (71) there is a marked difference in their most likely interpretation. We are likely to understand (71) to mean something like 'I've been to Tibet at some time in my life', but (70) as 'I've had breakfast today'. For relevance theorists, these two different interpretations can be explained in terms of what yields the first optimally relevant interpretation in each case. The 'this morning' meaning is part of the explicature in (70), and from there further implicated meanings are likely to follow. Note that in RT there is no sense of a temporal sequencing in the derivation of these interpretations or any suggestion that the explicature must in some way be fully elaborated before it can be input into further processing to reach implicatures: 'comprehension is an on-line process, and hypotheses about explicatures, implicated premises, and implicated conclusions are developed in parallel against a background of expectations which may be revised or elaborated as the utterance unfolds' (Wilson and Sperber 2004: 615).

Some recent work in RT has focussed on lexical issues in pragmatics: that is on the processes involved in deriving the particular interpretations of various different words and types of words in the contexts in which they occur. Relevance theorists point to words that are not indexical and are not semantically ambiguous, but may be used to express a range of different meanings in different contexts. Carston and Powell (2006: 344) suggest the following two sets of examples to demonstrate this:

72. a. Pat opened the curtains.
    b. Bill opened his mouth.
    c. Sally opened her book to page 56.
    d. The child opened the package.
    e. The carpenter opened the wall.
    f. The surgeon opened the wound.

73. a. The ironing board is flat.
    b. My back garden is flat.
    c. He had a flat face and sad eyes.
    d. Holland is flat.
    e. The sea was flat.

The linguistically encoded content of the word 'opened' is the same in all of the examples in (72). Yet in each case it describes a very different process. Carston and Powell describe this as a pragmatic process of 'narrowing': the linguistically encoded meaning is narrowed down to express a more specific concept. In the examples in (73), on the other hand, the meaning of the adjective 'flat' undergoes a process of 'broadening' to a different degree in the different contexts; the term 'flat' might be said to apply more broadly, or more loosely, in (73d), for instance, than in (73a).

For Horn the processes that are here described as narrowing and broadening are explained in relation to two different pragmatic principles: the Q- and the R-Principles respectively. For relevance theorists, however, they are both the result of a single pragmatic process: the constant attempt to maximize relevance in all interpretations. The processes of narrowing and broadening take place during the relevance-driven derivation of a propositional form; the linguistic semantic meaning of the words 'opened' and 'flat' is pragmatically enriched slightly differently in each of the examples in (72) and (73). That is, broadening and narrowing take place in the derivation of the explicature of the utterance, not as an implicature. As was the case with the relevance theoretic account of what Horn describes as 'scalars', discussed above, there is no place for preferred interpretations or for implicated meanings that arise by default. Each process of enrichment is individually licensed by context and occurs during the process of deriving a propositional, truth-conditional form. Recall that for relevance theorists the derivation of explicatures and implicatures occur together and in response to each other, guided by the principle of relevance. Carston and Powell outline the process of enrichment that would take place along these lines for one example:

74. Be careful. The path is uneven.

Probably every path could be said to be 'uneven' to some extent, in that it will diverge from being a perfect plane. What the hearer of (74) needs to establish is the degree of unevenness that applies in this case. In response to the first part of the utterance, the hearer will expect the second part to be relevant by explaining why he should take care. Given that he is looking for this implication, 'he will enrich the very general encoded concept "uneven" so that the proposition explicitly communicated provides appropriate inferential warrant for such implications of the utterance' as that he might trip, should tread cautiously and so on (Carston and Powell 2006: 345). He will arrive at an interpretation of 'uneven' which is contained within but is not uniquely determined by the linguistic semantic meaning of 'uneven'.

Carston and Powell suggest that even metaphorical uses of words can be explained in terms of broadening or loosening, so they don't need to be explained separately from other processes of lexical interpretation. Recall that for Sperber and Wilson the interpretation of metaphorical uses of language was to be explained in terms of relevance, rather than of truth as it is in a Gricean account. To use Carston and Powell's example, imagine that (75) is used to describe some long and difficult ordeal other than the running of an actual marathon:

75. It was a marathon.

For the Gricean, the hearer would need to recognize that (75) is literally false (if, for instance, it describes a lengthy and taxing business meeting) and, following the assumption that it was nevertheless uttered cooperatively, seek an alternative implicated meaning that in some way likens it to a marathon and is true. The relevance theorist, however, describes the process of interpretation in this case as a fairly radical broadening of the semantic meaning of 'marathon' which, driven by the search for relevance, proceeds until an explicature is derived that is in fact quite far removed from the much more specific semantic meaning of the linguistic expression.

Conceptual and procedural meaning

Sperber and Wilson acknowledge that a satisfactory pragmatic theory must account for the fact that, although speakers often use their utterances to make statements of fact and convey information to hearers, they also do a lot of other things too. As Austin noted, they can use utterances to make promises, ask questions, issue orders, offer advice, as well as performing a host of other acts. However, Sperber and Wilson don't espouse a speech-act theoretic account whereby different acts are classified into different categories, recognizable to speakers and hearers on the basis of their illocutionary force. Rather for them the intended force of an utterance, like other aspects of what is communicated, is recovered in accordance with the principle of relevance in the specific context of utterance. In *Relevance* they argue that 'illocutionary-force indicators such as declarative or imperative mood or interrogative word order merely have to make manifest a rather abstract property of the speaker's informative intention: the direction in which the relevance of the utterance is to be sought' (Sperber and Wilson 1995: 254).

They later discussed illocutionary force indicators as 'encoding procedural constraints' (Wilson and Sperber 1993: 22), and this is a notion that has played a significant role in RT. Certain aspects of the message of an utterance, it is argued, are concerned not centrally with the idea or meaning conveyed but with how the utterance itself is to be processed or interpreted: with what procedures the hearer should follow in seeking the optimally relevant interpretation. They argue that such features of utterances contribute to relevance by decreasing the amount of processing effort required. As the quotation above indicates, procedural constraints are actually encoded in the linguistic form of what is uttered. Sperber and Wilson contrast the procedural aspects of what is linguistically encoded with conceptual aspects. Conceptual meaning is concerned with the propositional content of the utterance. Procedural meaning offers guidelines on how that propositional content should be manipulated during the process of interpretation; it tells the hearer 'how to "take" the sentence or phrase' (ibid.: 11).

The type of procedural meaning that has received most attention from relevance theorists has not in fact been illocutionary force as indicated by features such as grammatical mood, but the type of meaning encoded by what are known as 'DISCOURSE MARKERS'. These are a disparate group of linguistic expressions, difficult to summarize in a definite list. As Diane Blakemore has noted, even the term 'discourse marker' itself has not been used consistently in linguistics; you will come across terms such as 'pragmatic marker', 'discourse particle', 'discourse connective', 'discourse operator' and 'cue marker' covering much the same range of expressions (Blakemore 2004: 221). The class of discourse markers are probably best explained in relation to some typical members of that class: expressions such as 'well', 'but', 'so', 'indeed', 'in other words', 'as a result' and 'now'. Such expressions have become a considerable source of interest in recent pragmatics. They might in general terms be described as not contributing to the information conveyed by an utterance that contains them, but rather indicating something of how that information fits into the context or relates to the discourse in which the utterance occurs:

76. *A*: Is John happy in his new job?
    B: Well, he was whistling as he walked to the station yesterday morning.
77. *A*: I've just bought a new dress.
    B: But you bought a new dress last week.
78. *A*: I'm looking forward to going home tomorrow.
    B: In other words, you're not enjoying your holiday at all.

The discourse markers in B's utterances in (76)–(78) above are 'well', 'but' and 'in other words'. They function in relation to the context in which B's message is communicated. In informal terms, we could paraphrase (76B) as saying that the speaker is providing what information she can that might point towards an answer to A's question, (77B) as suggesting some element of contrast or apparent incompatibility between what A said and what B is contributing, and (78B) as indicating that what she is saying is an interpretation of or an inference drawn from what A has said. A Gricean interpretation of such expressions would rely on the notion of conventional implicature. The meanings introduced by expressions such as 'but' and 'well' could be said to be dependent on the linguistic properties of the expressions themselves, but not to contribute to truth-conditional content. Because truth-conditional meaning has traditionally been equated with semantics and aspects of utterance meaning that don't affect literal truth or falsity with pragmatics, the meanings introduced by such expressions have been seen as pragmatic in nature.

For relevance theorists such as Blakemore, the distinction between truth-conditional and non-truth-conditional meaning doesn't equate to the distinction between semantic and pragmatic meaning, and nor does it align neatly with their distinction between conceptual and procedural meaning. Decoding the linguistic form doesn't give a truth-conditional meaning, but merely a conceptual representation that can be developed by pragmatic inferencing to something that is truth-conditional, namely an explicature. Discourse markers do encode semantic meaning. But the meaning they encode is not conceptual; it is a set of directions for how the conceptual representation should be processed. That is, discourse markers illustrate 'the ways in which linguistic form may contribute to the inferential process involved in utterance understanding'; they encode procedural meaning (Blakemore 2002: 185).

5.3 Semantic autonomy and pragmatic intrusion

Right back in Chapter 1 when we were looking at possible definitions of pragmatics, we considered one account of pragmatics as being concerned with meaning that is not truth conditional. Perhaps the most influential exposition of this account is that by Gerald Gazdar back in the late 1970s: 'pragmatics has as its topic those aspects of the meaning of utterances which cannot be accounted for by straightforward reference to the truth conditions of the sentences uttered. Put crudely: pragmatics = meaning – truth conditions' (Gazdar 1979: 2). This position can be taken as equating more or less closely with Grice's two-level analysis of meaning, allowing for the unresolved imprecision of his account of the relationship between literal meaning and 'what is said'. The meanings of sentences are determined by the semantics of the words they contain and by the rules for combining these. As a direct result of semantics, sentences express propositions which specify conditions for their truth and which indeed can be evaluated for truth once a sentence is uttered in a context. This truth-conditional proposition may seriously under-determine, or may be different from or even contradictory to, what the speaker intends to communicate. The difference between literal and communicated meaning will depend on a range of pragmatic principles. The meaning these add to literal content may well be crucial to explaining what a speaker intended to communicate, but it will not have any effect on what would make what the speaker said literally true or false.

As we have seen, this version of the relationship between literal and intended meaning has been rejected by many working in modern pragmatics on the grounds that it is too simplistic. Perhaps most strikingly, relevance theorists have argued that linguistic semantics is generally not enough to give any truth-conditional meaning at all. Literal meaning must be filled out in accordance with the principle of relevance before an identifiable propositional meaning, an explicature, can be reached. Levinson's account, although it differs in many significant ways from RT, is similar in its insistence that semantics needs assistance from pragmatics in establishing even a minimal propositional meaning.

There is a variety of other contributions to recent debates over the nature of the interface between semantics and pragmatics that has tackled this question of the relationship between pragmatic principles and truth-conditional meaning. In general these have been concerned with the question of whether semantics can be autonomous: that is whether it can operate in isolation to establish a truth-conditional proposition, even a basic or minimal one, that can then be input into various pragmatic processes of interpretation. A closely related question is whether pragmatic principles must intrude into semantic description or whether they can operate in series with semantics, applying only after truth-conditional form has been specified. We will briefly survey a few of these approaches in conclusion of this chapter. First we will consider two versions of what has generally been termed 'contextualism' in semantics. Then we will consider two approaches, 'insensitive semantics' and 'minimal semantics', that renew the case for autonomous semantics, delivering a complete and truth-conditional, if minimal, propositional meaning for every sentence. In making the case for the separate functioning of pragmatic principles, accounts such as these could be seen as returning to a more Gricean explanation of linguistic communication.

Contextualism

Contextualism is a general term used to describe a range of linguistic theories that argue that meaning, even literal or semantic meaning, is always dependent on context. There are various different versions of contextualism. One that has played a particularly prominent role in recent pragmatics is that associated with François Recanati; Recanati has engaged in debate with both neo-Griceans and relevance theorists. But an earlier argument for contextualism can be found in the work of John Searle, the philosopher responsible for the development of Austin's ideas into a theory of speech acts and for the introduction of the notion of 'indirect speech acts'.

Searle argued that semantic meaning is always relative to context: that, in effect, it isn't possible to discuss the literal meaning of a sentence until certain facts have been established about the context in which it is uttered. That isn't to say that he argued that there was no such thing as the literal meaning of a sentence; he was adamant that sentence meaning should properly be distinguished from pragmatic meaning. What he was arguing against was just the idea that a sentence could properly be said to have a meaning that was independent of context. For many sentences, this notion of a meaning independent of context is vacuous because, whether we are aware of it or not, when we think about the meaning of the sentence we actually do so in relation to a host of background assumptions about the types of context in which it is most likely to be uttered.

Some aspects of contextually dependent meaning are fairly obvious and include the resolution of the reference of expressions such as pronouns. But Searle considers a sentence that looks like it ought to have a clear literal meaning, independent of context, such as:

79. The cat is on the mat.

Even here, some of the aspects of meaning that are dependent on context are, as Searle puts it, 'already realised in the semantic elements of the sentence' (Searle 1978: 121). The exact identity of 'the cat' and 'the mat', for instance, and the time referred to by the present tense verb 'is', will vary depending on the contexts in which the sentence can be uttered. But Searle argues that even aspects of the sentence meaning that don't appear to make allowances for context, that is even non-deictic elements, are actually dependent for their meaning on context-dependent assumptions. He discusses a range of possible if outlandish sounding contexts of utterance to challenge the idea that a sentence such as (79) has an identifiable meaning independent of context. He argues that our understanding of the meaning of (79) actually depends on a series of assumptions about cats and mats, together with expectations about the operations of gravity and of other physical laws. In possible contexts where such assumptions don't hold, it may be necessary to revise what we would consider to be the truth conditions expressed literally by an example such as (79). Precisely because these assumptions are so familiar to us, it is difficult to detach them from our interpretation of a sentence and examine them. Such assumptions are distinct from the content of the sentence, although they contribute to determining what makes particular uses of it literally true. This context-dependent literal truth can still be clearly distinguished from the meaning a speaker intends by a particular utterance of the sentence in context: 'the distinction, for example, between literal sentence meaning and metaphorical or ironical utterance meaning remains intact' (ibid.: 133).

Recanati has developed his position from the late 1980s onwards, explaining it in terms of what he sees as a fundamental opposition between contextualists and anti-contextualists. 'Natural language sentences, according to [contextualists], are essentially context-sensitive, and do not have determinate truth conditions' (Recanati 1994: 157). For Recanati, there is an erroneous assumption in the philosophy of language and in pragmatics that the anti-contextualists have won the argument. He notes that many anti-contextualists regard Grice's theory of conversation as having defeated contextualism once and for all, but argues that the victory was apparent rather than actual. According to the Gricean account, what is literally said by any linguistic form doesn't change with context; any differences in interpretation between one context and the next are to be explained in terms of various types of conversational implicature, not in terms of a variation in the propositional content of what was said. This gives the Gricean account the apparent advantage of avoiding having to say that linguistic meaning varies from one context to the next; it obviates the need for multiple semantic ambiguity.

For the contextualist, what is literally said does depend to a large extent on the context of utterance. But, Recanati argues, this is not at all the same thing as admitting that the contextualist is committed to a potentially unlimited variation in the linguistic meaning of the sentence, or to multiple semantic ambiguity. On the contrary, for the contextualist the proposition expressed on any occasion is in part dependent on, but is by no means wholly defined by, linguistic meaning. Linguistic meaning alone isn't sufficient to give a fully propositional form, but must be supplemented in various ways by information dependent on context in order to determine the proposition expressed, or 'what is said'.

Recanati therefore proposes a 'what is said' that is further removed from linguistic meaning than Grice's version and is concomitantly much more dependent on contextual features. 'What is said' combines with what is implicated to give the full significance of what is communicated, and for Recanati both of these elements must be accessible to conscious scrutiny. One of his arguments with Grice is that the Gricean 'what is said' often seems to be at odds with what naive hearers will understand to have been communicated. He considers familiar examples such as (80):

80. I have had breakfast.

As we have seen, a traditional account of what was literally said in (80) would be that the speaker has had breakfast at some time in her life. However, the speaker is generally understood as communicating that she has had breakfast within a relevant time period: most likely on the same day on which she is speaking. The Gricean account of 'what is said' is often, as in this case, in contravention of Recanati's 'Availability Principle': ' "what is said" must be analysed in conformity to the intuitions shared by those who fully understand the utterance – typically the speaker and the hearer, in a normal conversational setting' (Recanati 2004a: 14). Sentence meaning, a purely linguistic and technical matter, need not be available to conscious scrutiny. But 'what is said', the proposition literally expressed in any context, must be apparent and recognizable to ordinary language users.

For Recanati, 'what is said' is derived from linguistic meaning by the application in context of various principles of interpretation, all of them pragmatic in nature. Like Searle, he allows that some of these are driven by the semantic elements of the sentence itself. If 'the meaning of the sentence contains something like a "slot" requiring completion or a "free variable" requiring contextual instantiation', then a pragmatic process known as 'saturation' is necessary to provide this extra information (Recanati 2004a: 7). The most obvious examples of such slots are pronouns and other deictic expressions. So in example (80) above, a process of saturation will provide the referent of the pronoun 'I'. Other examples of expressions that trigger saturation suggested by Recanati are 'he' and 'John's book'.

Saturation is mandatory, in that it is triggered by linguistic form; if an expression such as a pronoun is present then a process of saturation is necessary before a complete propositional form can be reached. Recanati draws attention to further pragmatic processes, which also operate on linguistic form to give a propositional 'what is said', but which unlike saturation are optional in nature. They are independently motivated in context rather than required by linguistic form. Recanati terms the three optional pragmatic processes 'enrichment', 'loosening' and 'semantic transfer'. Enrichment occurs when some information that is part of what is said is not strictly included in, or even directly motivated by, linguistic form:

81. Mary took out her key and opened the door.

We understand that Mary opened the door mentioned in the second conjunct with the key mentioned in the first conjunct. Because this interpretation is intuitively available, the availability principle states that it must be part of what is said. However, it isn't part of the explicit content of the sentence. Hence it is to be explained in terms of the operation of a pragmatic process of enrichment, prior to the derivation of the propositional content of the utterance.

Recanati's second optional pragmatic principle – loosening – can be seen as an opposite process of enrichment. That is, an element of meaning that would normally be attached to a particular linguistic form is dropped, or loosened, in a particular context:

82. The ATM swallowed my credit card.

In the context of having 'ATM', an inanimate object, as its subject, some of the usual requirements for a true use of 'swallowed' are relaxed; we get a wider application than usual of the verb. Finally, in 'semantic transfer', the interpretation derived by pragmatic processing is simply different from the usual semantic meaning of an expression, although related to it in some systematic way:

83. The ham sandwich left without paying.

Because of the semantic anomaly apparent in (83), 'the ham sandwich' will, through a process of semantic transfer, be interpreted as referring to 'the person who ordered the ham sandwich'.

The pragmatic processes of saturation, enrichment, loosening and semantic transfer operate on semantic form to give a fully propositional 'what is said', intuitively accessible to speaker and hearer. They don't of course tell us everything about what may be communicated in context. Once 'what is said' is established a hearer may well draw a variety of contextual implications from it that can't be explained in terms of these processes; further and different pragmatic processes are needed to explain these. In fact, Recanati groups together saturation, enrichment, loosening and semantic transfer as the class of 'primary pragmatic principles'. These are distinct from various 'secondary pragmatic principles' that operate once 'what is said' has been established. Primary pragmatic processes apply before any proposition at all is established. Secondary pragmatic processes then add to this further to give a full 'what is communicated'. Secondary pragmatic processes give rise to inferences that are intuitively available to the hearer and, Recanati concedes, are something roughly equivalent to Gricean conversational implicature.

In order to illustrate the operation of Recanati's pragmatic mechanisms, let's return to example (80) above, reproduced here for ease of reference as (84):

84. I have had breakfast.

The sentence meaning of (84) is a technical linguistic phenomenon that needn't be thought of in terms of a propositional form and that isn't available to intuitive inspection. Primary pragmatic processes work on this to reach a propositional 'what is said', intuitively available to both speaker and hearer. In particular, the presence of the personal pronoun 'I' triggers a process of saturation by which this is given a reference. A process of enrichment fills out the meaning of the predicate so that 'what is said' includes a specification of the relevant time scale, most likely 'this morning'. Once 'what is said' has been established, secondary pragmatic principles, concerned with contextual inferences, operate to give a full 'what is communicated'. Depending on the specifics of the context these may be, for instance, that the speaker isn't hungry, that she doesn't want the piece of toast she is being offered, or she doesn't want to hear a particularly gruesome story.

Recanati's pragmatic theory differs from Grice's most significantly in that for him pragmatic principles operate in order to produce 'what is said', itself a pragmatic level of meaning. For Grice the processes that contribute to 'what is said' beyond semantic decoding are reference assignment and disambiguation, both driven solely by linguistic form. Recanati's 'saturation' is this type of process, but the other pragmatic processes that contribute to 'what is said' are, as he puts it, 'pragmatically controlled pragmatic processes' (Recanati 2004a: 95). As we have seen, in Levinson's neo-Gricean theory and also in RT there is scope for pragmatic intrusion into the specification of a propositional meaning for 'what is said' (for relevance theorists, an explicature). But in these approaches the pragmatic principles at play in deriving the proposition expressed are the same as those involved in generating contextual implicatures. For Levinson the relevant pragmatic principles are his Q-, I- and M-Principles; for relevance theorists it is simply the cognitive drive towards relevance. For Recanati, however, primary pragmatic processes operate to produce a propositional form while quite different secondary pragmatic processes operate on this propositional form to generate the total significance of what is communicated in context.

Insensitive semantics

Recanati's contextualism extends the role of contextually motivated pragmatic principles beyond Grice's original conception. Pragmatic processing no longer operates on fully specified literal meaning in order to explain what is non-truth-conditionally implicated. Rather, it plays a fundamental part in establishing the truth-conditional proposition that forms 'what is said'. Other recent accounts, however, have argued for a much more limited scope, therefore in a sense a much more traditional role, for pragmatic processes. They have maintained that pragmatics shouldn't intrude into the establishment of literal meaning, but should indeed operate only once the process of semantic interpretation is complete. At the same time, they have urged linguists not to expect too much of literal, semantic meaning. Pragmatic processes are capable of operating on, indeed must operate on, very minimal meaning, highly under-determined in relation to the full significance of what is communicated in context.

Herman Cappelen and Ernie Lepore take issue with Recanati's 'Availability Principle' and also with Sperber and Wilson's notion of pragmatically enriched explicature as the propositional content of any utterance. They argue that it is perfectly possible to envisage pragmatic principles as operating on a very slight, indeed a non-propositional, semantic form, provided that there is no expectation that semantic form should be intuitively recognized by ordinary language users or that it should go a long way towards explaining what a hearer understands from an utterance in context. In direct opposition to contextualism, they propose that there is a very specific and very limited set of natural language expressions that are semantically sensitive to context. These are easy to spot and correspond to intuitive expectations about the dependence of meaning on context. Cappelen and Lepore draw attention to, for instance: personal pronouns such as 'I', 'he' and 'they'; demonstrative pronouns such as 'that' and 'this'; adverbs such as 'here', 'there', 'yesterday' and 'today'; as well as certain nouns such as 'foreigner' and 'native' and certain adjectives such as 'local' and 'imported'. All other linguistic expressions have complete meanings independent of context of use. 'Beyond fixing the semantic value of these obviously context sensitive expressions, the context of utterance has no effect on the proposition semantically expressed' (Cappelen and Lepore 2005: 2). A linguistic expression may, it is true, be used to refer to a range of different things or express a range of different ideas in different contexts. But its linguistic meaning remains constant, and is in fact not hard to identify. The linguistic meaning of an expression is that element of meaning that all different utterances of the expression have in common. For instance, there is a common relation that A, B and C stand in to their various projects if A is ready to commit a bank robbery, B is ready to eat dinner and C is ready to take an exam. That common relation is the semantic meaning of 'ready'. For Cappelen and Lepore semantics is 'insensitive', in that it operates independently of, or is not sensitive to, any features of individual contexts of utterance. They endorse what they describe as 'semantic minimalism'. The semantic meaning of a sentence may be very impoverished in comparison with what an utterance of that sentence can communicate in context, and may in fact be minimal, but it nevertheless has an independent and self-sufficient existence. It expresses a complete, truth-conditional proposition.

Hand in hand with Cappelen and Lepore's 'semantic minimalism' goes their 'speech act pluralism'. They argue that philosophers and linguists have been hampered by the mistaken idea that every utterance in its context must express one particular proposition or perform one particular speech act. They label this 'speech act monism' (ibid. : 133). The emphasis has then been on determining what that proposition or that speech act is and establishing how it can be explained by semantic and pragmatic principles. This idea needs to be replaced by the realization that an utterance in context can express a number of different propositions at one and the same time. One of these will be the semantic meaning of the sentence uttered. The others will be derived from it and related to it in a range of different ways, dictated in context by various different pragmatic principles. The sentence meaning is constant across contexts; this particular proposition will be expressed every time the sentence is uttered. It is an aspect of what was said when a particular sentence was uttered that we can understand even if we know nothing about the context in which the utterance took place. That isn't to say that it will necessarily, or even most likely, be the most important proposition communicated. As Cappelen and Lepore put it: 'in most regular-life contexts, the semantic content is not what is focussed upon. We're interested in all the extra stuff; that's typically where the juice is' (ibid. 2005: 207).

Here is an illustration of semantic minimalism and speech act pluralism from Cappelen and Lepore (2005: 145). Consider an utterance of the sentence (85):

85. She is happy.

This contains two expressions that are deictic and therefore contextually sensitive: the pronoun 'she' and the present tense element of the verb 'is'. In context these can be related to the female 'b' and the time of utterance as 't'. The proposition semantically expressed is, therefore, <b, t, happy> . Now in context, (85) could of course be used to express a host of other types of propositions, for instance that b's medication is working or that she is ready to meet her sister or, if it is being used ironically, that she is in a bad mood. These, however, needn't be explained in relation to the linguistic meaning of (85). In fact, it seems that for Cappelen and Lepore they may not be available for systematic explanation at all: 'we suspect that it just isn't the sort of subject matter that lends itself to any kind of serious, or rigorous, theorizing' (ibid.: 146). In Gricean pragmatics these types of meaning would be described as particularized conversational implicatures and explained in relation to the maxims of cooperation. For Cappelen and Lepore they are at best marginal to a systematic account of meaning.

Minimal semantics

Cappelen and Lepore's 'insensitive semantics' is one of a number of recent theories of meaning that have sought to reinstate linguistic semantics as the source of complete, if minimal, propositions, and to keep pragmatics quite separate. In such theories pragmatics principles operate on semantic output, filling out these propositions in context to give a full specification of what is communicated. Emma Borg argues for 'the retention of a level of propositional content divorced from current speaker intentions' (Borg 2006: 264); semantics operates independently of, and prior to, any actual use of linguistic expressions by speakers for the purposes of communication. In defending this position she takes issue with what she calls 'dual pragmatics', singling out in particular Sperber and Wilson's RT and Recanati's version of contextualism. 'Dual pragmatics' encompasses any theory in which pragmatic principles apply twice, once in tandem with linguistic semantics in order to establish a truth-conditional proposition as sentence meaning, and then subsequently to enrich this proposition to give full utterance meaning. We can dispense with dual pragmatics, Borg argues, if we don't have unduly high expectations of semantics. The role of semantics is simply to explain formal linguistic meaning, and it's a mistake to expect it to give a full account of the nature of meaning or indeed to explain communication. A host of factors to do with context and speaker intention are certainly necessary for a sufficient account of communication, but that doesn't mean that they have any place in semantic theory itself.

Borg acknowledges that in many cases a sentence might appear not to specify enough semantic material to produce a truth-conditional proposition. This is what has led proponents of dual pragmatics to argue that information must be supplied in context before a sentence can be properly truth-evaluable. But she argues that closer attention to the formal properties of the various elements of the sentence will reveal that such information is in fact accounted for even in the absence of any context. A case in point is Borg's example, reproduced here as (86):

86. Jill can't continue.

Out of context, (86) doesn't seem to express a complete proposition. People can't be simply able or unable to continue; they are able or unable to continue *something*. In response to this example, a relevance theorist would argue that information from a context of utterance, selected in accordance with the general cognitive quest for relevance, must be added to linguistic content to yield a truth-conditional explicature. Recanati would claim that the primary pragmatic process of enrichment must take place, adding information about what it is that Jill can't continue, in order for (86) to express a propositional 'what is said'. Borg, however, maintains an entirely formal semantic account of the proposition expressed in (86), drawing an analogy with (87):

87. John kicks.

'Kick' is a transitive verb. This is a linguistic fact about that particular word, so one of its formal semantic features is that it specifies a subject slot and a direct object slot. The semantic form of (87) is therefore actually 'John kicks something'; a minimal proposition, certainly, but containing enough information to be truth-evaluable. A similar explanation can be offered for (86). It is a semantic fact about the verb 'continue' that it possesses an object slot. Hence no information is needed from context to explain that the semantic form of (86) is actually 'Jill can't continue something'. An utterance of (86) in a particular context is of course likely to express something much more specific than this, but that more specific information needn't be seen as part of the proposition specified by the semantics of (86). This is consistent with Borg's general claim that 'because a speaker means a proposition, p, by her utterance of a sentence, s, this does not necessarily mean that the sentence uttered should be treated as having the semantic value that p', an insight that she attributes back to Grice (Borg 2004: 247).

Borg's position is at odds with the idea that literal meaning must be psychologically available to ordinary language users. In general, advocates of minimal semantics reject the claim that speakers' and hearers' intuitions are relevant to theories concerned with the distinction between semantic and pragmatic meaning. Defenders of versions of Gricean pragmatics have also dismissed the significance of such intuitions. Jennifer Saul argues that it's quite possible for speakers and hearers to be wrong about 'what is said' on any particular occasion, although she herself is keen to stress that this position doesn't commit her to semantic minimalism (Saul 2002: 357 n.).

Kent Bach has argued explicitly against using intuitions about semantic form as a way of discriminating between theories of meaning. It's not possible to be confident, he argues, that judgements of meaning are really about semantics and not about pragmatically determined understanding. Furthermore, 'intuitions are tainted' by the fact that when people are asked to think about the meaning of a sentence they often, unwittingly, imagine it in stereotypical context (Bach 2007: 39). There is in fact no need for people to have intuitions about semantics in order to communicate successfully: 'in the course of speaking and listening to one another, we generally do not consciously reflect on the semantic content of the sentences we hear or on what is said in their utterance. We are focussed on what we are communicating and on what is being communicated to us' (Bach 2001: 26). For Bach, unlike for Borg or Cappelen and Lepore, 'what is said', which is entirely semantic in nature, can be so minimal that it doesn't even express a proposition, but linguists needn't worry about this. Semantics is concerned with the formal property of encoded meaning. It is the job of pragmatics to explain the difference between this and what we understand when a sentence is used communicatively in context.

EXERCISES

1. Consider the following extract from *Gaudy Night* by Dorothy L. Sayers (1935). Harriet Vane is staying as a guest in her former Oxford all female college. Padgett is the college porter. The decorators have been brought in to repair damages to the new library that occurred last night, and that must have been caused deliberately by someone inside the college.

   > Some time later, Harriet and the Dean, decorously robed and gowned, found themselves passing along the East side of Queen Elizabeth Building in the wake of Padgett and the decorators' foreman.
   >
   > 'You ladies,' Padgett was heard to say, 'will 'ave their larks, same as young gentlemen.'
   >
   > 'When I was a lad,' replied the foreman, 'young ladies was young ladies. And young gentlemen was young gentlemen. If you get my meaning.'
   >
   > 'Wot this country wants,' said Padgett, 'is a 'Itler.'
   >
   > 'That's right,' said the foreman. 'Keep the girls at 'ome. Funny kind 'o job you got 'ere, mate. Wot was you, afore you took to keepin' a 'en 'ouse?'
   >
   > 'Assistant camel 'and at the Zoo. Very interesting job it was, too.'
   >
   > 'Wot made you chuck it?'
   >
   > 'Blood-poison. I was bit in the arm,' said Padgett, 'by a female.'
   >
   > 'Ah,' said the foreman decorator.

   How might Horn's Q- and R-Principles explain the ways in which the two speakers communicate more than they literally say? How would the analysis of this passage differ if instead we used Levinson's Q-, I- and M-Principles?

2. Recall the extract from George W. Bush's final press conference that we considered in Chapter 2:

   Bush: Yes, Suzanne. Finally got your name right, after how many years? Six years?

   Q: Eight years. (Laughter)

   Bush: Eight years.

   How would a relevance theorist explain what is communicated in this exchange, particularly in relation to the 'explicatures' and the 'implicatures' of the utterances?

3. Contrasting RT with Gricean pragmatics, Robyn Carston comments that 'there is no generalized/particularized distinction, but a continuum of cases from the very frequent to the one-off; the system runs on a single communicative principle, so all implicatures are necessarily relevance implicatures' (Carston 2002: 142). Is what

Carston is describing here a simpler pragmatic theory, and is it therefore a better one? Is anything lost if pragmatics dispenses with the notion of GCIs or default implicatures?

4. Consider the following paragraph from the introduction to Jennifer Saul's (2002) paper:

> Relevance theorists, I will suggest, systematically misunderstand Grice by taking him to be engaged in the same project that they are: making sense of the psychological processes by which we interpret utterances. Notions involved with this project will need to be ones that are relevant to the psychology of utterance interpretation. Thus, it is only reasonable that relevance theorists will require that what is said and what is implicated should be psychologically real to the audience. (We will see that this requirement plays a crucial role in their arguments against Grice.) Grice, I will argue, was not pursuing this project. Rather, I will suggest that he was trying to make sense of quite a different notion of what is said: one on which both speaker and audience may be wrong about what is said. On this sort of notion, psychological reality is not a requirement. So objections to Grice based on a requirement of psychological reality will fail.

Discuss the implications of this passage. Do you agree with Saul that Gricean pragmatics and RT are not in fact incompatible with each other?

5. Recanati's 'Availability Principle' states that '"what is said" must be analysed in conformity to the intuitions shared by those who fully understand the utterance – typically the speaker and the hearer, in a normal conversational setting' (Recanati 2004a: 14). How convincing do you find this?

6. Carston (2004: 652) comments on Borg's minimal semantics that:

> one might have qualms about the apparent prediction of this approach that sentences such as *Mary can't continue, John's book is on a shelf, It's night-time* are virtually always true (so what one 'says' in uttering them is inevitably true), and that others, such as *Everyone was sick, The door is closed, It isn't night-time* are always false. One might also have qualms about the consequence that quite often every proposition the speaker communicates/means by uttering a linguistic expression is an implicature; that is, she communicates nothing explicitly.

Do you share these qualms?

FURTHER READING

Neo-Griceans

The main primary sources for Horn's Q- and R-Principles include Horn (1972, 1989, 2004, 2006, 2007) and for Levinson's Q-, I- and M-Principles Levinson (2000, 2004). Introductions to neo-Gricean pragmatics in textbooks include Huang (2007) Chapter 2, Grundy (2008) Chapter 5 and Ariel (2008) Chapter 3. Sbisà (2006) offers an overview of neo-Gricean pragmatics and a comparison between it and RT. Geurts and Nouwen (2007) and Geurts (2009) are interesting recent commentaries on scalar implicature, supporting a notion of it but challenging some of the details of Horn's account. Bach (2006b), however, argues that scalar 'implicatures' are not in fact true implicatures. Pelletier and Hartline (2006) address some specific issues raised by Horn's scalar analysis of 'or'. Huang (2004) discusses the significance of Levinson's pragmatics to anaphora.

Relevance theory

The main primary source for RT remains Sperber and Wilson (1995), along with more recent work such as Wilson and Sperber (2004), Carston (2002, 2004) and Carston and Powell (2006). The relevance theoretic approach to the distinction between conceptual and procedural meaning has been developed largely in the work of Diane Blakemore (see particularly Blakemore 1987, 2002, 2004, 2007).

Among textbooks on pragmatics, Blakemore (1992) is entirely devoted to RT, while there are discussions of it in Ariel (2008) Chapter 3, Huang (2007) Chapter 6 and Grundy (2008) Chapter 6. Cummings (2005) Chapter 4 takes a critical approach to RT, while Christie (2000) Chapter 6 gives a feminist perspective.

Burton-Roberts (2005) takes issue with RT in general, and in particular with Carston's account of many types of meaning previously taken to be GCIs in terms of basic-level explicatures. Saul (2002) comments on recent renewed interest in Grice's 'what is said', arguing that unlike RT Grice never aimed at psychological plausibility, and therefore that the two types of pragmatic theory are not necessarily in conflict.

Horn (2007) suggests that, despite claims to reduce Grice's maxims to a single principle, RT, like his own form of pragmatics, relies essentially on a balance between effort and effect. Ariel (2002) discusses the minimal meaning of utterances, or what she calls 'privileged interactional interpretations', which speakers are taken most centrally to be committed to, and argues that these don't necessarily correspond either to Gricean 'what is said' or to relevance theorists' explicatures.

Semantic autonomy and pragmatic intrusion

Searle's account of contextualism, including his highly imaginative discussion of his example 'The cat is on the mat', can be found in Searle (1978). The primary account of Recanati's version of contextualism is Recanati (2004a). Cappelen and Lepore set out their views on semantic minimalism and speech act pluralism in Cappelen and Lepore (2005) and contrast them with RT, in particular in Cappelen and Lepore (2007). Borg's chief account of minimal semantics is Borg (2004). See the essays collected in Preyer and Peter (2007) for various responses, both supportive and critical, to Cappelen and Lepore (2005). In particular Cappelen (2007) offers a summary overview of some of the approaches considered in this chapter, including RT, contextualism and minimal semantics. Borg (2007) argues that Cappelen and Lepore are in fact not minimal enough in their approach; the range of contextual features that are allowed to play a part in determining semantic context should be limited to formal and objective features, ruling out matters relating to speakers' intentions.

Textbooks that introduce the ideas discussed in section 5.3 include Huang (2007) Chapter 7 and Ariel (2008) Chapter 8. Thompson (2007) gives an overview of approaches within pragmatics to conventional or literal meaning.

Among other recent contributions to the debate that are not discussed here, Atlas (2005) defends the notion of literal, linguistic meaning but rejects the idea that it must be 'scrutable': that is, that every expression has a single, precise and intuitively accessible meaning. Jaszczolt (2005) allows that pragmatic information plays a role in determining truth-conditional content, that is the truth conditions of utterances. Truth-conditional content is formed by a process of merger of information from various sources, both semantic and pragmatic.

Applications of Pragmatics

6

The last two chapters have been concerned with early and more recent pragmatic theories. We have considered the most significant data that have been discussed, compared treatments of these by different pragmaticists and looked at some of the main areas of current debate. Of course there is a lot more to be said about pragmatic theory. The debates continue and the literature surrounding them is vast and ever expanding. We haven't attempted to survey the whole field or even to touch on every current pragmatic theory. But hopefully we have seen enough to understand the central concerns of theoretical pragmatics and the main differences between its major branches. In this chapter we are going to do something different. We are going to consider some of the ways in which pragmatics has impacted on the study of language more generally. That is, we will be looking at some of the ways in which pragmatic theory has been applied to the analysis and understanding of data from various different types of language use.

There are two main reasons why those studying pragmatics should take an interest in its applications. The first is that it is here that pragmatics becomes relevant to the study of language and its use in what we might call the 'real world'. Some of the debates in pragmatics, even the very notion that there is something identifiably distinct about pragmatic as opposed to linguistic meaning, might begin to appear a little esoteric or of marginal interest to the study of real language. But in a number of areas, including those we will be considering here, pragmatic theory has in fact provided an illuminating framework for the consideration of language and of various ways in which it is used. Secondly, these topics offer the chance for pragmaticists to test out their theories in relation to various types of 'real life' data, as opposed to the invented data subjected to intuitive interpretation that has been current throughout much of the history of theoretical pragmatics. As we will see, opinion is divided among pragmaticists about what sort of data is appropriate to testing their theories and even as to whether pragmatic theories can legitimately be compared in relation to such data at all. But for many pragmaticists these applications are valuable evidence of the relevance and of the empirical testability of pragmatic theory.

The five different applications we will be concerned with in this chapter all represent ways in which pragmatics interacts with another area of study, either within or outside of linguistics. The first topic, politeness, is centred on the interaction of pragmatics with sociolinguistics and with sociology more generally; it is concerned with how and why the type of indirect or non-literal meaning that pragmatics is concerned with is negotiated in social situations. The data under investigation is drawn from real conversation and other kinds of talk. The second topic, literature, has obvious connections with fields such as stylistics and literary criticism. The data can broadly be defined as literary texts. The third section of this chapter is concerned with the relationship between pragmatics and language acquisition, bringing pragmatics into contact with psycholinguistics and developmental psychology more generally, and confronting it with data drawn from observations of children's early use of language. The next section, on clinical pragmatics, is concerned with the pragmatic aspects of clinical linguistics and of language pathology and neurology. It draws on both experimental and observational data. Finally we will consider experimental pragmatics, a relatively new development. Here, pragmatics interacts with experimental psycholinguistics. The data are largely collected in laboratories, in experiments designed to find out about how people process and interpret relevant linguistic examples.

6.1 Politeness

The study of politeness in linguistic interaction, or what is sometimes known as 'politeness theory', draws heavily on the pragmatic theories that we have been considering, particularly on speech act theory and Grice's account of conversational implicature. The link is perhaps obvious; speech act theory is concerned with how we negotiate and perform various different acts, including those that might be socially difficult, while implicature is concerned with the ways in which we convey messages indirectly or without being blatant. When he proposed the notion of indirect speech acts, John Searle suggested that 'in directives, politeness is the chief motivation for indirectness' (Searle 1975a: 36). And when Paul Grice contemplated his own account of the maxims of conversation he suggested that 'there are, of course, all sorts of other maxims (aesthetic, social, or moral in character), such as "Be polite", that are also normally observed by participants in talk exchanges, and these may also generate nonconventional implicatures' (Grice 1975: 28). He conceded that he had restricted his discussion to those maxims most centrally concerned with the exchange of information and that ideally 'the scheme needs to be generalized to allow for such general purposes as influencing or directing the actions of others' (ibid.).

Politeness theory takes account of these other general purposes. It also interacts with ideas drawn from sociology to try to explain the social motivations for speaking to each other as we do. That is, it is centrally concerned with how people behave, not with the more abstract or logical aspects of meaning. It was originally developed at least in part as a theory explaining invented data of the type familiar in pragmatics. But from very early on politeness theorists also drew on isolated examples from attested language usage. Increasingly now linguistic politeness is discussed in relation to more extended pieces of linguistic interaction.

Why politeness?

In its ordinary everyday use, the term 'politeness' is used to describe behaviour that shows respect and consideration for others, or ways of talking that avoid rudeness or abruptness. But it would be mistaken to believe that linguistic politeness is simply the study of why people say 'please' and 'thank you', or of when they avoid taboo or potentially offensive expressions, although these issues are certainly relevant. There are many different versions of politeness theory and many different linguists working in the field today, but they are generally all keen to point out that it is not a formalized way of explaining how people choose to be nice to each other or to obey social etiquette. Rather, it is a theory of meaning that puts language fully in its social context. If Grice's theory of conversation and other more recent pragmatic theories are attempts to explain how a speaker's meaning on any occasion is often different from the literal meaning of the words uttered, then politeness theory is an attempt to explain why this is the case, or what it is about the use of language in social contexts that leads us to choose certain forms of expression.

Some of the earliest contributions to the development of politeness theory came from Robin Lakoff who published two short but very influential articles on the subject in the early 1970s. She was impressed by Grice's theory of conversation, which he had first presented just a few years earlier, and by his attempt to explain systematically how words can convey more than their literal meaning, but she proposed to discuss this in terms not so much of conveying information as of establishing and maintaining social relationships. Lakoff's more general motivation was to argue that the formal rules of the semantics and syntax of a language, however carefully expressed, could never do the full job of explaining the differences in acceptability and interpretation between different utterances. To do so 'it is essential to take extralinguistic contextual factors into account: respective status of speaker and addressee, the type of social situation in which they find themselves, the real-world knowledge or beliefs a speaker brings to a discourse, his lack of desire to commit himself to a position, etc.' (Lakoff 1972: 926).

Lakoff went on to suggest that there are two basic rules of pragmatic competence, namely 'Be clear' and 'Be polite' (Lakoff 1973: 296). These two rules will often come into conflict; being as clear as possible might make it difficult or impossible always to be polite, while being polite will in some situations rule out being clear. Depending on the nature of the context, one or other of these rules will win or will overrule the other. In very formal or technical contexts the accurate conveying of information is generally prized highly. So in the courtroom, for instance, or the lecture theatre, clarity may be allowed to overrule politeness. But in many everyday conversations in various social settings, the establishing and maintaining of social relationships is more important than getting across any particular piece of information. So in the majority of cases of language use, the drive towards politeness wins out over the drive towards clarity.

Lakoff suggested that Grice's maxims of conversation were a pretty good account of the specific rules of clarity, under the general heading 'Be clear'. She proposed three specific rules of politeness under the general heading 'Be polite', namely 'Don't impose', 'Give options' and 'Make A [the hearer] feel good – be friendly' (ibid.: 298). We will look briefly at some of Lakoff's examples of these rules in operation, so as to see what sort of effects politeness has on how we express ourselves.

Rule 1, 'Don't impose', puts the onus on speakers not to make demands on hearers. For instance, in our society at least, it is considered rather an imposition to ask people questions relating to money and wealth; we are putting people on the spot or requiring them to impart information that they may be reluctant or embarrassed to give. This can explain examples such as the following:

1. May I ask how much you paid for that vase, Mr Hoving?

This seems unnecessarily lengthy and complex compared with a simple interrogative such as:

2. How much did you pay for that vase?

That is, (1) seems to be in breach of the pragmatic rules of clarity. But this can be explained by the speaker's observance of the more pressing rules of politeness; the hearer negotiates the social situation by apparently asking for permission to perform the difficult task. In general, of course, (1) will be interpreted and responded to not as a request for permission to ask the question, but as the question itself. Lakoff suggests that the rule 'Don't impose' can also explain examples where social distance between speakers is reinforced by a syntactically more complex form of expression. 'The proper butler says [3] not [4]' (ibid.: 298), because the passive construction in (3) creates a sense of distance between speaker and hearer, and therefore seems more polite:

3. Dinner is served.
4. Would you like to eat?

Rule 2, 'Give options', requires that the speaker give the hearer at least apparent options to interpret an utterance how he chooses or to avoid an interpretation that might be in some way unpleasant. It tends to steer speakers away from blunt expressions of opinion or fact. In some situations a speaker might choose the form of expression in (5), even if (6) better represents her views:

5. Nixon is sort of conservative.
6. Nixon is an arch-conservative.

Rule 2 also explains the preference in some situations for euphemisms over literal expression of taboo subjects. We might talk about someone being 'hard up' in preference to describing them as 'poor'. The euphemism is less clear than the literal term but it is more polite because it at least purports to offer the hearer the option of not reaching the unpleasant interpretation. In fact, in cases of euphemism the hearer does necessarily reach the unpleasant interpretation every time, but nevertheless euphemisms can be seen as conventionalized ways of acting as if one is trying not to require the hearer to contemplate something unpleasant.

Finally, rule 3 enjoins the speaker to 'make A feel good' or to produce a sense of camaraderie or friendship between speaker and hearer. Lakoff points out that, again, this may well be more a matter of convention than of genuine warm feeling. Nevertheless, it offers a further explanation of why we often depart from absolute clarity when speaking in social situations, particularly of why we often seem to use more words than are strictly necessary to get our message across. Such extra words include using the hearer's first name or alternatively a marker of camaraderie such as 'mate' or 'love'. They also include expressions such as 'like', 'you know' and 'I mean', whose function is not informative but rather to involve the hearer in what is being said.

Politeness and face

Early work on linguistic politeness, such as Lakoff's, focussed on the ways in which social pressures towards politeness influence how people express themselves. It suggested that such pressures are often at least as significant as the demands on a speaker to be clear in the interests of imparting information. Insights such as these formed the basis of the theory of politeness developed by Penelope Brown and Stephen Levinson. Brown and Levinson's politeness theory was developed from the early 1970s onwards, was for some time predominant in the field, and, even now, after recent questioning and criticisms, remains one of the main frameworks within which linguistic politeness is discussed. Brown and Levinson introduced the notion of 'FACE' into politeness theory, which allowed them to describe a much more formalized and systematic account of the different ways in which the demands of politeness shape our utterances. They based their account of face on work dating from the 1950s by the sociologist Ervine Goffman, in which he explored ways in which individuals relate to and present themselves in social interaction. For Goffman, 'the term *face* may be defined as the positive social value a person effectively claims for himself by the line others assume he has taken during a particular contact', where 'line' refers to a pattern of behaviour which expresses the individual's view of the situation and evaluation of himself (Goffman 1955: 319). Goffman noticed that people's conduct in social situations is often geared towards maintaining that positive social value, a norm of behaviour which he describes as the rule of self-respect. However, at the same time there is an onus on individuals in social situations to be aware of the desire of others to maintain their face or to act in a way that supports their positive social value; Goffman describes this as the rule of considerateness. 'The combined effect of the rule of self-respect and the rule of considerateness is that the person tends to conduct himself during an encounter so as to maintain both his own face and the face of the other participants' (ibid.: 323).

Brown and Levinson took on board Goffman's point that social participants need to pay attention both to the needs of their own face and to the needs of the faces of others. They discussed this in terms of the 'face wants' of the participants in any interaction (Brown and Levinson 1987: 13). But they divided the notion of face into two distinct categories, labelled respectively 'positive' and 'negative' face, reflecting the fact that people's concerns about social standing take two distinct forms. Positive face is something close to Goffman's account of positive social value; it is the desire of the individual to look good or to appear to be liked and appreciated. Negative face is close to Lakoff's earlier insight that politeness requires speakers to give their hearers options and not to impose on them; it is the desire of the individual not to have their actions impeded or more informally not to be pushed around.

With two participants involved in any interaction (the speaker and the hearer) and with two types of face to be considered for each, we end up with four different types of pressures on how the speaker expresses herself, driven by four different types of 'face wants'. It might help to think about the restrictions on the speaker imposed by these face wants in terms of the following table:

	Face of speaker	*Face of hearer*
Positive face	(a) Look good	(b) Make hearer look good
Negative face	(c) Don't give in too easily	(d) Don't push hearer around

Not uncommonly in our everyday experience as speakers, we find ourselves in a position of wanting to do something that might potentially go against the restrictions outlined above. If we all just went round saying nice things about each other and trying not to have any effect on each other's actions we would be very limited in terms of what we could do. Moreover, some of the requirements of politeness are actually in conflict with each other. For instance, if a speaker attended exclusively to the hearer's negative face wants and avoided trying to impose her wishes on his actions, conforming to requirement (d) above, she might end up infringing the requirement (c) above by giving in too easily to what the hearer wants, and therefore ignoring her own negative face wants. So for various reasons we often need to do things that have the potential to damage one of these four face requirements: that is, we have to perform an 'intrinsically FACE THREATENING ACT' (ibid.: 65). Examples of acts that might threaten the speaker's positive face (a) include confessions and admissions of guilt, such as:

7. I have spilled red wine all over your presentation notes.

Threats to the speaker's negative face (c) would include examples where the speaker needs to accept an offer or invitation from a previous speaker, thereby being in danger of putting herself in debt, and possibly also of giving in to another's wishes too easily:

8. *A*: Will you come out for a drink with me this evening?
   B: Yes!

Threats to the hearer's positive face (b) include any act that might suggest that the speaker doesn't care about the hearer's wants or feelings. These arise when the speaker wants to criticize the hearer in some way, complain to him or disagree with him:

9. You made a complete idiot of yourself this evening.

Finally, threats to the hearer's negative face (d) arise when the speaker apparently doesn't intend to avoid impeding the hearer's freedom of action, as when she performs acts such as orders, requests or advice:

10. Lend me ten pounds.

Examples (7)–(10) are all cases of face threatening acts performed 'on record' and 'baldly'. That is, the speaker makes no attempt to disguise what she is doing or to make amends for the possible face damage. Face threatening acts are by no means always performed in this way. Brown and Levinson discuss a range of options that are available to a speaker who finds herself in a situation where she wants to perform a face threatening act. She may choose not to perform that act at all or, if the potential for loss of face is not too great, to go ahead and perform it. If she does perform it and if the potential face damage is not too great she may perform it on record, but she may also choose to perform it 'off record'. That is, she presents what she wants to say in a manner that allows for more than one possible interpretation, so that the hearer is at least superficially given the option of not interpreting what she has said in a manner that is face threatening. Examples (11)–(14) are possible 'off record' performances of the same acts as were performed 'on record' in (7)–(10):

11. There has been a little accident involving some red wine and your presentation notes.
12. *A*: Will you come out for a drink with me this evening?
    B: I think I'm free.
13. You weren't at your best this evening.
14. I've arranged to go out for a drink and I've just realized my wallet is empty.

If the speaker decides to take the risk and perform her act on record, she still has some options. She may perform it baldly, as in examples (7)–(10) above, or she may take some 'redressive action', that is she may add material to her utterance that is designed to make up for the face threatening act by 'giving face': by indicating that despite possible evidence to the contrary the speaker does recognize that the hearer has face wants. The redressive action may be orientated towards either positive or negative face. That is, an intrinsically face threatening act such as (10) above could be redressed by giving either positive or negative face, depending on the situation and the relationship between speaker and hearer. Redressive action concerned with the hearer's positive face wants involve adding a reassurance that the speaker likes the hearer or considers him to be in some ways the same as or on the same side as herself. The speaker indicates that, despite the fact that she needs to perform a face threatening act, she nevertheless wants the fulfilment of the hearer's positive face wants:

15. Would you help out a friend in trouble? Lend me ten pounds.

Redressive action concerned with the hearer's negative face wants indicates that the speaker is not willingly imposing on the hearer or impeding his actions. If the act performed baldly in (10) were instead performed with redressive action with regard to the negative face of the hearer, we might get something like:

16. I'm really sorry to trouble you, but could you lend me ten pounds?

Brown and Levinson suggest that the decision of how to produce a face threatening act depends on an assessment by the speaker of how serious the act is, or more technically on a calculation of its weightiness. The options for the speaker outlined above can be understood in terms of a hierarchy of ways of performing a face threatening act in response to this weightiness. If such an act is very weighty the speaker may avoid producing it altogether. If it is not too weighty to avoid but still quite weighty she will produce it 'off record'. If it is not so weighty as to go off record she may choose to produce it on record but with some form of redressive action. Finally, if the weightiness of the face threatening act is slight, there may be no motivation for the speaker not to produce it on record and without redressive action, or baldly. Potentially face threatening acts may also be performed baldly in cases where the urgency of the situation overrides the needs of politeness. You are more likely to shout 'run!' than 'I wonder if I could trouble you to run?' if you are crossing a field with a companion and see a bull charging at you.

The weightiness of a face threatening act depends on a number of sociological variables which, Brown and Levinson claim, can be identified and assessed in relation to each other. They label these sociological variables 'D' for social distance between speaker and hearer, 'P' for the relative power of speaker and hearer, and 'R' for the ranking of impositions within the relevant culture. They suggest (Brown and Levinson 1987: 75) the following equation for the calculation of the weightiness of a face threatening act, where 'W' stands for weightiness, 'x' for any particular face threatening act, 'S' for speaker and 'H' for hearer:

$$Wx = D(S, H) + P(H, S) + Rx$$

In effect, the weightiness of a particular face threatening act is determined by the extent of the social distance between speaker and hearer, combined with the degree of power that the hearer has over the speaker, together with the extent to which that particular face threatening act is deemed to be an imposition in that culture.

Both of the ways in which a speaker may choose to lessen the impact of a face threatening act, that is both producing an act off-record and employing redressive action, involve the speaker in some apparent breach of the maxims of conversation. That is, the speaker is less clear or more wordy than is appropriate for the simple business of getting her message across. However, the fact that the speaker has put more effort into producing a longer and more complex utterance than was strictly necessary for informative purposes ensures that she is seen to be striving to satisfy face wants.

Universality and impoliteness

Linguistic politeness has been an extremely prolific area for the application of pragmatic analysis, particularly over the last couple of decades. Brown and Levinson's seminal account has certainly not been abandoned, but it has been joined by various others accounts of politeness and subjected to various criticism and revisions. In this section we will consider briefly two types of criticisms of Brown and Levinson and the theories of politeness that have developed from them: criticisms in terms of claims for universality and in terms of the need for linguists to be able to account not just for politeness, but also for impoliteness.

As we saw in the last chapter, Grice's apparent belief that the cooperative principle identified a general norm in human behaviour led to some criticism that his theory applied in fact just to one specific type of society. This in turn gave rise to some discussion as to whether the theory of conversation was ever intended, and therefore whether it could fairly be judged, as a generalized account of human interaction in all societies. Brown and Levinson were much more explicit in their claim for general application of their theory. In fact, the full title of their 1987 book is *Politeness: Some Universals in Language Usage*. This claim has some empirical backing. The data for their study was drawn from three languages and cultures chosen in part because they are unrelated: Tamil as spoken in Southern India, Tzeltal as spoken by Mayan Indians in Mexico, and also English as spoken in the USA and England. But critics have questioned whether this range is really sufficient to justify a claim to have identified universal trends in human behaviour. Just two years after the book was published, Yoshiko Matsumoto produced a study of politeness phenomena in Japanese, noting that 'a socially and situationally adequate level of politeness and adequate honorifics must obligatorily be encoded in every utterance even in the absence of any potential face threatening act' (Matsumoto 1989: 207). This suggested a challenge to Brown and Levinson's claim that politeness phenomena typically accompany only potentially face threatening acts. Soon afterwards Watts et al. challenged Brown and Levinson's formulation of negative face in terms of an individual's desire to be unimpeded in relation both to maintaining material possessions and to freedom of action, asking: 'how is negative face to be understood in a culture in which the possessions of individuals are at one and the same time the possessions of the community, or in which the individual's right to act depends crucially on the consent of the community?' (Watts et al. 1992: 10). Since then much work on other world languages has contributed to the challenge posed to Brown and Levinson's claims for the universality of the particular politeness strategies they identified. Lakoff and Ide have questioned whether universality in politeness theory is either possible or desirable. They caution against any hasty claims to having discovered universals in language use, especially if these are based on observations by those who are outsiders to the cultural context under study (as Brown and Levinson were cultural outsiders to the non-Western languages from which they drew data). 'Until native participants are in a position to construct their own systematicities without pressure from Euro-based models, every allegedly universal system is open to suspicion' (Lakoff and Ide 2005: 10).

As well as a growing interest in how politeness is manifest in a variety of different languages and cultures, there have been a number of recent studies of linguistic exchanges in which politeness is not in fact a determining factor: in exchanges that are hostile, argumentative or conflictual. Such studies are generally identified by the heading 'impoliteness theory'; a central claim is that Brown and Levinson, with their focus on how politeness is maintained and potentially face threatening acts are mitigated, are unable to account for or explain impolite interactions.

Impoliteness theory focusses on how and when impoliteness is triggered and how it can be resolved. It also considers how impolite acts are sequenced within a particular exchange (see, for instance, Bousfield 2008: 2). In all of this, the notion of 'face' remains central. But here the emphasis is on how a speaker may express her contribution to a conversation so as deliberately to threaten or damage the hearer's face wants (Culpeper 1996). Impoliteness theory also pays attention to wider social context and particularly to the interaction between impoliteness and power. This is of course a relationship that Brown and Levinson were aware of; relative power of speaker and hearer was one of the factors in their equation for measuring the weightiness of a potential face threatening act. But power is not central to their model, whereas impoliteness is 'inextricably tied up with the very concept of power because an interlocutor whose face is damaged by an utterance suddenly finds his or her response options to be sharply restricted' (Bousfield and Locher 2008: 8–9).

Because impoliteness theory focusses on argument and other kinds of conflict, including how it is initiated, how it progresses and potentially how it is resolved, its data tend to consist of longer stretches of naturally occurring conversation than were traditionally used in politeness studies. Brown and Levinson's theory is illustrated with both invented and real-life data, but almost exclusively with examples that stretch no further than one turn in a conversation (Bousfield 2008: 3). In drawing on the analysis of longer stretches of data, impoliteness theory is in line with developments in studies of linguistic politeness more generally. Politeness theorists now tend to deal with transcribed conversations or conversational extracts. This brings into the discussion of politeness both a greater range of contextual features and conversational features such as intonation, gesture and gaze.

Recent studies in both politeness and impoliteness have also suggested ambitions towards more specific applications than was the case in earlier work in politeness theory and indeed in pragmatic theory in general. Brown and Levinson's main purposes were to understand the operations of politeness in verbal interaction, to say something systematic about these, and hopefully also to identify something universal in human interactive behaviour. More recent studies have suggested that politeness and impoliteness theory might have something to contribute to how people actually interact in their day-to-day lives. Bousfield suggests that: 'when one is placed in a confrontational, non-harmonious situation, a powerful tool in neutralizing aggression can be had by having the knowledge of (1) the types of impoliteness that may be used, and (2) the effective linguistic "management" and "defence" options that are available within the discourse and the situational context in which one is operating' (ibid.: 4). Lakoff and Ide have even suggested that a better understanding of linguistic politeness, particularly with reference to cross-cultural aspects, might be able to contribute to global understanding and to American sensitivity after 9/11 (Lakoff and Ide 2005: 12).

Nowadays it is common among pragmaticists working in this area to describe the field as '(im)politeness theories', reflecting the fact that there are a plurality of frameworks and approaches, based around similar types of data and motivations to explain them. Politeness theory was always one that crossed the boundaries of pragmatics and other related disciplines, but according to present-day accounts it is increasingly a multidisciplinary field. Lakoff and Ide (2005) see the present day study of linguistic politeness as drawing from features and principles of both pragmatics and sociolinguistics. Bargiela-Chiappini sees the future as even more interdisciplinary: 'a future, much needed, multi-disciplinary enquiry into the nature of face and impolite behaviour is sure to lead linguists, pragmaticians, sociologists and social psychologists to share insights on the very essence of the social order' (Bargiela-Chiappini 2003: 1467). According to Xie '(im)politeness cannot, and can never be confined to one branch of linguistics; rather, (im)politeness is an area of multidisciplinary, interdisciplinary or even transdisciplinary nature' (Xie 2003: 817).

6.2 Literature

The various concepts and frameworks for analysis developed within pragmatics have proved useful tools for the analysis of literary texts. This is of course not surprising; pragmatics is all about studying language in use, and creating and reading literary texts are important and interesting examples of language use. Monika Fludernik has suggested that the emergence of pragmatics in fact made possible the application of serious linguistic analysis to literary texts: 'the recent paradigm shift within linguistics towards a pragmatic model of language use ... has made it possible to bridge the divide between the literary and the linguistic approaches to language' (Fludernik 1996: 585). The increased interest in language use within linguistics has allowed for an emphasis in the linguistic analysis of literature not just on the formal properties of literary texts but on their contextual and intertextual properties.

The central frameworks of classical pragmatics, speech act theory and conversational implicature were quickly recognized as potentially valuable to the study of literary texts. More recently, politeness theory and RT have also been applied to literature, although neo-Gricean pragmatic theories have not been widely used in this area. The pragmatic theories have provided valuable insights into various aspects of the texts studied. In addition, particularly in the case of RT, the process of analysing literary texts has in turn fed back into the development and the exposition of the pragmatic theories themselves.

Broadly speaking, there are two main focusses for those interested in the relationship between pragmatics and literature. Firstly, there is the application of pragmatic theory to the analysis of the language of individual literary texts, in order to illustrate some aspect of how meaning is conveyed, how characters interact or how the author or narrator of a text interacts with the reader. That is, these approaches take some aspect of pragmatic meaning as their method and some literary text or texts as their data. Secondly, the resources of some pragmatic theories have been applied to more general questions about the nature of literature itself. Pragmatics has been employed in the discussion of what actually constitutes a literary text or a literary reading – that is, of the question 'what is literature?' The theory of speech acts has proved particularly significant in this area of study. For this reason, we will leave the consideration of the relationship between speech act theory and literature until we focus on this question in the final part of this section.

Implicature

Some of the earliest attempts to apply pragmatics to literary texts involved Gricean analyses. Soon after 'Logic and conversation' was first published, linguists with an interest in literary texts began to consider the question of whether Grice's account of interaction in conversation also applied to interactions between writers and readers of literary texts. Teun van Dijk suggested that the maxims 'partly concern the structure of the utterance itself, and might therefore be called "stylistic"' (van Dijk 1976: 44). In this, he was suggesting an affinity between Grice's work and stylistics, the linguistic analysis of the language of literary texts. He argued that literature needs to be explained by its own set of maxims. These would be similar in nature to the maxims of cooperation, but different in detail. Mary Louise Pratt, however, argued that it ought to be possible to explain literature alongside other types of discourse, without recourse to a separate set of maxims. In literary texts the cooperative principle is particularly secure between author and reader, and therefore 'we can freely and joyfully jeopardize it' (Pratt 1977: 215). This means that flouting and the resultant conversational implicatures are particularly characteristic of literary texts, although they are properties shared with all communicative uses of language.

Pratt uses the opening sentence of Jane Austen's *Pride and Prejudice* as an example of the cooperative principle operating in the discourse between author and reader:

17. It is a truth universally acknowledged that a single man in possession of a fortune must be in want of a wife.

Pratt suggests a list of possible interpretations of this, but puts forward the following as the most likely explanation. The reader believes neither the 'truth' nor the claim that it is universally acknowledged. The reader also believes that the author of the novel is aware of this. Therefore, it is reasonable to assume that Austen is deliberately flouting the maxims of Quality; she is saying something that is blatantly false for communicative effect, rather than trying to deceive the reader into believing what she says. The most obvious implicature in this example of flouting Quality is that the opposite of what is stated is actually the case: that is, an interpretation of the statement as ironic. However, as Grice has pointed out, irony has not just propositional but emotive meaning (Grice 1978: 53). The reader is encouraged towards a mocking attitude to those who hold either belief. Furthermore, the reader is being made aware right from the start that an ironical attitude will be useful to understanding and evaluating what is to come.

Other analyses of literary texts within a Gricean framework have concentrated on conversational exchanges represented within literary texts. For example, the introduction to a collection of essays edited by Culpeper, Short and Verdonk contains a short but compelling analysis. The editors argue that Grice's theory of implicature can tell us things that the 'poetry analysis tool kit', or the basic skills of formal linguistic analysis, can't. They consider the following brief exchange from Shakespeare's *Henry IV (Part 2)*, in which the new King is deliberately snubbing his old companion Falstaff as he turns his back on his former, carefree lifestyle and takes on the responsibilities of his new office:

18. *Falstaff*: My King! My Jove! I speak to thee, my heart!
    King: I know thee not old man. Fall to thy prayers.

Culper et al. suggest that formal linguistic analysis can reveal features such as the syntactic patterning in this passage, the phonological parallelism and the pun on 'Falstaff'. But we need Gricean analysis fully to explain the snub. Falstaff's 'I speak to thee' flouts the maxims of Quantity by stating information that is obvious to the hearer. It therefore introduces an implicature that the King's behaviour is marked in ignoring Falstaff and that the King should acknowledge his friend. In turn, the King's 'I know thee not' flouts the maxims of Quality; the King is saying something that is clearly known to both speaker and hearer to be false. The implicature is that the King wants nothing more to do with Falstaff (Culpeper et al. 1998).

Other studies of literary texts in relation to Gricean implicature include Gilbert (1995) who looks at Shakespearean monologue, and Gautam and

Sharma (1986) and Herman (1994) who study dialogue in *Waiting for Godot* and *Finnegans Wake* respectively. Cooper (1998) analyses implicated meaning in *The Taming of the Shrew*, with an eye to the interpretations available to the audience and the widely different interpretations in fact reached by critics. More recently Blake (2002) has used Gricean implicature to discuss editing decisions and reconstructing original textual features in Shakespeare's plays.

Relevance Theory

Sperber and Wilson outlined an analysis of various features of language use typically associated with literary texts, including metaphor, when they first introduced RT. In doing so, they included a discussion of what makes some metaphors particularly creative or 'poetic'. Although they did little with this idea in relation to literature, many linguists and stylisticians have subsequently used RT as a framework for the analysis of specific literary texts. Some of these have continued the discussion of metaphor, while others have looked at further aspects of how literary texts convey meaning and how they are interpreted by readers.

Sperber and Wilson (1995) draw attention to the notion of weak implicature to explain how some uses of language achieve what they describe as 'poetic effects'. The contextual effects of an utterance can, as we saw in the last chapter, be divided between those aspects of meaning that are communicated explicitly and those that are communicated implicitly. Sperber and Wilson's contention is that implicatures are not all of the same status, and are not all equally licensed by what the speaker has said and predictable as to how the hearer will interpret what he has heard. Rather, implicatures can be seen as existing along a continuous scale ranging from the very strong ones that are most clearly invited by what the speaker has said to the progressively weaker ones that may be the result of individual preoccupations on the part of the hearer, which couldn't have been known in advance by the speaker. Sperber and Wilson use the following examples to illustrate this point:

19. *Peter*: Would you drive a Mercedes?
    Mary: I wouldn't drive ANY expensive car.
20. Mary wouldn't drive a Mercedes.
21. Mary wouldn't drive a Rolls Royce.
22. Mary would not go on a cruise.

For Sperber and Wilson, (20)–(22) are all implicatures of Mary's utterance in (19). Indeed many other propositions might potentially be implicated as well as these three. But (20)–(22) differ in terms of their strength, becoming progressively weaker as we go down the list. That is, (20) is clearly licensed by what Mary has said, given that the most relevant interpretation of her utterance for Peter will be as an answer to his question. If he chooses to continue processing her utterance after he has arrived at (20), that is if he sees it as appropriately relevant to do so, he may well arrive at the interpretation in (21); Mary might reasonably be assumed to realize that he might reach this conclusion and to have sanctioned it. However, if Peter continues to search for implicatures beyond this and, based on his own assumptions about wealth and lifestyles, arrives at the interpretation in (22), then the link between his interpretation and the explicit content of what Mary actually committed herself to is relatively weak; Mary could hardly be said to have encouraged Peter to reach this conclusion.

Sperber and Wilson define a 'poetic effect' as 'the peculiar effect of an utterance which achieves most of its relevance through a wide array of weak implicatures' (Sperber and Wilson 1995: 222). In relation to metaphor, they suggest that the more poetic or more creative metaphors may be those that allow for a wide range of potential but unpredictable weak implicatures. We considered example (24) below in relation to Sperber and Wilson's account of metaphor in Chapter 5. In fact, they present it on a scale (23)–(25), the metaphors becoming progressively more poetic or creative:

23. This room is a pigsty.
24. Robert is a bulldozer.
25. His ink is pale.

The very strong implicature of (23) is that the room is filthy and untidy. Example (24), in contrast, conveys no single obvious strong implicature, but rather a host of slightly weaker implicatures concerning Robert's persistency, obstinacy and so on. The hearer must take some responsibility in reaching an interpretation. Example (25) is a translation of a scathing comment made by Flaubert on the poet Leconte de Lisle. For Sperber and Wilson 'the only way of establishing the relevance of this utterance is to look for a wide range of very weak implicatures' (ibid.: 237). These will vary from one interpreter to the next, depending on their existing knowledge of the poet and of poetry in general, and on their imagination. Flaubert is to be given credit for creating a metaphor that has the potential to generate such a wide and creative range of weak implicatures.

RT became a fruitful and, for a time at least, a controversial vehicle for stylistic analysis. It was applied particularly in the discussion of poetry: for instance of Browning (MacMahon 1996) and Frost (Pilkington 1991). Pilkington analysed Frost's *Stopping by Woods on a Snowy Evening*, with particular focus on the final stanza:

26. The woods are lovely, dark and deep,
    But I have promises to keep,
    And miles to go before I sleep,
    And miles to go before I sleep.

Pilkington argues that the metaphorical potential of the poem causes readers to access their individual encyclopedic entries for particular prominent words and to explore a range of possible weak implicatures that they may give rise to. This explains differences in subjective interpretations. For instance, the repetition of the final line makes the word 'sleep' particularly prominent. There is no determinate way to identify what interpretation this will give rise to, but readers who are encouraged to explore their knowledge of the associations of the word 'sleep' may well eventually establish a link between this word and death.

The controversy surrounding the application of RT to literary texts arose during the late 1990s, advocates of RT including Clark (1996), Pilkington et al. (1997) and Pilkington (2000) and opponents including (Green 1997, 1998) and Toolan (1998a, 1999). The central question was whether readings such as Pilkington's of Frost really added anything to existing mechanisms for poetic interpretation. Critics of RT claimed that such analyses simply rewrote subjective responses to literary texts using new technical vocabulary, rather than offering anything new. The relevance theorists replied that they were not in the business of offering interpretations: as Pilkington (2000) puts it of solving crossword clues set by the poet. Rather, the business of RT was to explain poetic or rhetorical effects, determining the value of a work in relation to its potential for weak and strong implicatures. RT was a good tool for this, the relevance theorists argued, because it allowed for a continuum of implicatures from fully determinate to very indeterminate. In effect, the wider the range of potential weak implicatures the more poetic the message and therefore the text.

Politeness

The various accounts of how politeness operates as a shaping force in the interactions between language users have been applied to the analysis of literary texts. As was the case with Gricean implicature, two types of interaction are available for such analysis: broadly the interactions between the characters within the text, and the interaction that readers themselves enter into more generally in reading the text. Perhaps because it is an area of pragmatics specifically targeted at explaining spoken discourse, the types of literary texts most frequently discussed in relation to politeness are scripts from plays and films. For instance, Simpson (1989) analyses the relationship between the two central characters in Ionesco's play *The Lesson*, and how it changes during the course of the play, with reference to Brown and Levinson's politeness theory. Culpeper (1998) describes the changes in terms of impoliteness strategies that take place in the two central characters in the Hollywood film *The Scent of a Woman*. He comments on the light that such an analysis sheds on character development, on the relationships between characters, and on dramatic tension. Norman Blake makes a similar point in relation to Shakespeare, commenting that 'changes in levels of politeness may be significant in an understanding of the motivation of a character and in assessing the tone of a scene' (Blake 2002: 325).

Work on the applications of politeness theory to the interpretation of novels and of poetry has tended to focus on the relationship between the implied author and the reader. This is an instance of interpersonal communication like any other and so, the argument goes, it ought to be amenable to analysis in terms of politeness phenomena. Sell (1985) argues that 'if we feel that Dickens can be cheeky, or George Eliot importunate, or Pope politely impolite, it would be worth trying to pin these impressions down' (see also Sell 1991b). Simpson (1989) suggests that positive politeness might provide a valuable tool for revealing fictional attitudes and predispositions. He proposes that his readers might try to compare the passage from Charlotte Brontë's *Jane Eyre* quoted in (27) with the opening passage from J. D. Salinger's *The Catcher in the Rye* quoted in (28) in this light:

27. Gentle reader, may you never feel what I then felt! May your eyes never shed such stormy, scalding, heart-rung tears as poured from mine. May you never appeal to heaven in tears so hopeless and agonized as in that hour left my lips: for never may you, like me dread to be the instrument of evil to what you wholly love.

28. If you want to hear about it, the first thing you'll probably want to know is where I was born, and what my lousy childhood was like, and how my parents were occupied and all before they had me, and all that David Copperfield kind of crap, but I don't feel like going in to it, if you want to know the truth. In the first place, that stuff bores me, and in the second place, my parents would have about two hemorrhages apiece if I told anything pretty personal about them.

As a first start on this exercise, we could note that these passages are both first person narratives, therefore purporting to contain utterances addressed from a central character to the reader. Example (27) is marked by many terms that register positive politeness on the part of that character. For instance 'Gentle reader' is a term of endearment or praise and the list of wishes that begin with 'may you never feel what I then felt!' are explicit expressions of hope for the good of the reader. In general, the use of metaphor and of syntactic patterning demonstrate an interest in making the story interesting and pleasing for the reader, again a marker of positive politeness.

Example (28), in contrast, is marked by a series of face threatening acts, which are in general not redressed. References to 'my lousy childhood' and so on indicate that the character doesn't care about presenting himself in a good light, and therefore that he doesn't care about the reader's opinion of him. Use of taboo language such as 'crap' is a threat to the speaker's positive face. 'I don't feel like going in to it' demonstrates the character's blatant refusal to comply with the assumed wishes of the reader. 'That stuff bores me' continues the refusal, and also expresses unmitigated disagreement with the assumed interests of the reader. Notice, however, that this passage is not devoid of positive politeness. The tone is humorous and mocking of literary conventions, which makes the passage interesting and potentially amusing for the reader.

The nature of literary texts

As well as various ways of analysing what happens within specific literary texts, pragmatics holds out the possibility of being able to say something about the distinctive characteristics of literary texts themselves, particularly in relation to the ways in which readers interact with literary texts or the type of discourse that characterizes an engagement with a literary text. Much of the early work in this area concentrated on the potential of speech act theory to explain literature, largely thanks to an article by John Searle (1974). We considered Searle's work on speech acts in Chapter 4. When he turned his attention to literature, Searle suggested that a formal account was not really possible. Literature was defined not by linguistic characteristics of a text but by 'a set of attitudes we take towards a stretch of discourse' (ibid.: 59). What counts as literature is therefore a subjective matter for individual readers and is not amenable to further analysis.

Searle did suggest, however, that is was possible to say something formal about what constitutes fiction, with the proviso that some although not necessarily all fictional texts are also literary texts. Searle considers a passage from a literary text: the opening of Iris Murdoch's novel *The Red and the Green*:

29. Ten more glorious days without horses! So thought Second Lieutenant Andrew Chase-White recently commissioned in the distinguished regiment of King Edward's Horse, as he pottered contentedly in a garden on the outskirts of Dublin on a sunny Sunday afternoon in April nineteen-sixteen.

Searle compares this with a non-fictional extract from a newspaper article. Both his examples are made up of declarative sentences. Searle argues that declarative locutionary acts are typically associated with the illocutionary function of giving some factual information. This situation holds in the case of the newspaper article, but not in that of the novel. Yet, Searle observes, we don't need to learn an entirely new language, or even a new way of using language, in order to read the novel. Searle's suggestion is that: '[Iris Murdoch] is pretending, one could say, to make an assertion, or acting as if she were making an assertion, or going through the motions of making an assertion, or imitating the making of an assertion. I place no great store by any of these verb phrases but let us go to work on "pretend", as it is as good as any' (Searle 1979: 65). Searle's claim is that in fictional texts the author is pretending to perform certain illocutionary acts, particularly the act of asserting information. It is a pretence recognized and willingly entered into by the reader. The locutionary act of stating is genuine, but the illocutionary act of describing the world is a pretence. Other studies to consider the merits and demerits of a 'pretence'-based account of fiction include Smith (1971), Armstrong (1971), Reichert (1977), Brown and Steinmann (1978), Beardsley (1978) and Currie (1985).

More recent work on the pragmatics of literature continues to consider the rules operating between text and reader, or the nature of the discourse involved. As MacMahon suggests in her overview of the field: 'much of contemporary literary pragmatics is concerned to define literature as having a special functional and communicative status, yet at the same time operating on principles recognizably similar to those of nonliterary discourses' (MacMahon 2006: 234). This work addresses the same questions as were addressed by theorists such as those mentioned above, but without the use of a speech act framework. MacMahon cites work which draws instead on the presuppositions that hold in literary and non-literary discourses; literature might be said to be a particular type of discourse characterized by a looseness of presuppositional constraints in relation to many other types of discourse (Chapman and Routledge 1999).

The characteristic discourse of literature has been defined within this framework as 'non-truth-committed discourse', because readers are committed neither to the truth nor to the falsity of what they read (Routledge and Chapman 2003). Others have considered pragmatics as a way of assessing the relationship between writer and reader (for instance Feng and Shen 2001, who discuss the relationship between playwright and audience).

6.3 Language acquisition

Much recent research into the acquisition by children of their first language has been dominated by the debate between Chomskyans and their opponents over the issue of the existence of an innate language faculty. This debate has mainly focussed on the acquisition of 'core' linguistic competencies such as syntax. But some studies of child language have focussed on the acquisition of pragmatic abilities, such as the ability to recognize indirect speech acts or to understand conversational implicatures. These studies may have a lot to tell us both about the nature of the pragmatic processes involved in these abilities and about the relationship between these pragmatic processes and linguistic knowledge more generally.

In an overview of studies of early pragmatic development, Haydeé Marcos has suggested that the general issues concerning the relationships between language, the functions it can be used to perform and the contexts in which it is used for communication are the same as in the study of pragmatics more generally, but that the specific questions raised in relation to these issues are different. Children must develop an ability to understand and distinguish the different social and physical aspects of any instance of communication. They must also develop an ability to use language to perform a variety of social functions and an awareness of the intentions of other communicators to do the same. The acquisition of language itself is also relevant to the study of developmental pragmatics because certain linguistic competencies must be in place in order for the child to perform the various communicative functions. 'In addition to studying these developments at the functional level, the pragmatic approach examines some of the mechanisms that contribute to language acquisition at the structural level, in particular the lexicon and syntax' (Marcos 2001: 210).

What's at stake?

The question of how children learn language has of course fascinated people for a very long time. But in the middle part of the twentieth century the ideas of Noam Chomsky polarized opinion in a way that had a profound effect on the subsequent development of the field. Whether or not experts on language acquisition were sympathetic to Chomsky's ideas they could hardly ignore them, and their work became at least in part categorized in terms of where they stood on the Chomskyan issue. Chomsky's central claim was that children don't learn a language in the same way that they learn many other skills, on the basis of imitation, trial and error or of direct teaching from adults. Rather children develop the ability to use and understand language because they are genetically programmed to do so. That is, all human beings have an innate predisposition to use language, which is manifest in part in an innate ability to learn language quickly and effortlessly.

Chomsky's claims were based not on actual observations of individual children's development of language, but on a rational appraisal of the nature of linguistic knowledge. He contemplated what it is that an adult speaker knows about the language once the process of acquisition is successfully completed. He labelled this the 'steady state'. The steady state was, he argued, a highly structured set of knowledge, which was quite unparalleled in complexity and unique in type among other forms of human knowledge. The steady state raised for Chomsky what he called 'the logical problem of language acquisition', or the problem of the 'poverty of input'. The actual evidence from which the steady state was derived, Chomsky argued, was simply inadequate to explain it. The language that children hear being used around them as they develop is full of mistakes, hesitations, false starts and self-corrections. Yet every normal person ends up with a fully developed knowledge of the language, including an ability to judge which sequences of words form grammatical sentences and which don't. Chomsky proposed that if the complexity of the steady state couldn't be accounted for by the input, then it must be explained in terms of the 'initial state', or the genetically determined and unobservable state of the mind of the human newborn. On the evidence of the nature of the steady state, and prompted by his views on the inadequacy of the linguistic input, Chomsky hypothesized that the initial state must include a specific capacity for the acquisition of human language, or a dedicated language faculty. In Chomsky's own words: 'the transition from the initial state to the steady state takes place in a determinate fashion, with no conscious attention or choice. The transition is essentially uniform for individuals in a given speech community despite diverse experience. The state attained is highly articulated and very rich, providing a specific interpretation for a vast array of sentences lacking close models in our experience' (Chomsky 1986: 51).

We saw in our discussion of Chomsky in Chapter 3 his interest in language was narrowly focussed on syntax and structure. This is true also of his interest in language acquisition. What he claimed to be innate was the ability to acquire the specific rules that make up the grammar of the language the child is exposed to. Within the Chomskyan model, the grammar of the language includes the rules that define its syntax, its semantics to the extent that this is dependent on syntax, and its phonological system. The ways in which the child would eventually use that grammar to communicate in context were of little interest to Chomsky. One implication of his theory would seem to be that knowledge of the structures of the language and knowledge of how to use those structures communicatively are two completely separate types of knowledge and the processes by which they are obtained need separate types of explanation.

Arguments against Chomsky's views on the innateness of language have been advanced from various sides. Some have been voiced on philosophical or theoretical grounds (e.g. Quine 1960, Putnam 1967, Goodman 1984). Researchers who studied the ways in which adult carers talk to very young children argued that Chomsky had made some wrong assumptions about the poverty of the input; what they identified as 'child directed speech' was in fact well suited to offering a reliable and accessible source of information about the language the child was acquiring (e.g. Snow 1986). During the 1970s, the 'functional' approach to the study of language acquisition developed some very different premises and reached some very different conclusions from Chomsky. This was based on a functional understanding of language, most closely associated with the linguist M. A. K. Halliday. On this approach, the structure of a language was intrinsically related to the different functions it could be used to perform in communicative situations.

One of the earliest and most significant accounts of the functionalist view of language acquisition was that developed in Halliday (1975). For Halliday, language was defined by the functions it was used to perform within a society, so the acquisition of language was in effect the acquisition of these functions. In explaining language acquisition the linguist needs to explain not just how children acquire structures but how they learn to use language to communicate successfully. Within the functionalist framework, the linguistic behaviour of children of a much wider age range is relevant to the study of acquisition than is the case in the Chomskyan framework. Chomsky's focus on structure meant that his ideas were used to explain the speech of children from the time when they began to combine words in what might be seen as a systematic way (roughly at two years) to the age at which the major structures of the language were judged to have been acquired (roughly at five years). Halliday argued that, on the contrary, the earliest indications of an intention to communicate, even in babies, were relevant because they marked the beginning of an awareness of the functions that language would eventually fulfil. Children's language should be studied considerably after the age of five, too, because they continued to develop their abilities to communicate successfully well beyond this point.

Some more recent approaches to language acquisition have steered a path between the radically innatist and the exclusively functional. For instance, Tomasello (2000) proposes a 'usage based' theory of language acquisition; the child's ability to imitate and to understand the adult's communicative intention, together with other cognitive abilities, explain how the structures of the language are acquired. However, the basic distinction between 'formal' and 'functional' accounts of language acquisition (associated respectively with Chomsky and with Halliday) still offers a good framework for explaining what is at stake when children's pragmatic abilities are studied. In the first, where the structures of the language and any actual communicative purposes to which they might be put are seen as totally separate phenomena, the expectation would be that the structures of the language would be acquired relatively effortlessly, while their use might be learnt though a process of imitation, practice and perhaps deliberate teaching on the part of an adult. The second, where language is in effect defined and determined by the communicative purposes to which it can be put, implies that it shouldn't be possible to detect any difference between the process of acquiring a language and the process of learning how to use the language successfully. As Eve Clark has posed the central question in developmental pragmatics: 'do children focus first on forms and later on uses, or do they acquire both together as they master a first language?' (Clark 2004: 562).

Of course the evidence available from children's language can't be expected to provide an uncontroversially self-evident answer to this question; the data are open to interpretation and their implications are subject to debate and argument. For a researcher such as Halliday, evidence from child language points towards the conclusion that 'the child learns language as a system of meanings in functional contexts, these contexts becoming, in turn, the principle of organization of the adult semantic system' (Halliday 1975: 9). That is, the adult language is built up from the different functions that children need to put it to as they learn to communicate. For a researcher such as Susan Foster, on the other hand, evidence from child language points to 'an innate basis for the grammatical aspects of language while at the same time allowing for an experimental basis for pragmatics' (Foster 1986: 247–8). That is, the structures of language are acquired through an innate process, largely independent of the separate processes that children go through in order to learn how to use those structures appropriately and successfully.

In the next two sections we will consider the implications of some of the central topics of pragmatics – namely speech acts, implicature and politeness – for the study of children's acquisition of language. Specific studies, together with their data, can be accessed by following up the references in the text or the Further reading section at the end of this chapter.

Speech acts

Speech act theories are concerned with speakers' communicative intentions. Their ambition is to explain how speakers achieve the range of things they can intend to do with words and, of course, how hearers are able to recognize those intentions. Studies of the language of very young children in relation to speech acts are therefore concerned with general questions about when the intention to communicate and the understanding that other people may also intend to communicate can first be recognized, as well as with more specific questions about the emergence of particular functional uses of language.

In general, stages of pragmatic development are less clear-cut than those of the development of the phonetic, lexical or grammatical aspects of language. Claims about when a particular pragmatic feature or ability typically first emerges can differ widely, even by several years. This is true too in the specific case of speech acts, with some widely divergent claims about when children first develop the ability to recognize, and first begin to produce, functionally different uses of language. In recent research, however, there is some consensus that the fundamental awareness of intentional communication arises remarkably early, perhaps in advance of the linguistic ability necessary to achieve those intentions. Children's very early conversations are based on their own desires to communicate and the willingness of the adults around them to collaborate: 'children communicate remarkably well, even when their linguistic resources are still very limited. They persist in expressing their intentions and adults cooperate in trying to arrive at appropriate interpretations' Clark (2004: 562–3).

Relatively early in the study of developmental pragmatics, during the 1970s, a number of researchers found speech act theory a useful model for analysing and explaining children's early intentional communication. Like Halliday, and working at much the same time as him, they argued that the process of learning a language is intrinsically bound up with the process of learning the social functions to which language use can be put. Unlike Halliday, they explained this within the specific framework of speech act theory, explaining the various functions children were able to perform in terms of the various speech acts available to them. Bates (1976), for instance, argued that the acquisition of language depended on, and followed after, the acquisition of the speech act functions to which it would be put. She suggested that the intention to communicate is constructed in the first two years of life, in preparation for language development. Moreover, functionally different speech acts could be identified in very early utterances, even before the recognizable appearance of grammatical structure. Even one-word utterances could be interpreted as speech acts. For instance, the use of 'give' by a child of 15 months can be seen as a demand for a pencil with three arguments: a giver, a receiver and an object.

Dore (1974) identified nine 'primitive speech acts' in the very early vocalizations of young children: labelling, repeating, answering, requesting (action), requesting (answer), calling, greeting, protesting and practising. Single word utterances could be ascribed to a variety of different categories depending on how the child intended them, or what Dore called their 'primitive force'. So, for instance, the single word 'mama' could be a 'label', a 'question (of ownership)' or a 'call'. In later work Painter (1984) argued that two word utterances such as 'want bread' could be interpreted as speech acts, namely demands. Like some of the earlier researchers, she suggested that speech acts may in fact be found even earlier. She also offered evidence that she claimed demonstrated that children may sometimes 'rehearse' speech acts not for specific communicative purposes but for their own sake, getting them ready for use. More recently, Clark has indicated research that suggests that early versions of speech acts may be identifiable even before recognizable linguistic development: 'pointing and reaching, typically present before the first words, have been documented by many researchers, and are generally viewed as proto-versions of the speech acts of asserting (points) and requesting (reaches)' (Clark 2004: 569–70).

However, the claims of those who analyse language from very early childhood in terms of speech acts raise the question of the legitimacy of using what is essentially an adult system of communication to explain a developing version of that system. It could be argued that the adult system is just too powerful to explain these early instances of communicative behaviour, which may in fact consist of little more than naming or labelling. Certainly, the analysis of one-word utterances as primitive speech acts involve a lot of interpretation on the part of the adult researcher, interpretation which can only be speculative. Arguably, analyses involving such adult interpretation fail to focus on the intention of the speaker, essential to the correct application of speech act theory, precisely because the intentions of very young children can't be known for certain. Susan Foster has even suggested that in cases where reaching towards an object was interpreted by mothers as meaning that the child was communicating a desire for the object 'it can be argued that the acquisition of the adult meanings for these behaviours comes about after the emergence, probably as a result of the interpretative activities of the adult' (Foster 1986: 245).

Wide variety can also be found in the claims that are made in relation to children's developing understanding and production of indirect speech acts. It is generally accepted that indirect forms such as 'would you like to shut the door' are treated initially as questions, but that somewhere around the time that they start school children learn to treat these as requests or orders. For instance, Carrell (1981: 341) finds that 'children aged 4 to 7 years are able to comprehend a wide variety of indirect request types'. Some researchers, however, have suggested that children may be able to use and respond to indirect orders from a pre-school age, although the younger children display a preference for direct requests. Garvey (1975) studied play sessions involving 36 pairs of pre-school children, concentrating on evidence of the children's ability to convey and respond to requests for action. She found that direct requests predominated 'but it was clear that they could also mean something other than what they said, i.e. they could convey a request or a refusal indirectly' (Garvey 1975: 62). Marcos and Bernicot (1997) have located the awareness of the different potentials for performing speech acts even earlier, concentrating on children as young as two and a half years old. Looking at how children were able to reformulate assertions and requests, they argued that the children were able to adapt their communicative behaviour to their addressee's attitude. More than that, the children used different means to adapt when asserting and when requesting. 'Thus, children appear to differentiate between the two speech acts and to act accordingly' (ibid.: 796).

Other work has focussed on children's awareness of the potentials of language use more generally. Ely and McCabe (1994) have suggested that awareness of the non-literal and the playful possibilities of language are generally present before school age. Bernicot and Laval (1996) studied the awareness of the various felicity conditions for promises (discussed in Chapter 4) among three-year-olds, six-year-olds and ten-year-olds. They concluded that 'the importance of the promise fulfilment conditions is clear by the age of 3, the sincerity condition seeming to play an earlier part than the preparatory condition (regarding the listener's wishes)' (ibid.: 120).

Implicature and politeness

Studies of first language acquisition have also focussed on the emergence of the ability to recognize and to communicate implicated as opposed to literal meaning. Here, researchers have again been interested in the questions of when in the process of language acquisition these abilities can be said to appear, and of whether they can best be seen as distinct from or intrinsically linked to the acquisition of more core linguistic skills. Just as researchers have been interested in scrutinizing children's use of language in relation to their ability to understand aspects of speech acts such as preparatory and sincerity conditions, so too they have looked for evidence of the emergence of pragmatic principles such as the maxims of cooperation suggested by Grice.

There is evidence of some rudimentary awareness of cooperation in even very young children, particularly in relation to the need to make the contributions relevant to what has been said before. Children are able to use this awareness to communicate more than they literally say. The following short data extracts from Painter (1984) illustrate a child (Hal) who at less than two years of age is able to make contributions to his conversations with his mother (M) that are relevant at the level of what is implicated, or that respond to implicated meanings. Painter has suggested the implicated meanings in brackets after each utterance; in each case, she claims, this is derived because of the maxim of relation. (*Italics are used to indicate intonational prominence.*)

30. (22 months)
    M: Shall we throw the teddies to Daddy?
    H: Teddy on table <=so we can't, until we fetch it>

31. (22 months)
    M: Oh, don't bite my pillow.
    H: *Hal* pillow <=so I can>

32. (23 months)
    M: Which book do you want Hal?
    H: (looking round) Where's [the] new one? <=that's the one I want>

33. (23 months)
    M: Oh you found your slippers <?=where were they?>
    H: Slippers in [the] cupboard.

As well as a conception of relevance, children must develop an understanding of the need to provide information, indeed an appropriate quantity of information, in order for their conversational contributions to be cooperative. As in the case of speech acts, some researchers have claimed evidence for this skill very early; one word utterances or even prelinguistic pointing can be analysed as directing attention to aspects of a situation that are salient because they are new. At a slightly later stage of development, intonational prominence has been taken to provide evidence of an awareness of, and an ability to express, a distinction between what is given and what is new. Again, Painter (1984) provides some relevant data, which is presented below. Hal seems to place intonational prominence consistently on what is new:

34. (22 months)
    M: That's *Matthew's* big man, isn't it?
    H: *Hal* big man.

35. (22 months)
    M: Where's *Daddy*?
    H: *There's* Daddy.

36. (23 months)
    H: Put [the] bib *on*.

> *M*: (out of sight) Put *what* on?
> *H*: Put [the] *bib* on.

37. (23 months)
> *F*: Put the drink down *there* (indicating table).
> *H*: Put it on *new* table (takes it to other, new table).

See also Ochs and Schieffelin (1976), who describe the abilities of very young children to distinguish between what is given and what is new information in a particular context.

However, at the early stages of conversational interaction there is no evidence of deliberate flouting to produce implicated meaning. Bates (1976) suggests that the ability to make full use of implicature needs awareness along the following lines: 'I know I mean X. The listener will hear Y but has sufficient additional information to know that I mean X'. In other words, full use of implicature involves an awareness of the state of mind of others and of the fact that this is different from the state of mind of self. The ability to see someone else's point of view, and therefore the awareness of what is shared knowledge and what isn't, is something that the child needs to develop. Again, there is a wide range of estimates as to when this takes place. Some researchers claim that in a limited respect at least it may emerge as early as between two and a half and three years. Others put it as late as between five and eight years.

Perner and Leekam (1986) studied young children's ability to adjust the content of what they say according to their knowledge of what their hearer knows. They concluded that 'as young as 3;0 [three years and no months] children preferred to mention the most informative item for their listener first and avoid mention of redundant items already known to their listeners as prescribed by Searle's preparatory conditions for sincere assertions and Grice's Maxim of Quantity' (ibid.: 313). Bernicot et al. (2007) have studied children's understanding of non-literal language and suggested that there is a discernible order in which different types of non-literal meaning are apparent to children. They conclude that 'our findings (semantic-inference implicatures were easy to understand, sarcastic-inference implicatures were difficult) validate our predictions, which were derived from the idea that the greater the complexity of the cognitive-social inference required to bridge the gap between "what is said" and "what is meant", the later the acquisition' (ibid.: 2128).

As Clark (2004: 574) has pointed out, the skills that children must master in relation to politeness are very varied and include the linguistic forms that mark different degrees of politeness, the conditions on doing various things in conversation that include factors such as the age and status of the person you are addressing, and 'what the costs and benefits are of gaining (or losing) face in relation to others'. Such factors of course cross over with other topics in pragmatics, such as speech acts. Indeed, much work that addresses issues of politeness in children's conversations has been centrally concerned with their use of indirect forms when making requests (see, for instance, Pedlow et al. 2004).

Brown and Levinson (1987: 37) themselves, surveying some of the studies of politeness in children's language that had been conducted to date, conclude that the studies 'suggest children begin acquiring strategic variation in utterance formation naturally, along with the acquisition of language, and that formal markers of politeness (honorifics, address variables) come later and are more explicitly taught'. They tentatively suggest that this may offer support to their claims that some politeness phenomena are universal while some are language specific. That is, the ability to adopt different strategies to perform potentially difficult acts in context may be a human universal, while the skill of producing the appropriate forms to demonstrate politeness in particular social settings may be more specific to individual languages and cultures.

6.4   Clinical linguistics

One of the types of data that brings pragmatics most strikingly into contact with real issues concerning language and language use is that drawn from studies of various language disorders and pathologies. Here, pragmatics comes into contact with clinical linguistics and clinical and neurological practice more generally. People's ability to communicate and interact successfully using language can go wrong in a huge variety of different ways, resulting in a very wide variety of types and subtypes of language disorders. In relatively recent years, the insights of pragmatic theory have been applied to the analysis and study of some of these disorders.

The implications, and the potential benefits, of the application of pragmatic theory to clinical studies of language pathology are twofold. Firstly, clinicians themselves stand to gain a deeper understanding of some language disorders. Earlier clinical studies were sometimes hampered by the lack of a clear descriptive framework of language use with which to describe the problems that patients were presenting with. They lacked, for instance, an understanding of how the knowledge and abilities employed in using language might be of complex and diverse types, involving both linguistic and extra-linguistic elements. They also lacked a clear and theoretically motivated terminology to describe the different aspects of language use that might be affected in a particular disorder. Pragmatics has offered a framework within which to describe, diagnose and perhaps even treat some types of language disorder. As one team of researchers have noted, 'Gricean pragmatics has provided a theoretically meaningful framework for examining the discourse of individuals with communication disorders' (Bloom et al. 1999: 554). McDonald (1992) reports on ways in which pragmatic theory has been utilized for the assessment of language disorders. These include a 'Pragmatic Protocol' designed to assess the nature and extent of language problems following brain damage. 'The protocol, designed within a speech-act theory framework, was used to classify attributes of spontaneous conversation, including the interactional behaviour between speakers. Language was deemed appropriate or inappropriate to the context' (ibid.: 285). A further checklist was devised using Grice's maxims of conversation.

Secondly, pragmaticists themselves stand to gain because clinical studies offer a wealth of well documented and potentially revealing data. Studying what can happen when our communicative abilities go wrong can potentially offer a unique insight into how those abilities operate successfully in normal situations, or into how they are made up of different types of individual skills and knowledge. The main focus of interest for pragmaticists is in the possibility that our ability to use language can be selectively impaired. That is, that in different types of language disorders some aspects of communicative ability can be disrupted while others are left untouched. It would be interesting if selective impairment suggested that core linguistic or semantic abilities and knowledge might be separate in type and operation from pragmatic abilities. It would be even more interesting if the nature and effects of pragmatic impairment might suggest something about the nature of normal pragmatic ability.

Despite these exciting possibilities, data from clinical linguistics needs to be treated with caution. Language disorders don't necessarily fit into neat and distinct categories, with clearly established properties. The very fact that language use draws on so many different types of knowledge and ability means that it can be difficult to establish exactly what problems a particular patient is experiencing. Sometimes semantic and pragmatic abilities appear to be impaired together, and sometimes they appear to be impaired separately. There is also often a difference to be described between patients' receptive ability in understanding language and their productive ability in producing it. In what follows we will briefly survey some of the claims that have been made, and some of the tentative conclusions that have been reached, in relation to two broad areas in the study of language disorders. First we will consider a range of linguistic impairments and the extent to which they may be linked to or separate from other types of cognitive impairment. Then we will concentrate on the more specific question of what differences in language ability, if any, can be detected in patients with brain damage, depending on whether that damage was sustained in the left or the right hemisphere.

Linguistic and cognitive impairments

Cognitive impairments that are either present from birth or develop later in life can have a vast range of different effects on communicative abilities. Although all clinical data needs to be treated with caution, they do suggest some evidence for the selective impairment of semantic and pragmatic abilities, and we will survey them very briefly here.

Perhaps the fullest study of a case of cognitive impairment from a linguistic point of view is the book-length study of an autistic individual called Christopher, published by linguists Neil Smith and Ianthi-Maria Tsimpli in 1995. Christopher is a language savant. Despite difficulties with many of even the most basic everyday tasks, to the extent that he is not able to look after himself and live independently, he shows a remarkable ability to learn languages. He is able to read, write and speak somewhere between 15 and 20 languages, and learns new words and new languages with ease and speed. The difference between Christopher's general cognitive capabilities and his linguistic abilities would be striking enough in itself, suggesting that there is something unique and autonomous about the human capacity for language. But it is even more striking that his abilities to understand aspects of meaning associated with language in use and with context are poor, like his general cognitive abilities, and not advanced like his linguistic ones. As Smith and Tsimpli (1995: 74) comment, Christopher's 'linguistic decoding' is as good as anyone else's but he can't handle irony, metaphor or jokes, suggesting a distinction between linguistic and non-linguistic impairment. Christopher's case seems to suggest some support to the idea that while language is a specific and separate human ability, pragmatic awareness of the use of language is in turn distinct from linguistic ability, perhaps more closely related to general cognitive ability.

Further studies of the communicative abilities and problems of children and adults with autism support the idea that pragmatic abilities are separate from linguistic and semantic ones, and may be impaired separately. People with autism are often over-literal in their interpretations, perhaps because of problems related to understanding the point of view and therefore the likely communicative intentions of others. This manifests itself in, for instance, problems with the comprehension of indirect requests among autistic adults (Paul and Cohen 1985) and in detecting utterances that violate Grice's maxims among children with autism (Surian 1996).

Much recent work has focussed on the various manifestations of what clinicians describe as 'specific language impairment' (SLI), a group of disorders that manifest themselves in relation to children's abilities to use and understand language. One subtype of these disorders has become known as 'semantic-pragmatic disorder' or 'semantic-pragmatic deficit syndrome'. Children with this syndrome typically display symptoms such as poor conversational skills, poor topic maintenance and an inability to provide relevant answers to questions (Cummings 2005: 268). The linguistic symptoms of semantic-pragmatic disorder are similar to those of autism, however, and some clinicians have argued that it should be classed as a form of autism. The issues surrounding this question are surveyed in Rapin (1996) and further discussed in Bishop (2000).

Schizophrenia is an acquired disorder, in that it generally manifests itself in adolescent or adult life. Like many disorders, it takes a variety of different forms, each with different implications for the types of problems with communication. In at least one type, thought disorder, there is evidence that, without experiencing any significant problems with language structures, patients can demonstrate difficulty adhering to the conversational maxims (Thomas 1997). Reviewing some of the literature on tests involving schizophrenic patients, Cummings identifies some differences in the findings in relation to the type of schizophrenia involved. In some studies schizophrenics made many more errors than control subjects in identifying and explaining implicatures relating to the maxim of relation. In a study where schizophrenics with paranoid delusions were compared to those without, however, the two groups were found to perform differently: 'subjects with paranoid delusions often failed to respond in polite fashion, but performed at a similar level to controls on stories involving the Gricean maxims' (Cummings 2009: 102).

Langdon et al. (2002) is an example of a study of schizophrenia using a particular pragmatic framework, in this case RT. They claim that the problems some schizophrenic patients encounter with non-literal meanings, specifically with metaphorical examples, can be explained in relation to the relevance theoretic account of utterance interpretation, in particular the operations on encoded meaning that generally give people access to metaphorical interpretations.

Left and right hemisphere brain damage

Many patients who experience difficulty with some aspect of the communicative use of language do so as a result of some specific incident that has caused physical damage to the brain. Such damage is typically caused either by a stroke or by some severe blow to the head, such as in a traffic accident. In such cases it's generally possible for clinicians to identify a specific localized area of brain damage. This has very interesting implications because it opens up the possibility of trying to link the specific types of language impairment that result from the injury to the location of the injury in the brain, perhaps even of trying to relate different types of cognitive ability to different physical areas in the brain.

It is generally acknowledged that, for the majority of people, at least the bulk of linguistic ability is located in the left hemisphere of the brain. Damage to this hemisphere often results in aphasia, the impairment or even complete loss of language. There is some evidence to suggest that, while core linguistic ability is located in the left hemisphere, pragmatic ability concerning the appropriate use of language in context may be located in the right hemisphere and may be selectively impaired by damage to that region. Such evidence is certainly very appealing to pragmaticists searching for support for the idea that linguistic and pragmatic abilities are separate from each other, but it must be treated with caution. It would certainly be far too simplistic to claim that all linguistic ability is clearly located in the left hemisphere and all pragmatic ability in the right hemisphere. Damage to one area of the brain can have a range of consequences for linguistic ability that are often hard to disentangle from each other and classify neatly. And it isn't necessary for linguistic and pragmatic abilities to be located in separate hemispheres of the brain, or even to have identifiably different physical locations at all, for them to be cognitively different.

Aphasia, like many language disorders, manifests itself in a number of different forms, with differing types and degrees of impairment. Because the impairments involved are often so complex an informed awareness of different types of linguistic ability, including pragmatics, has proved particularly valuable to the understanding of and response to aphasia. In their study of the relationship between linguistics and aphasia, Lesser and Milroy (1993: 29) claim that pragmatics, along with psycholinguistics, has 'been applied to the study of aphasia in ways which are transforming not only our understanding of the nature of this phenomenon, but also therapists' approaches to helping aphasic patients'. They focus particularly on the insights offered by Grice's theory of conversation. They are wary of an over-simplistic application of the theory to the explanation or diagnosis of aphasia, but admit some connection. They quote the following data, concerning a conversation between an aphasic patient (P) and a therapist (T), which was initially cited as evidence that aphasic comprehension problems could be at the level of speaker meaning, as explained by Grice:

1. T. is it raining today.
2. P. er (cough) it's quite (cough) pardon/ no it never put me off (uhuh) no I was quite happy (right) even if it was raining and then I'd see it would cloud away and would be blue (OK) and you're happy (yes) all over again I always used to feel good about things
3. T. OK and the last one/ is it Monday today
4. P. Monday/ that's the beginning (right) it is *the* beginning
5. T. is it Monday today
6. P. it's a Monday
7. T. is it Monday today
8. P. oh this one you mean
9. T. Today
10. P. oh now this is fourth fifth February/ its about the fourth fifth is it now ...

(Thirteen more turns follow on the topic of days of the week.)

Lesser and Milroy (1993: 139) allow that 'the patient's first response, while addressing the general topic of the weather, is not quite cooperative in the Gricean sense. More specifically, the maxim of Quantity seems to be violated, since the patient answers the next question at quite unreasonable length, possibly understanding the word *Monday* but not the rest of the utterance'. In general, the problems with producing appropriate conversational contributions that the patient displays during this conversation can be explained to a considerable extent as a 'failure to converse with due regard to the co-operative principle' (ibid.: 140).

More concrete proposals about the relationship between aphasia and the maxims of conversation have been put forward by Elizabeth Ahlsén who argues that 'implicatures based on the maxims of Quantity and Manner cannot be made in the same way as in the case of nonaphasic patients' (Ahlsén 1993: 61). She observes that aphasic patients often use politeness as a way of compensating for these communicative deficiencies, in effect taking the blame for their problems in responding appropriately and apologizing for them in order to indicate that despite them their intentions are cooperative.

Speech act theory, too, has had a role to play in the analysis of aphasia: 'because of its attention to the mismatch between linguistic form and communicative function, speech act theory has attracted attention from researchers investigating *functional communication* in aphasia' (Lesser and Milroy 1993: 148). Left-brain damaged patients 'seem to be impaired in their ability to link social and previous textual information in such a way as to derive inferences' (ibid.). However, Lesser and Milroy express their awareness of the limitations of speech act theory as applied to real-life conversational data, and therefore as a framework to explain aphasic speech.

There has been less research into the effects on communication of damage to the right hemisphere of the brain. This is perhaps because early studies, working with the assumption that language is controlled chiefly by the left hemisphere, saw right hemisphere damage as of little relevance to clinical linguistics. Beginning a few decades ago, some clinicians began to argue that the right hemisphere seemed to play a more important role in language processing than had previously been thought, although this role seemed to be largely concerned with relating language to context. A study published in 1983 noticed that right-hemisphere-injured patients often had problems with understanding the 'point' of a conversation. It concluded that 'although less intimately involved with the traditional building blocks of language, the right hemisphere seems pivotal in the processing of extra- or paralinguistic facets of language – facets which contemporary students of language would designate as part of pragmatics or the discourse functions of language' (Gardener et al. 1983: 173; see also Moscovitch 1983; Caplan 1987).

More recent studies, more closely informed by pragmatic theory, have pinpointed the types of problems typically encountered by patients with right hemisphere damage more specifically. Cummings (2009: 98) reports on studies that identified problems such patients encountered with producing coherent narratives, responding to violations of Gricean maxims, and selecting appropriate deictic expressions for personal reference. Further, some studies have been conducted with reference to specific pragmatic frameworks, with the intention being at least in part to support the validity of a framework or to compare the success of two competing frameworks. For instance, Dipper et al. (1997) analyse the communicative problems of patients with right hemisphere damage within the framework of RT and conclude that the right hemisphere is essential to the processing of language in context, including drawing inferences. They argued that the patients they studied were deriving contextual effects from the utterances they heard, but not the contextual effects that were intended by the speaker, or would be reached by the majority of hearers. The effects available in the intended context were being blocked or overridden by effects from a different, alternative context. 'The results of this study suggest that the RHD [right hemisphere damaged] subjects are unable to use the linguistic information from the text in the deductive system, and have an over-reliance on encyclopaedic memory. A consequence of this is their difficulty in using the procedural information provided by discourse connectives – this is because discourse connectives have no encyclopaedic entry in the deductive system' (ibid.: 228).

However, pragmatic studies involving clinical data from patients with right hemisphere damage are not universally supportive of RT. McDonald (1999) concentrates on the problems patients with right hemisphere damage encounter in comprehending sarcasm. Comments that are clearly not true, especially those that contradict information already given verbally in the context, are particularly problematic for such patients. She contrasts the Gricean account of sarcasm – in terms of a blatant flouting of the expectations of Quality leading to an implicated meaning, with the relevance theoretic account – in terms of an echoic utterance that conveys explicitly both a contradiction of something said or implied before and an attitude of disapproval. She concludes that identifying the blatantly counterfactual nature of sarcastic utterances as a clue to processing does seem to correspond to clinical findings, while there is no evidence to support the idea that sarcastic comments function as echoic mentions of previous actual or potential utterances. The specific problems that patients with right hemisphere damage encounter in processing sarcastic comments suggest that 'such nonliteral comments have a special status and require additional cognitive processing. This finding needs to be addressed by relevance theory, which currently implies that the literal and nonliteral meanings of a given remark are processed with equal ease in the appropriate context' (McDonald 1999: 499). McDonald does not, however, see the clinical finding as straightforwardly supportive of the Gricean view. Right-hemisphere-damaged patients have also been assessed in relation to problems they have with interpreting metaphor (see for instance Bryan 1988; Tompkins 1990).

Some recent studies of the specific communication problems faced by patients with right hemisphere brain damage, particularly those that are closely informed by pragmatic theory, might seem to lend support to the hypothesis that, while specifically linguistic knowledge and ability is generally restricted to the left hemisphere, pragmatic abilities that allow language to be appropriately produced and interpreted in context are localized in the right hemisphere. However, the picture is far from clear-cut, and any such conclusions must be drawn tentatively and cautiously. We have already seen evidence, for instance, that patients with aphasia caused by damage to their left hemispheres often also encounter problems with interpreting and producing implicatures. Many clinical linguists remain sceptical about the idea that the hemispheres are specialized for language and for pragmatics respectively. Asa Kasher, together with a team of researchers, devised a battery of tests for pragmatic ability, drawing on the insights of both speech act theory and Grice's theory of conversation, and designed to test both productive and receptive abilities. They conclude that the picture is far more complicated than a simple distinction between the hemispheres in terms of the type of processing involved: 'in conclusion, both hemispheres appear to be involved in the pragmatic processing of implicatures, but the responsible cognitive mechanisms appear to be rather different on each side. The verbal and nonverbal implicatures were not selectively lateralized to the LH [left hemisphere] and RH [right hemisphere], respectively. The RH seems to incorporate a mosaic of specific processors, whereas the LH activates a more general processor'. The 'mosaic' of processors based in the right hemisphere overlapped with functions that were not related to language more than did the general processor in the left hemisphere, but 'neither side shows strong anatomical localization of implicatures' (Kasher et al. 1999: 588–9). Borod et al. conclude even more starkly that 'deficits in pragmatic appropriateness are shared equally by both brain-damaged groups' (Borod et al. 2000: 118). Such scepticism is not, of course, the same as a belief that pragmatic ability is not properly separate from linguistic ability, or that no distinction can be drawn between semantic and pragmatic abilities in language use. An autonomous pragmatic faculty doesn't necessarily entail an autonomous physical neurological location.

It's worth noting before we conclude that, despite the general enthusiasm with which pragmatic theory has been adopted into clinical linguistics, and conversely the potential for the advancement of pragmatics that clinical data suggests, not everyone working in clinical linguistics is unconditionally enthusiastic. Perkins (2000: 8) argues that 'the direct and unmodified application of frameworks and concepts from linguistic pragmatics to the study of communicative impairment has introduced an overly narrow linguistic bias which, despite the undoubted insights it provides, has so far been of limited clinical value'.

6.5 Experimental pragmatics

The relatively new field of experimental pragmatics has received a lot of interest and seen a proliferation in published books and articles during the past few years. Experimental pragmatics isn't in itself a new account of pragmatic meaning, but is rather a collection of methodologies designed to shed new light on the range of existing pragmatic theories and approaches. It is where pragmatics overlaps with psycholinguistics; it utilizes some of the equipment and techniques that psycholinguists have developed to investigate how language is processed in the mind and applies these to issues concerning the relationship between linguistic and pragmatic aspects of meaning.

Experimental pragmatics has been used to compare the relative merits of the major different pragmatic theories that we considered in Chapters 4 and 5. The results produced are certainly interesting but, as we will see, not always clear-cut or easy to interpret. This in turn has raised some important questions about the nature of pragmatic theories themselves, whether they are amenable to empirical testing, and if so what sort of tests and what sort of experimental findings might be used to choose between them. Experiments have been designed that are based on many of the major types of data discussed in pragmatics. Here we will concentrate on just two, as representative of the types of questions raised in experimental pragmatics and of the types of experiments devised in an attempt to answer them: that is, scalar implicatures and metaphor. But other areas of study that have been investigated using the methods of experimental pragmatics include, for instance, indirect speech acts (Bernicot and Laval 2004) and indirect replies (Holtgraves 1998, 1999).

The aims of experimental pragmatics

Experimental pragmatics is centrally concerned with an issue that we have been aware of throughout our exploration of pragmatics: namely, the question of what forms the most appropriate data against which to develop and evaluate pragmatic theories. As we have seen, for many pragmaticists who rely on 'invented' examples, the knowledge or the intuitive judgements of language users, including those of pragmaticists themselves, provide sufficient data. For others, particularly those working in areas of pragmatics that are closely linked to sociolinguistics, such as (im)politeness, the most appropriate data are examples of the actual behaviour of speakers and hearers in real communicative contexts: that is, recordings and transcriptions of naturally occurring conversations. In experimental pragmatics, too, actual behaviour provides the data, but in this case it is behaviour that is manipulated, recorded and measured with scientific accuracy in laboratory conditions. It is generally the behaviour of those interpreting and responding to language that is measured and analysed: those usually labelled 'hearers' in discussions of pragmatics, although in effect in laboratory tests they are more often readers of written input. The reception and processing of language is the focus of inquiry.

The aims of experimental pragmatics are focussed on pragmatic theory itself. So unlike in the cases where pragmatics interacts with the study of language acquisition or with clinical linguistics, pragmatic theory isn't being used to shed light on some aspect of language use, but is itself in the spotlight. Experimental pragmaticists are generally interested either in testing out the validity of the explanation that some pragmatic theory offers in relation to a specific type of data, or else in comparing the validity of two alternative theoretical explanations. Because of their prominence in the development of pragmatics the theories that are most frequently investigated or compared are Gricean pragmatics, either in its original form or in some neo-Gricean variety, and RT. Evidence from the laboratory offers the potential for carefully controlled and accurately recorded and measured data against which to test these theories. But it also brings with it some potential problems and points to issues that need to be addressed. These problems and issues have been widely discussed in the literature of experimental pragmatics.

Firstly, there is the problem that there is necessarily something artificial about subjects responding to linguistic input in a laboratory situation. However carefully designed to test responses to a certain type of linguistic example, such experiments are far removed from the ways in which people usually encounter and respond to language. Recorded and transcribed naturally occurring data may be haphazard, difficult to work with and rather hit-and-miss in terms of collecting instances of particular types of examples, but at least it gives a record of how language is used in its natural environment: that is, in free-flowing, spontaneous and communicative conversation. As experimental pragmaticists have observed, 'when you bring language into the laboratory you are forced to strip it of its everyday features – often in unknowable ways' (Clark and Bangerter 2004: 26). It is of course impossible ever to get away entirely from this problem, but experimental pragmaticists try as far as they can to be aware of the issues it raises and where possible to use technology 'to bring more of the world into the laboratory', such as exposing subjects to recordings of naturally occurring conversation (Coulson 2004: 202).

The second issue that the possibility of laboratory data brings with it is the question of what exactly should most appropriately be measured. In order to test out some scientific theory or hypothesis it is necessary to determine what the theory predicts will happen in a particular set of circumstances and then observe whether this does actually happen when the circumstances are created or modelled in the laboratory. Take for instance the theory that all substances in the world around us are made up of molecules. Add to this the claim that water is denser than oil because water molecules are closer together than oil molecules. These claims together predict that oil will float on top of water rather than mixing with it or sinking into it. A scientist can perform an experiment in a laboratory in which oil is added to water and can observe what happens. The oil floats on the water; the theory has made an accurate prediction. The scientist can't of course go so far as to claim that the theory has been proved conclusively to be true. There may be other reasons that no one has thought of as to why oil floats on water, reasons which are nothing to do with molecular structure. But the scientist can certainly say that the experiment has lent support to the theory, or that the theory has survived that particular experiment, because its predictions were proved accurate.

But it is far from a straightforward matter to establish what predictions are made by pragmatic theories. These need to be concrete, testable predictions about how people will respond to particular types of language use in particular contexts. Experimental pragmaticists are generally of the opinion that pragmatic theories should be testable. For instance, Raymond Gibbs (2004: 69) has stated that 'I strongly embrace the belief that the best ideas in linguistic-pragmatics are those that can be experimentally examined and potentially falsified (where failing to falsify allows one to claim scientific evidence in support of a hypothesis)'. But some experimental pragmaticists have questioned whether pragmatic theories are in fact testable in this way, or whether they are all equally testable. For instance, Ira Noveck has claimed that it is hard to derive specific predictions from Grice's theory of implicature. If 'what is implicated' is derived by the application of pragmatic principles to 'what is said', then this might suggest that people should take longer to understand supposedly implicated meanings than literal meaning. On the other hand, if some implicatures arise by default unless cancelled by context, it might be the cancellation, in other words the lack of an implicated meaning, that should take longer to process (Noveck 2004: 301). Furthermore, experimental pragmaticists need to identify not just testable predictions made by pragmatic theories, but predictions that distinguish them from each other. Most pragmatic theories allow for some distinction between linguistic and context-dependent meaning, and most also agree on how particular expressions will be interpreted in particular contexts. Where they differ is in terms of where they draw the distinction between the linguistic and the context-dependent, and how they explain the unobservable mechanisms which link the two. Experimental evidence that supports a particular pragmatic theory but can also be shown to be compatible with another pragmatic theory 'provides only weak support' for the theory under investigation (van der Henst and Sperber 2004: 141). So it is necessary to identify not just testable predictions made by a particular pragmatic theory, but testable predictions that distinguish it from all other pragmatic theories; and this is no slight matter.

Thirdly, experimental pragmatics needs to address the issue of how the predictions of pragmatic theory are to be tested, or what in the language receiver's behaviour is to be measured. Because pragmatic theories generally have something to say about how language is processed and how interpretations are reached, the length of time it takes a subject to respond to some linguistic input is perhaps the most common factor to be measured in experimental pragmatics. Experimenters can't of course observe what mental processes the subject is engaged in, but they can at least measure how long those unobservable mental processes take to perform, for instance by measuring how long it takes a subject from seeing a sentence displayed on a screen to pushing a button to indicate whether that sentence is true or false. But some experimental pragmaticists argue that reaction time is not a very helpful type of evidence, and that information about the subject's eye movements – giving information about what parts of the linguistic input they paid most attention to or returned to during the process of interpretation – is more revealing: 'eye movement data provide an on-line record of processing as it unfolds over time' (Bezuidenhout and Morris 2004: 269). The practice of electrophysiology actually attempts to measure brain activity during interpretation, to try to get even closer to the cognitive processes involved; electrodes are hooked up to subject's scalp to measure electrical activity in the brain during comprehension. This is arguably more illuminating than reaction time data because it can tell more about the intensity of the processing effort involved: 'reaction times are typically interpreted as reflecting processing difficulty, yet it is quite possible for two processes to take the same amount of time, but for one to recruit more neurological resources' (Coulson 2004: 181).

Scalar implicatures

The way in which people process and reach an interpretation of examples that involve so-called scalar implicatures has generated a lot of experimental work. This is perhaps because here is one case where two competing pragmatic approaches offer explanations of the same phenomena that are easy to distinguish and that might be said to make distinct testable predictions. Scalars are the type of generalized implicature that we considered in Chapter 5 in relation to the work of neo-Gricean Laurence Horn, where the use of a particular word seems to implicate by default the negation of a semantically related but stronger word:

38. Your essay was good.
39. Your essay wasn't just OK.
40. Your essay wasn't excellent.
41. Your essay was good; in fact it was excellent.
42. Your essay was good; it wasn't excellent.

Someone hearing (38) is likely to understand it as conveying (39), and on Horn's account 'not just OK' is part of what 'good' actually means. But the hearer is also likely to understand (40), and for Horn this is an implicature rather than an entailment. The use of 'good' implicates 'not excellent' because of the Q-Principle. 'Excellent' is stronger and therefore more informative than 'good'. If the speaker has been in a position to say 'excellent' the Q-Principle tells us that she would have done so. The fact that (40) is an implicature is illustrated by the fact that in context it can be cancelled, as in (41), without any sense of contradiction or incongruity, or reinforced, as in (42), without any sense of redundancy.

The account of such examples in RT is completely different. Remember that in relevance theory there is no place for default implicatures; every aspect of utterance interpretation, whether explicature or implicature, must be independently licensed in context. So 'good' offers something like an indication of a judgement of quality, to be filled out in context into a more precise explicature, one which may but will not necessarily include the meaning 'not excellent'.

These two positions might seem to make different testable predictions about how such examples would be processed. If the implicature from 'good' to 'not excellent' arises by default it should be reached without much processing effort, but the process of cancelling it, requiring a complete rethink, should be cognitively more difficult than the process of reinforcing it: (41) should take longer to interpret than (42). If, however, the meaning of an expression such as 'good' is filled out in context – the same principles of interpretation operating whether an explicature of 'not excellent' or an explicature of 'including excellent' is reached – there should be no such processing difference to observe. Here we will look at a couple of experiments that have been devised to test which theory makes more accurate predictions. As we will see, the findings tend to point more towards a relevance theoretic than a neo-Gricean explanation, although there are reasons why we must treat any conclusions that might be drawn from this with caution.

Breheny et al. (2006) compared what they describe as 'default' and 'context-driven' accounts of scalar implicatures, in effect general descriptions of the neo-Gricean and relevance theoretic style of explanation respectively. They concentrated on the interpretation of 'or'. Remember that for Horn 'or' exists on a semantic scale with 'and', such that the use of 'or' implicates by default the negation of the semantically stronger 'and'. For relevance theorists, the application of the principle of relevance in context will determine whether the explicit interpretation will include the meaning 'not and' or the meaning 'and'. They measured how long the participants in their experiment took to read a 'trigger-containing segment' (a phrase including 'or') when it was presented to them in a context that favoured the 'not and' interpretation, and also when it was presented in a context where the 'not and' interpretation was not so obviously available, because not so obviously relevant. The context in which the supposed implicature to 'not and' was encouraged was labelled the 'upper-bound context':

43. John was taking a university course and working at the same time. For the exams he had to study from short and comprehensive sources. Depending on the course he decided to read the class notes or the summary.

The context in which the supposed implicature wasn't encouraged they labelled the 'lower-bound context':

44. John heard that the textbook for geophysics was very advanced. Nobody understood it properly. He heard that if he wanted to pass the course he should read the class notes or the summary.

The test subjects watched computer screens where they were presented with a variety of examples of these two types, in a randomized order and mixed up with other types of examples that didn't involve interpreting 'or'. They were asked to answer a yes/no question about some of the examples presented to them by pressing the left mouse button for 'yes' and the right mouse button for 'no'. The questions in fact had nothing to do with the comprehension of 'or', but they enabled the researchers to gain an accurate measure of when the participants were ready to offer their interpretation of the examples: in other words, of how long they had taken to process them. They concluded that their findings supported the 'context-driven' rather than the 'default' explanation of interpretation:

> As predicted by the Context-Driven approaches, reading time was significantly longer in the condition where the implicature is warranted by the context, indicating that implicatures are generated only in such cases. If implicatures were generated in contexts that did not warrant them and were subsequently cancelled, this should have manifested as longer reading time on the lower-bound context condition or at least equal reading time between conditions. (Breheny et al. 2006: 445)

Their conclusions are negative in relation to a neo-Gricean style analysis of the meaning of words such as 'or' in terms of default generalized implicatures, but tentative in relation to an alternative, relevance-theoretic analysis. They argue that more work would be needed in order to determine whether such an account is justified.

Bezuidenhout and Morris (2004) produced their own generalized descriptions of the neo-Gricean and relevance-theoretic approaches to scalar implicatures, calling them the DM (default model) and UM (underspecification model) respectively. In their experiments they concentrated on the interpretation of 'some', which in the scalar model gives rise to a default implicature negating the semantically stronger item 'all'. Like Breheny et al. they measured processing time for examples containing the target expression, but they also measured their subjects' eye movements, in order to ascertain how long they spent looking at each part of an example and which parts they returned to during interpretation. Their 24 participants were presented with pairs of sentences such as the following on a computer screen, where a sentence containing an expression of the form 'Some N were/had P' was followed by a sentence which explicitly cancelled the supposed implicature 'Not all N were/had P':

45. Some books had colour pictures. In fact all of them did, which is why the teachers liked them.

They argue that the DM would predict that in (45) 'some' at the beginning of the example would trigger an implicature of 'not all'. The occurrence of 'all' in the middle of the example would be the first encounter with the idea that this is not the appropriate interpretation, but the implicature would not be definitely ruled out until 'them were/did' was reached. The 'all' might be introducing a new and different entity, so the subjects wouldn't abandon the default 'not all' interpretation until they reached 'them were/did', meaning that this part of the example should take the most time to process.

Bezuidenhout and Morris further suggest that the UM would predict that when subjects read 'some' they don't commit themselves to an interpretation of 'not all' straight away, but are prepared to develop their interpretation over time, depending on what information is offered in the context. The encounter with 'all' provides information that points towards an interpretation of 'some and possibly all' and so is highly significant, suggesting that it should attract extra attention and processing time. After that, by the time participants get to 'them were/did', they are only receiving information that is consistent with their current interpretation ('some and indeed all'), meaning that 'them were/did' isn't particularly significant and won't attract noticeable attention.

The participants in the experiment were asked to read the examples and then to demonstrate their comprehension by answering a yes/no question. They were monitored in relation to the time they spent reading 'some N' in the initial sentence, the time they spent reading 'all' and then 'them were/did' in the cancellation sentence, and also the number of times they looked back to 'some' during their interpretation. Bezuidenhout and Morris discovered that participants generally spent extra time looking at 'all', but not at 'them were/did', suggesting that it was at 'all' that they did most of the interpreting of 'some'. They didn't look back to 'some' during reading of the cancellation sentence, suggesting that there was no need to reassess an earlier default interpretation. They interpreted their results as consistent with the predictions of UM and not DM.

Other researchers to challenge the account of scalars as default implicatures include Chierchia et al. (2004), who argue that the occurrence of so-called scalar implicatures always depends on the specific properties of context. Comparing data from children and adults responding to sentences that include 'or', they conclude that test subjects either produce or fail to produce interpretations predicted by scalar implicature based entirely on the content of the example sentence itself. They use their findings to support not RT but their own 'semantic core model', in which 'semantic and pragmatic processing takes place in tandem' (ibid.: 284).

Noveck (2001) also compared adults with children and found that whereas adults react to implicated meaning associated with scalars, children are more likely to respond to logical meaning. He concluded 'not only that these Gricean implicatures are present in adult inference-making but that in cognitive development these occur only after logical interpretations have been well established' (ibid.: 183). Noveck's study could certainly be read as support for a broadly Gricean explanation, indicating that such implicatures exist and even that they are learnt later than literal or linguistic meaning. But in a later article Noveck acknowledged that his findings could support either a Gricean or a relevance-theoretic framework because 'Relevance Theory would suggest that children and adults use the same comprehension mechanisms but that greater cognitive resources are available to adults, which in turn encourages them to draw out more pragmatic inferences' (Noveck 2004: 307). This time he was inclined to favour an explanation of his data that supported RT.

Metaphor

The account of metaphor associated with Grice's theory of conversation has also been the focus of considerable experimental interest, perhaps because in this case too there seems to be the prospect of testable predictions. Again, the results of such experiments are generally interpreted as weighing against Grice, although not in every case. Remember that according to Grice metaphors such as (46) are literally false:

46. You are the cream in my coffee.

The blatant falsity is a cue to the hearer to find an alternative, implicated meaning. The maxims of Quality, specifically the injunction 'do not say what you believe to be false', indicate to the hearer that the speaker must be intending to convey something other than a straightforwardly false statement, and he therefore reanalyses it to reach a metaphorical interpretation. This model, where the literal meaning is accessed and found to be wanting, triggering the process of calculating a conversational implicature, suggests a 'double processing' for metaphors, and might be taken to suggest that metaphorical examples should take longer to process than literal ones.

Experimental results don't in general show evidence of extra processing time for metaphorical examples. Gibbs (1999, 2002) argues against the Gricean concept of 'what is said' on the grounds that experimental findings provide no evidence that people first access literal meaning and then go on to derive a metaphorical interpretation: 'people can read figurative utterances ... as quickly, sometimes even more quickly, as literal uses of the same expressions in different contexts or equivalent nonfigurative expressions' (Gibbs 1999: 468). Giora (1999) disagrees with Grice on metaphor interpretation because of evidence that the salient, rather than the literal, meaning has priority in their interpretation.

Glucksberg (2004) presented his subjects with what he describes as literally false, but metaphorically true, statements, such as the following:

47. Some roads are snakes.
48. Some offices are icebergs.

He asked his subjects explicitly to respond only to literal meaning and measured their reaction times in judging whether such examples were true or false. The average length of time that the subjects took to reject such examples suggested that 'people had difficulty in judging that metaphors were literally false' (ibid.: 76). For Glucksberg, this indicated that Grice's account of the interpretation of metaphors was not psychologically accurate.

Winer et al. (2001) also concluded that people are most likely to spot an inferred, rather than the literal meaning, even in cases that involve metaphorical interpretation. However, for them this offers potential support for the Gricean position which they see as predicting that people will recognize not what was literally said but what was intended. They compared the responses of adults and children to a series of questions with apparently straightforward and obvious answers, such as:

49. Do you see with your fingers?

They found that adults were more likely to make 'errors', for instance by answering (49) with 'yes' rather than 'no'. They suggested that adults are reluctant to interpret what they are presented with as having a literal but trivial meaning and therefore search for an alternative metaphorical and non-trivial meaning, for instance identifying that the sense of touch might be seen as in some ways metaphorically similar to seeing. Children are more ready to take utterances at face value and give them a literal interpretation. 'Our interpretation, supported by the experimental manipulations of both experiments, is based on a Gricean analysis. Presumably the answers to the questions were so obvious to adults, that the adults responded with something other than a literal interpretation, i.e., they interpreted the question metaphorically' (ibid.: 495–6). Their interpretation suggests that the adult subjects were able to access the literal meaning, judge it to be trivial and seek an alternative implicated meaning, while the children, less practised in interpreting different sorts of utterances, stopped once they had reached the literal meaning. The fact that for Winer et al. the interpretative primacy of the metaphorical meanings can be construed as support for Grice, whereas for others such as Giora and Glucksberg it is evidence against him, is interesting in itself. It is also an illustration of why it's necessary to be cautious about the conclusions drawn in experimental pragmatics and why they remain controversial. We will consider the reasons for this next.

Conclusions?

The conclusions that can be drawn from individual studies in experimental pragmatics, and indeed more general conclusions about the success of experimental pragmatics itself, must necessarily be tentative ones. This is not to say that the findings of experimental pragmatics are not valuable sources of information in pragmatics. It seems clear that evidence about how people respond to and interpret a range of the types of examples that have been central to pragmatics is highly interesting and potentially highly illuminating. But as we have seen the evidence remains open to interpretation. Much evidence from recent studies seems to point more towards the model of interpretation developed within RT, for instance, than within Gricean pragmatics. But the evidence doesn't all point in that direction, and researchers don't always agree on the implications of their findings for pragmatic theories, and may even change their own minds about this over time.

There is a further reason why the conclusions of experimental pragmatics are open to question, and it has to do with an issue that we considered in Chapter 5 when we compared RT with Grice's theory of conversation. This is the question of whether or not pragmatic theories should aim at, and should be judged in terms of, psychological plausibility. Experimental pragmatics aims to find out about the actual cognitive processes involved in language processing.

These can't be directly observed, but they can be measured in terms of their duration and perhaps the intensity of the scrutiny that subjects apply to particular aspects of the input. Some pragmatic theories, of course, explicitly aim at explaining just these cognitive processes. Perhaps most notably, RT is presented as an account of cognition as well as of communication. But it is far from clear that accuracy in terms of cognitive processes is a main goal for other pragmatic theories. For Grice concepts such as 'what is said' and 'what is implicated' are part of an attempt to offer a formal explanation of specific aspects of meaning. This of course raises the further question of whether pragmatic theories ought to be judged in terms of psychological plausibility: of whether that should be a deciding factor in distinguishing between them, regardless of the intentions of the theorists who developed them. For many pragmaticists success in explaining a range of facts about language use, and not evidence about the psychological activity of subjects in a laboratory, is the appropriate evidence against which to evaluate pragmatic theory.

Bezuidenhout and Cooper Cutting, for instance, have argued that measuring reaction times isn't a very helpful way of testing Grice's theory. For Grice, saying one thing may give rise to an implicature of something else, and this suggests that a hearer must recover 'what is said' and then work out what is implicated. But it is possible for Griceans to deny that his claim commits him to any view about the actual order of processing. 'Grice was interested in giving a conceptual analysis of the concepts of saying, meaning, and so on, and not in giving a psychological theory of the stages in utterance processing' (Bezuidenhout and Cooper Cutting 2002: 443). As we have seen, evidence has been offered against Grice on the grounds, for instance, that the processing of metaphors doesn't in fact seem to proceed from an understanding of a literally false meaning to a metaphorically true one. But this offers a genuine challenge to Grice only on the assumption that 'what is said' must be more salient or more apparent to the hearer than 'what is implicated', a claim that Grice never made.

This last point is closely related to the question of whether literal meaning, or in Gricean terms 'what is said', must be empirically accessible to ordinary language users. As we saw in Chapter 5, the claim that 'what is said' must be intuitively available is of central importance to some pragmatic theories; it forms the basis of Recanati's Availability Principle, for instance. But not all pragmaticists agree that ordinary speakers need to be able to recognize literal as well as intended meaning, or even to be aware of the distinction between the two. Many recognize that sentence meaning is 'an abstraction' and that 'only linguists and philosophers of language have a clear and distinct notion of, and an interest in, sentence meaning proper' (Sperber and Noveck 2004: 2). Ordinary language users' interpretations can't be taken uncritically as evidence relevant to Gricean pragmatics. It's always possible that intuitions about implicated meaning – what Handley and Feeney (2004: 229) describe as 'Gricean errors' – will intrude on what subjects claim about literal meaning.

For all these reasons, then, data concerning people's reactions to and interpretations of the types of data discussed in pragmatic theory need to be treated with caution. There are those working in pragmatics who claim that ordinary speakers do hold the key to evaluating pragmatic theories, but the view is not universally accepted. Data from experimental pragmatics certainly has much to contribute to present day pragmatics but it is seen, even by those working with it, as providing a useful complement to other types of data. Evidence relevant to pragmatics is appropriately drawn from intuitive speculation, from experiments and from naturally occurring conversation; or, as Clark and Bangerter (2004: 25) put it, from 'armchair, laboratory, field'.

FURTHER READING

Politeness

Textbooks that introduce politeness theory include Thomas (1995) Chapter 6, Christie (2000) Chapter 6, Grundy (2008) Chapter 9 and Huang (2007), the latter also providing an overview of some of the arguments against Brown and Levinson on the grounds that their claims about politeness lack universality.

Leech (1983) outlines a version of politeness theory not discussed here. He proposes to introduce a Politeness Principle, with a variety of accompanying maxims, to complement Grice's Cooperative Principle.

As well as the sources cited and quoted in section 6.1, the following books are relevant to recent debates in the field of politeness theories: Eelen (2001), Watts (2003), Watts et al. (2005) and Christie (2010).

Literature

Mey (2000) and Black (2006) are textbooks that explicitly link pragmatics to the study of literary texts. Toolan (1998b) is a more general introduction to the application of linguistic analysis to literary texts, but it includes a discussion of the analysis of literary texts in terms of speech acts in Chapter 8. MacMahon (2006) offers a good overview of the application of pragmatics to specific literary texts and to the nature of literature more generally. Clark (2009) surveys work that relates inference in general and RT in particular to literary texts.

Language acquisition

Much of the work relevant to the relationship between pragmatics and language acquisition is presented in individual published articles. A small sample of these are referenced and quoted in section 6.3 above. There are also studies of topics in pragmatics not discussed there, for instance of the development of the appropriate use of pronouns and of deictic expressions more generally (see for example Hickmann 1987).

Some relatively old book-length studies of language development are still very pertinent in relation to pragmatics and offer some useful data from child language. These include Hayes (1970), Cruttenden (1979) and Ochs and Schieffelin (1979) as well as the work of Halliday (1975), Bates (1976) and Painter (1984) which are discussed here.

Foster (1990), especially Chapter 4, offers an interesting alternative to the more functional explanations of pragmatic and linguistic development. Clark (2004) is a good introduction to and overview of the field.

Clinical linguistics

Cummings (2005), a general introduction to pragmatics, includes a discussion of the relationship between pragmatics and clinical linguistics in Chapter 9. Cummings (2009) offers a much fuller treatment of the subject. Perkins (2007) is a further useful overview of the subject, which argues for the integration of theoretical and clinical interests in pragmatics. Lesser and Milroy (1993) is concerned with linguistics and aphasia, and focusses particularly on the implications of pragmatics. Crystal (1981) is a good introduction to clinical linguistics, but doesn't specifically discuss pragmatics, which hadn't made much impact on clinical practice at the time of publication.

Experimental pragmatics

The findings of experimental pragmatics to date are generally reported in individual research articles. A useful collection of such articles is to be found in Noveck and Sperber (2004) and the introduction to this collection (Sperber and Noveck 2004) is a good survey of the field. Noveck and Sperber (2007) gives an overview of experimental work on scalars, with many references.

Pragmatics and Language in Context

7

Right at the start of this book we tentatively adopted a working definition of pragmatics as the branch of the study of language concerned with 'meaning in context'. The last six chapters have all been concerned with questions of what is involved in studying meaning in context, what theories and frameworks have been advanced to explain how language operates in context, and how these theories and frameworks might be applied to different types of data and compared and evaluated. But pragmatics isn't the only discipline which is concerned with the relationship between language and the contexts in which it is used. There are many working in present-day linguistics who might be said to be concerned with language in context who don't use, or at least who aren't primarily concerned with, the models and terminologies developed in pragmatics.

In this final chapter we will briefly survey four other fields that are concerned with language in context: conversation analysis, discourse analysis, sociolinguistics and corpus linguistics. Like pragmatics, these are all relatively recent developments in the study of language and all can be seen as distinct from more core areas of linguistic study, such as the formal analysis of syntax, semantics or phonology. They have, of course, some features in common with pragmatics and with each other, but each is a unique and distinct approach to the study of language. In the following sections we will consider briefly what distinguishes each of these fields of study from pragmatics in terms, for instance, of the types of data they deal with and the types of question they ask about that data. We will also consider areas in which pragmatics overlaps with these other fields, particularly where insights or forms of analysis developed in pragmatics have proved useful in other areas of the study of language in use.

Some working in other fields of language study may have found pragmatics useful, but not everyone agrees that it is a legitimate way to study language in context at all. There are many present-day critics of pragmatics who see its goal of modelling how language interacts with context in order to understand the principles used in communication by speakers and hearers as misguided or ill conceived. In very general terms we can see such objections as focussing on the general reliance in pragmatics on some notion of literal, core or linguistic meaning, a reliance that goes right back to Austin and his distinction between 'form' and 'meaning'. For some linguists, it is an unwarranted abstraction to regard some particular utterance by a speaker in a context as having a 'linguistic' and a 'pragmatic' component. For instance, in the approach to linguistics known as integrationism, any communicative event must be treated as a unique and holistic entity. Integrationists resist the idea found in pragmatics that a single linguistic form can occur in different contexts with different communicative significances: 'whereas pragmatics is interested in identifying communicative patterns which are to be found in similar situations (and which constitute the sameness between these situations), integrationism is interested in the uniqueness of each communication situation' (Gretsch 2009: 341).

Roman Kopytko (1995) criticizes theoretical pragmatics, or what he calls 'rationalistic pragmatics', on the grounds that it is based on assumptions about what would constitute optimally rational or logical behaviour, rather than on empirical studies of actual communication. He argues that rationalistic pragmatics makes the limiting assumptions that the use of language is driven by the intention to fulfil certain communicative goals, that the context for any utterance can be neatly modelled and that the mechanisms of interaction can be, or should be, summed up in a finite set of principles based on logic and reasoning. For Kopytko, these assumptions mean that rationalistic pragmatics 'is more concerned with the question of how "rational agents" should use their language to meet the standards of rationality and predictiveness than with describing how language is actually used by the speakers' (ibid.: 489). We saw in Chapter 4 that Grice's concentration on 'cooperation' in conversation left him vulnerable to criticisms of idealizing over how speakers ought to behave rather than describing how they do actually behave. For Kopytko, such criticisms apply to rationalistic pragmatics as a whole.

7.1   Conversation analysis

Conversation analysis, often abbreviated to CA, is an area of social studies that is particularly concerned with the structures, patterns and regularities of naturally occurring conversation. It was developed during the 1960s and 1970s by a number of researchers, most prominently by the sociologists Harvey Sacks and Emmanuel Schegloff.

As a discipline that is concerned entirely with how language is used in context, CA might at first appear to have a lot in common with pragmatics. Certainly, there are areas of overlap, for instance in a shared concern with how language can be described in terms of the different functions it can fulfil. But there is in fact a major difference in emphasis between pragmatics and CA, in terms of the type of data each is centrally concerned with and, even more significantly, the type of question that each asks about that data. Very generally, pragmatics is concerned with questions of how speakers communicate and hearers interpret meanings that can't be explained simply in relation to the linguistic forms used. CA is concerned with how linguistic forms are structured into interactive sequences and how both linguistic and others features of conversation operate as mechanisms of social behaviour. Let's consider the type

of data that conversation analysts concern themselves with, as shown by this
example from an article by Emmanuel Schegloff:

```
 1. Shane:    [·hehh huh       ·hhhh Most wishful thinkin
 2.           hey hand me some a'dat fuckin budder willyou?
 3. ?Shane:   °°Oh::yeah°°
 4.           (1.1)
 5. Nancy:    C'n I have some t[oo
 6. Michael:                   [mm-hm[hm:
 7. Nancy:                     [hm-hm-↑h[m    [↑he-ha-]ha·hehh]
 8. Vivian:                              [Ye[h [I wa]nt]sometoo]
 9. Shane:                                   [N[o:  ]  [( ) -
10. Shane:    No.
11.           (0.2)
12. Shane:    Ladie[s la:st.
```

Notational key

:::	colons indicate stretching of the preceding sound, proportional to the number of colons
[	left brackets connecting two lines indicate simultaneous onset of
[	what follows the brackets
ta̲ble	underlining indicates slight overstress on the underlined item
(1.1)	numbers in parentheses indicate silence in tenths of a second
°°	words between degree marks are markedly softer that surrounding talk in proportion to the number of degree marks

(Data and key from
Schegloff 1999: 410, 428)

This, of course, is an extract from a naturally occurring conversation that has
been recorded at the time at which it took place and subsequently transcribed
for the purposes of analysis. Such transcripts aren't the most usual form of data
in mainstream theoretical pragmatics. But as we have seen some pragmaticists
do use transcribed conversational data, so the type of data in itself doesn't
clearly distinguish CA from pragmatics. But look at the level of detail that is
included in the transcription. The analyst is able to access information about
where speakers overlapped with each other, where they lengthened sounds or
pronounced words other than in a standard manner and where and for how
long there were pauses in the conversation. Transcriptions used in CA also
typically include information about other conversational features such as when
speakers have made a 'repair' in their utterance by restarting and correcting it
and where someone has provided 'backchannelling' to a speaker – by nodding,
smiling or saying things such as 'yeah' or 'mm' while the speaker is talking – in
order to show interest in what is being said. These facts about the conversation

wouldn't be of much interest to most pragmaticists, but they are central to the concerns of conversation analysts who are interested in drawing up as full a picture as possible of what goes on in conversation.

CA was motivated, and remains driven, by the insight that casual conversation, although apparently a free-flowing and spontaneous form of human behaviour, is far from random and is certainly far from chaotic (Sacks et al. 1974). Sacks and his fellow researchers noticed, for instance, that although it isn't decided in advance who will talk in which order and for how long, conversations generally proceed smoothly with surprisingly little overlap and strikingly few pauses. Conversation is 'locally managed', in that its structure and shape is determined as it proceeds through the active collaboration of the speakers involved, rather than being planned in advance or controlled by a single umpire. Sacks et al. therefore became interested in the mechanisms that, although they are generally not consciously noticed, allow participants in a conversation to judge when it is appropriate to speak and not to speak, and when someone who is currently speaking is about to pass the conversational floor over to someone else. The notion of the 'turn' in conversation became central. A turn is basically a stretch of speech produced by a single speaker until speaker change occurs and a different participant in the conversation becomes the speaker. It became apparent that there are certain generalizations that can be made about the structures of turns that help to explain how conversations work. In particular, turns contain what are known as 'transition relevance places'. These are marked by a combination of factors including intonation, semantic completeness, lengthening of syllables and so on. They are points at which if another speaker chooses to she may successfully start talking and gain the turn.

CA is concerned not just with the structure to be found within turns but also with the ways in which different turns in a conversation are structured together to form coherent wholes. One structural unit of conversations that has been identified is the 'adjacency pair' (Schegloff and Sacks 1973). Adjacency pairs are groups of two utterances defined by their function in the interaction. They begin with a certain type of utterance that forms the 'first pair part' and typically requires a different speaker to produce a 'second pair part' of a particular type. Examples of adjacency pairs include: greeting – greeting, invitation – acceptance/refusal, question – answer/disclaimer, and offer – acceptance/decline. As can be seen from these examples, it is sometimes possible that a particular first pair part may license more than one type of second pair part, or may allow for a choice between two different second pair parts. If a speaker asks a question it is usual for a different speaker to answer it, but it's also possible that the second speaker might issue a disclaimer, indicating that for some reason she is not in a position to answer. Similarly, an offer is generally followed by an acceptance, but a speaker may instead choose to decline. In cases where there are two possible types of second pair part, it is possible to describe one as the 'preferred response' and one as the 'dispreferred response'. In the case of a question, the preferred response is an answer and the dispreferred response is a disclaimer. In the case of an invitation the preferred response is an acceptance and the dispreferred response is a refusal, and so on. Labelling a response as 'preferred' or 'dispreferred' is not a judgement about the attitudes or wishes of individual speakers in particular social situations. Rather, it is a statement about what is normally expected in particular types of sequences and therefore what type of turn it will be relatively easy or difficult for a speaker to produce. Speakers generally put in more effort when they need to produce a dispreferred rather than a preferred response. Refusals, for instance, generally take longer to produce than acceptances and may include hesitations, apologies and explanations as to why the invitation can't be accepted.

In CA the data, the recorded and transcribed extracts of conversations, take central place. Generalizations such as the identification of adjacency pairs as structural units of conversation must all be built up from successive observations of much data. As Deborah Schiffrin explains, 'CA views the empirical conduct of speakers as the central resource out of which analysis must develop. Furthermore, "what is said" provides not only the data underlying analysis, but also the evidence for hypotheses and conclusions: it is participants' conduct itself that must provide evidence for the presence of units, existence of patterns, and formulation of rules' (Schiffrin 1994: 236). Here then is another striking difference from pragmatics. In theoretical pragmatics, at least, data are used to illustrate the operation of particular principles rather than as a basis on which patterns and rules are constructed.

In part because of the centrality of data to everything that goes on in CA, the process of collecting and transcribing data, and the decisions that are made in producing a transcription, are themselves topics of central importance. Analysts have choices to make in terms of how 'broad' or 'narrow' to make their transcriptions. A very broad transcription would include just the basic information about who said what in what order and would be inadequate for most purposes in CA. A very narrow transcription would contain precise details about every aspect of the linguistic and extra-linguistic features of the conversation. Potentially any of these might prove important and might show up significant regularities and patterns, but an excessively narrow transcription can become difficult to decipher. Conversation analysts also face questions about how far from the original event of the conversation a transcription takes them. A transcription is of course not the same thing as the conversation itself. It is necessarily to some extent a representation, or an interpretation, of what took place in a particular communicative situation.

One further significant feature of CA is summed up in this comment by Stephen Levinson (1983: 295): 'the data consist of tape-recordings and transcripts of naturally-occurring conversation, with little attention paid to the nature of the context as that might be theoretically conceived in sociolinguistics or social psychology (e.g. whether the participants are friends or distant acquaintances, or belong to a certain social group, or whether the context is formal or informal, etc.)'. Although it is sociological in its origins and orientation, CA doesn't concern itself with the specifics of individual social situations. This is because its main concern is to identify the overarching structures and regularities of conversational interaction, of which individual conversations are specific examples or occurrences. These structures and regularities may themselves have a lot to tell the analyst about social organization and human social behaviour, but only because they are generic rather than specific. Schegloff suggests that we should 'think of structures of interaction as the recurrent structures of sociality, which recruit constantly shifting cohorts of participants to staff the episodes of conversation and other forms of talk-in-interaction which they organize' (Schegloff 1999: 427).

7.2 Discourse analysis

Discourse analysis (DA) is harder to define than CA. This is in part because it is a much broader discipline, incorporating a wide range of types of data and analyses. It is partly also because the term itself has sometimes been used in a very broad way indeed to cover any of the many ways in which language use is analysed. But at the same time there is also a use of the term that restricts it to a relatively autonomous branch of linguistic analysis. So in the broad definition 'discourse analysis' might be said to be compatible with, indeed to include, both pragmatics and conversation analysis. But according to the narrower definition it is separate from them and indeed differs from them in a number of significant ways. Here, we will try to make sense of this narrower definition of DA, so as to be able to recognize in particular how it is distinct from and where it borders pragmatics.

The development of DA in the 1960s and 1970s was driven by the ambition to perform linguistic analysis on stretches of authentic language use that extended beyond the sentence. There was dissatisfaction with the Chomskyan approach, then dominant in mainstream linguistics, in which the emphasis was on the analysis of syntactic structure and the data were almost exclusively invented examples of single sentence length. As Ruth Wodak (2001: 5) has observed, this feature of Chomskyan linguistics was at the time shared by pragmatics. It is in fact still a feature of much of the work that goes on in theoretical pragmatics today. Early pioneers of DA argued that it was artificial to deal with data that had no attested occurrence in the practice of actual language use and to restrict analysis to single sentences, when language was normally actually used in much longer spoken or written texts. The assumption behind DA is that, just as sentences are structured and patterned and can be analysed in terms of formal categories, so too longer stretches of text display patterns and structures that occur across sentences. DA is concerned with identifying the distinctive linguistic features, the structural patterns and also the functions of stretches of naturally occurring language use, both written and spoken. Unlike in CA, information about the social context in which language use is produced and interpreted is crucial. Also unlike CA, in which analysis is always driven by what is found in the data, DA is concerned with developing theoretical frameworks for describing how texts are constructed and interpreted.

Much work that is central to DA draws on the functional approach to language developed by Michael Halliday. We considered Halliday's functional approach in Chapter 6 in relation to theories of language acquisition. For Halliday, language is defined and shaped by the communicative functions it is used to perform. This is reflected in his functional grammar (Halliday 1985) which sees the shaping influences on language as being the meanings it is used to express, rather than autonomous structural forms. Functional approaches to discourse have often focussed on the concept of 'cohesion' (first identified by Halliday and Hasan 1976): the ways in which sentences within a text can be linked and related together, features that can of course only fully be analysed by looking beyond the individual sentence. Cohesive devices include conjuncts such as 'and', 'nevertheless', 'so' and 'finally'. They also include referring terms which direct the interpreter elsewhere, either outside or inside the current text, for their interpretation. These can include both pronouns such as 'these', 'it' and 'he', and also forms that either repeat previous expressions ('John won the lottery. John was happy') or co-refer with them ('John won the lottery. The man was happy'). This type of DA found particular applications in language teaching. Becoming competent in a foreign language is not just about learning the vocabulary and grammar that form the sentences of that language, but also about how those sentences are appropriately joined and structured into different kinds of texts.

The analysis of cohesion within texts largely involved the analysis of written texts, but another development within DA at much the same time was exclusively concerned with the analysis of stretches of spoken discourse. This is the analysis of the typical patterns of classroom discourse in terms of the types of acts it contains and the ways in which these acts are structured into larger units (Sinclair and Coulthard 1975; Coulthard 1977). Sinclair and Coulthard focussed on the exchange as a significant building block of classroom discourse. An exchange is a structural unit of discourse concerned with a single piece of behaviour or information and typically, in the case of classroom discourse, made up of three separate moves: an opening move produced by the teacher, an answering move produced by one or more of the pupils, and a follow-up move from the teacher. Moves themselves are made up of one or more acts. Coulthard makes it explicit that 'the category *act* is very different from Austin's illocutionary acts and Searle's speech acts. Acts are defined principally by their interactive function' (Coulthard 1977: 126). They have very general definitions in terms of what function they perform in the interaction. For instance, an 'elicitation', a very frequent type of act in classroom discourse, functions 'to request a linguistic response'.

Here is an example of just one exchange from Sinclair and Coulthard's data:

> *Teacher*: Who knows anything about these What do we call them? Er, kings of Egypt We don't call them kings really. They have a special name.
> *Pupil*: Pharaohs.
> *Teacher*: They were Pharaohs.

> (Sinclair and Coulthard 1975: 81)

The teachers opening move here is an 'elicit', and therefore the exchange type as a whole is analysed as an elicit. But the opening move in fact contains three separate acts: a starter ('Who knows anything about these'), an elicitation

('What do we call them? Er, kings of Egypt') and a clue ('We don't call them kings really. They have a special name'). The pupil's answering move consists of just one act, a reply ('Pharaohs') and the teacher's follow-up move also consists of one act, an evaluate ('They were Pharaohs'). In the classroom, the repetition of a suggested answer is recognized as an acceptance and a positive evaluation of the answer.

A more recent development in DA, one that continues to attract a lot of interest and generate a lot of research is critical discourse analysis (CDA). Like DA in general, CDA is based on the assumption that the analysis of language should proceed in relation to larger units of text. Also like DA in general, it assumes that these texts must be analysed in relation to their social context of production and interpretation. However, the particular emphasis of CDA is how discourse can present language users as either powerful or powerless. It is therefore concerned particularly with forms of discourse that address, establish or reinforce different types of social inequality. Its aim is to reveal by analysis the underlying and often implicit assumptions of texts such as political speeches, newspaper articles and advertisements.

As just one example of the types of features that might be commented on in CDA, consider Norman Fairclough's comparison of the wording of a report of the House of Commons Home Affairs Committee on hard drug abuse, and an article about that report in *The Sun* newspaper. The report contained the following passage:

> The Government should consider the use of the Royal Navy and the Royal Air Force for radar, airborne or ship surveillance duties. We recommend ... that there should be intensified law enforcement against drug traffickers by HM Customs, the police, the security services and possibly the armed forces.

Here is the beginning of the article in *The Sun*:

> *Call Up Forces in Drug Battle!*
> The armed forces should be called up to fight off a massive invasion by drug pushers, MPs demanded yesterday.

Using the abbreviations 'S' for *The Sun* article and 'Report' for the House of Commons Home Affairs Committee report, Fairclough notes that:

> S uses vocabulary items wholly absent from the Report (*Call up, battle, fight off, massive, invasion, pushers* and *forces* without modification). It also uses a (dramatic) imperative, in the headline. But S also changes the ideational meaning of the Report – it represents a cautious recommendation that armed forces might be involved as a demand for them to be involved. (Fairclough 1995: 58)

CDA seems to have a somewhat ambivalent attitude towards pragmatics. Those working with the CDA framework have found some aspects of pragmatic theory to be useful tools for analysis. For instance, Fairclough (1989: 157) draws attention to the relation between direct and indirect speech acts and expressions of power while Bloor and Bloor (2007) relate CDA to Gricean implicature and also to politeness theory. But explicit comments on pragmatics from within CDA are generally critical. Fairclough (1989: 9) comments that pragmatics concentrates on individual speakers adopting strategies to achieve goals and 'understates the extent to which people are caught up in, constrained by, and indeed derive their individual identities from social conventions'. Ruth Wodak (2001: 3) complains that in some of the research in pragmatics 'context variables are somewhat naively correlated with an autonomous system of language'.

Nowadays it is fairly widespread practice to refer to the field as a whole as (critical) discourse analysis or (C)DA. This acknowledges both that CDA is just one branch of the much wider discipline and also that it is a very significant presence within it.

7.3 Sociolinguistics

We have already considered the relationship between pragmatics and sociolinguistics. In Chapter 6 we looked at politeness theory as a field of study that draws on both disciplines; Brown and Levinson (1987: 2) describe the significance of their work in relation to pragmatics and also to sociolinguistics. Certainly, phenomena such as how speakers express degrees of politeness through the linguistic choices they make are matters of concern to both pragmaticists and sociolinguists, but the two branches of linguistics are nevertheless very different from each other, with different focusses, methodologies and motivations. Jacob Mey (2006: 1793) has summarized the difference as follows: 'pragmatics studies the use of language in the users, while sociolinguistics focuses on the linguistic aspects of the social use'.

Sociolinguistics is concerned with the relationship between language and society, and it investigates the various social factors that impact on the linguistic resources available to people and on how they use these resources. The social factors that interest sociolinguists are generally variables such as age, social class, gender and ethnicity. Sociolinguists are interested in discovering how these variables affect the way that people use language to interact in social settings. They are also interested in how people make particular choices about their language use in order to present themselves as having a particular type of social identity, sometimes in ways that differ between different social situations. These interests mean that the only legitimate data for sociolinguists to use must necessarily be drawn from instances of actual language use; invented examples just couldn't answer the questions of sociolinguistics in the way that they can arguably answer the questions of pragmatics. The data that sociolinguists use is often recorded and transcribed conversational data, but this isn't always the case. Data collected by interviewing speakers about their attitudes to language or what they consider to be their own normal linguistic practice, or by prompting speakers to utter particular words or expressions, are also commonly used in sociolinguistics.

The different questions that are asked in sociolinguistics compared to those that are asked in pragmatics mean that sociolinguists have their own terminology to discuss the features of language use that interest them, and in general there is little cross-over between these and the terminology of pragmatics. For instance, the concept of the 'linguistic variable' describes the way in which two or more linguistic units may have the same function but may alternate in interesting and measurable ways in different social contexts. But there are some ways in which sociolinguistics draws on aspects of pragmatic theory, and here speech act theory is particularly significant. The work of theorists such as Austin and Searle has informed discussions of power in relation to directness and indirectness and to questions such as who in a social situation has the power to perform certain types of speech act (see for instance Hall 2003). Meyerhoff (2006, Chapter 10) considers both speech acts and conversational implicatures to be tools for studying conversational interaction from a sociolinguistic point of view.

The term 'cooperation' is widely used in sociolinguistic studies of conversational interaction, but it's important to be aware that this use of the term is very different from Grice's and has different implications. In fact the difference between the concept of 'cooperation' in pragmatics and in sociolinguistics is an illuminating instance of the difference between the two fields. In pragmatics, of course, the cooperative principle is an attempt to define the general norms that describe the communicative use of language and the assumptions that people bring to linguistic interaction that enable them to derive intended from literal meaning. In sociolinguistics the term 'cooperative' is a description of a certain style of interactive behaviour or of how people may choose to present themselves and build their social relationships through conversation. It is particularly associated with discussions of the relationship between gender and conversational interaction. Feminist linguistics have claimed that women's talk is generally cooperative, while men's is generally competitive. That is, women tend to consider the needs of the group as a whole and to support each other in a conversation, whereas men tend to assert their own needs and the validity of their own contributions. This sociolinguistic notion of cooperation is made up of a number of types of conversational behaviour, rather than by generalized principles. Jennifer Coates, for instance, has described cooperative conversation in terms of topic (women tend to choose topics concerned with people and feelings and to build on each other's contributions to these topics), minimal responses (women tend to use responses such as 'yeah' and 'mhm' to show that they are listening and to support each other), hedges (women tend to use a lot of hedges to mitigate the force of what they are saying and to encourage others to participate), questions (women tend to use questions not to seek information but to invite others to participate and to check for agreement) and turn-taking (women often talk at the same time as each other but in order to support each other and construct the conversation collaboratively rather than to interrupt and claim a turn for themselves) (Coates 1993: 138; see also Tannen 1998).

As an example of the type of data that is of interest to sociolinguists, and of the type of observations they make about it, consider the following extract from an all-female conversation:

Meg: we did the interviews for the – you know I'd been shortlisting and there were twenty-four and un inCREDibly well-qualified and the twenty-four that applied for er nine places. all had um good degrees in psychology I mean and some of them had . M- MPhils and DPhils and um .hh PhDs. you know they were very well qualified and . all- virtually all of them had done some . proper ongoing research into child abuse or -

Mary: what's the course?

Meg: the M- it's called the MClinPsychol it's the qualification I did [masters in clinical

Mary: [yes

Meg: [psychology

Mary: [mhm

Meg: um . anyway we interviewed them on two days running Thursday and Friday and ((something)) really funny happened . one was an extremely pretty girl that's doing . um er er- what's the diploma? a- a- a Master's in Child Development at Newcastle with Professor Newton and she got a SPLENdid reference from Professor Newton

Jen: You used to have Professor Newton [didn't you?

Meg: [yeah yeah but s- and saying things like- can't remember the girl's name Nicola I think saying um you know 'She's academically u- u- unimpeachable she's absolutely superb she's also an extremely nice girl and she's the sort that joins in well at the party and is always- has al-always there- er also there for the washing up'
<LAUGHTER>

Meg: that was a nice little domestic note anyway um-

Helen: they wouldn't have said that about a bloke   [((xx))

Sally: [I was going to [say

Meg: [well
there WAS that um . anyway during the interview um . it went okay . um she's- she's the sort of- she has a very pleasant manner and she answered quite competently and at the end um David Blair said to her . um 'You've been working with autistic children [...] he said to her . um 'Do you believe um there's any relationship between dyslexia and autism?' and she absolutely panicked

Bea: heavens

Meg: and it was TERRible for us to watch

Helen: mhm

(Adapted from Coates 1998: 316–17)

Coates in fact uses this example to discuss how women portray themselves when they are in a position of power, such as being on an interview panel, but we can see in it examples of the types of cooperative behaviour she identified as typical of women's conversations. The topic is a particular job applicant and her appearance, personality and emotional responses. The women support the main speaker, Meg, with various minimal responses such as 'yes' and 'mhm'. Meg herself includes hedges such as 'you know', 'I mean' and 'sort of', while questions put to her such as 'what's the course?' and 'you used to have Professor Newton didn't you?' are designed to encourage her in her story. Simultaneous speech such as 'I was going to say' reinforces what other participants are saying rather than challenging it. A pragmaticist looking at the same data, however, would be interested in a different notion of 'cooperation' and would therefore focus on different aspects of the conversation. These might include, for instance, what meaning Meg conveys by implicature about the candidate or about the nature of her reference by including the apparently irrelevant statement 'also there for the washing up'.

7.4 Corpus linguistics

Corpus linguistics is of relatively recent origin but is now flourishing as a branch of linguistics, or perhaps as a methodology for various areas of linguistic study. Its history and rise are closely linked to developments in technology. Corpus linguists study large collections of naturally occurring language use. These collections are known as 'corpora'; they are stored electronically and read and sorted using various pieces of software. So as computer technology has developed it has become possible for corpora to be larger and for the methods by which they are analysed to become more sophisticated.

If corpus linguistics is of recent origin, then the use of corpus techniques to study discourse, or more specifically to look at pragmatic aspects of language use, is even more recent. Some of the reasons for this are discussed in Partington (2004). For instance, corpora have recently not only got bigger but also been able to include whole texts or longer stretches of language use, rather than text fragments, making more of the relevant context available. In addition, specialized corpora are increasingly being developed, concentrating on particular types or genres of language use. These specialized corpora include those of spoken language, which has been transcribed and often marked up for intonation and other interactional features.

Corpus-based studies of the pragmatics of spoken discourse have tended to focus on the most overtly interactional features, which might be said to belong to the social rather than the theoretical side of pragmatics. For instance, a recent issue of the *Journal of Pragmatics* that was concerned with 'pragmatic markers' included articles describing corpus-based studies of interjections such as 'oh', 'gosh', 'dear me' and 'goodness me' (Norrick 2009), of the occurrence of 'mind you' and its variant 'mind' (Bell 2009), of discourse markers in Catalan and Spanish oral narrative (Cuenca and Marín 2009) and of topic orientation markers such as 'incidentally', 'I want to return to' and 'speaking of' (Fraser 2009).

Corpus pragmaticists are also interested in analysing utterance functions on the basis of spoken corpora, and it is perhaps here that they come closest in their interests and terminologies to theoretical pragmaticists. Speech act theory, in particular, has proved a useful tool for the analysis of functions in spoken language. It is striking that one of the earliest founding theories of pragmatics is being given something of a new lease of life in relation to this most techno-logical of approaches to language study.

An analysis of speech acts in a spoken corpus by Almut Koester provides a good example of studies that bring together corpus linguistics and pragmatics, of the type of data with which such studies are concerned, and of the nature of the findings they present. The interests of the corpus linguist in looking at a phenomena such as speech acts are of course related to those of the pragmati-cists, focussing on how speakers achieve their communicative intentions and use language to perform different functions. But the findings of corpus linguis-tics tend to be descriptive of how particular speech acts are actually performed rather than to theorize over, for instance, the differences between literal and intended meaning. And corpus linguists often also have a more practical out-come in mind, particularly in relation to second language teaching.

Koester based his study on a corpus of 34,000 words of spoken discourse, drawn from conversations that had taken place in various workplaces. He searched the corpus for the following terms, chosen because they are performa-tive verbs or because they are what he calls 'metalinguistic verbs and nouns (discuss, talk, conversation) [that] make explicit the communicative function of the utterance' (Koester 2007: 235):

> *tell, talk, speak, conversation, discuss/discussion, understand/understanding, agree/disagree/agreement, explain, accept, chat, suggest/suggestion, apologize.*

Koester offers some interesting findings about the actual occurrence of such items. Explicit performatives are the exception rather than the norm in his cor-pus, and are generally restricted to situations that involve some type of conflict. They serve to offer token agreement before a disagreement:

> Right. ↑ <u>I agree</u> with that, but when- when they're- when we're carrying them for a hundred days?

or sometimes simply occur at face value as part of an argument:

> *Sid*: No I'm sorry, <u>I don't accept</u> all this. If you give someone an order, you give a- you give them an order with the sizes on it.
> *Val*: ↑ Well Sid, <u>it's no good talking</u> to me about it then.
>
> (Data from Koester 2007: 236; underlining indicates the element that makes explicit the communicative function of the utterance)

Speech acts are in fact much more likely to be performed using a variety of implicit devices, to take place over more than one turn in a conversation and to be interactive: a speech act of advising is generally completed, for instance, by an acceptance and evaluation from a different speaker (Koester links this observation to the notion of the adjacency pair, as developed in CA). Here is an example of a speech act which can be described only in relation to several turns in the conversation, and which has the structure '(a) advise (b) accept + evaluation':

Chris: I was thinking this also .. the: 'I was wondering' approach? Hehehehehehehehehehehe
Joe: Yeah 'I was wondering' Heh yeah I like that, okay,
Chris: Uhm ... an' a- an' maybe just a note at the end here [...]
Joe: Yeah. That's right. [...]
Chris: But- but you know, you can- after you've presented this to 'em, you can always listen to the conversations, an' an' say...
Joe: An' that- uh- that's excellent.

(Koester 2007: 238; the underlined parts here show where the pattern of advice, accept and evaluation takes place over several turns.)

Koester compares his findings to the models for performing various kinds of speech acts that are generally presented to learners of English as a second language which, he argues, overemphasize the use of direct speech acts. This emphasis might leave students in danger of sounding rude and of being unable to interpret speech acts directed at them which are not performed explicitly. Students need to be taught to use language in ways appropriate to the individual situation, using materials developed from spoken corpora.

The findings of corpus-based studies such as Koester's don't engage directly in the debates of theoretical pragmatics. They don't, for instance, take issue with Austin's account of language use as a series of speech acts with illocutionary forces composed of conventional and intentional elements, or with Searle's classification of those forces in terms of a complex series of felicity conditions. Austin observed that speech acts may be achieved using explicit performatives or may be produced more indirectly, but he made no claims about the pervasiveness, or the contextual appropriateness, of explicit performatives. But recent corpus-based findings can offer information that wasn't available to early speech act theorists about, for instance, how various types of speech acts are most frequently produced, or what aspects of the wider conversational context are typically relevant to their success. This most up-to-date of linguistic methodologies can offer some interesting information about actual language use that is complementary to Austin's original insight.

FURTHER READING

Conversation analysis

There are a number of good current introductory books on conversation analysis, including Liddicoat (2007), ten Have (2007), Hutchby and Wooffitt (2008) and Schegloff (2007).

Levinson (1983), although principally a textbook on pragmatics, devotes a whole chapter to conversational structure (Chapter 6). Grundy (2008), again a pragmatics textbook, links pragmatics to the techniques and data of conversation analysis in Chapter 10. See also Schiffrin (1994) Chapter 7.

Discourse analysis

Useful introductions to discourse analysis include Beaugrande and Dressler (1981), van Dijk (1981) Brown and Yule (1983), Cook (1989), Schiffrin (1994), Martin and Rose (2003) and Schiffrin et al. (2003). Levinson (1983: section 6.1) offers a discussion of the differences between CA and DA and a critique of DA. Introductions to critical discourse analysis include Fairclough (1989, 1995), and Bloor and Bloor (2007). Wodak and Meyer (2001) and Wodak and Chilton (2005) are collections of essays covering various aspects of the techniques of CDA and their applications to particular texts.

Sociolinguistics

Introductions to sociolinguistics include Spolsky (1998), Wardhaugh (1998), Holmes (2001) and Meyerhoff (2006). Sociolinguistic approaches to language and gender, including the notion of cooperative versus competitive conversational styles, are discussed in Coates (1993), Cameron (1998) and Holmes and Meyerhoff (2003).

Corpus linguistics

General introductions to corpus linguistics include Kennedy (1998), McEnery and Wilson (2001) and Meyer (2002). Adolphs (2008) is concerned with the application of corpus linguistics to the analysis of spoken language. Collections of essays specifically concerned with the relationship between corpus linguistics and pragmatics, or the analysis of discourse more generally, include Partington et al. (2004), Hoey et al. (2007), Teubert and Krishnamurthy (2007), Romero-Trillo (2008) and Jucker et al. (2008).

Glossary

When a term that has its own separate entry is used it appears in *italics*.

Acceptability   A property of an utterance that is concerned with whether it can be interpreted successfully, regardless of its *grammaticality*. Chomsky's example 'Colourless green ideas sleep furiously' is a perfectly grammatical sentence according to the rules of the English language, but is nevertheless unacceptable because it makes no sense. Unlike grammaticality, acceptability is sometimes relative to context.

Constative   In Austin's version of speech act theory, a term for utterances that are used to make a statement of fact and that can be judged to be either 'true' or 'false'. Examples include 'The Earth revolves around the Sun' and 'My Aunt is in Ibiza for the summer'. Austin noted that constatives account for only one small part of what speakers do with language; many utterances are *performative* in nature.

Conventional implicature   A type of *implicature* identified by Grice that is determined by the conventional meaning of a particular word but doesn't contribute to '*what is said*' and therefore to *truth-conditional* meaning when the word is used. The word 'but', for instance, conventionally introduces an implicature of contrast. Saying 'He's a banker but he's quite nice really' commits the speaker to the truth of the two facts that he is a banker and that he is quite nice really, but it conventionally implicates that it is in some way surprising or unusual that these two facts should both be true. The notion of conventional implicature has been and remains controversial; some pragmaticists have argued that such examples should instead by seen as involving types of *presupposition*.

Conversational implicature   A category of *implicature* that is central to Grice's theory of conversation. Unlike *conventional implicatures*, conversational implicatures are not determined by conventional meaning, but instead depend on general features of language use, summarized in Grice's maxims of cooperation. For discussion and examples see separate entries for *generalized conversational implicature* and *particularized conversational implicature*.

Deixis   The property of particular words and expressions that indicate some aspect of situation and therefore require information from context to be understood fully. Deictic expressions include those that express person deixis (such as 'I', 'you', 'he' and so on), those that express time deixis (such as 'today', 'tomorrow', 'on Friday', 'in one year's time') and those that express place deixis (such as 'here', 'there', 'bring', 'take').

Discourse markers   Expressions that indicate how an utterance relates to its context or fits into the discourse in which it occurs. Examples include 'well', 'but', 'therefore' and 'on the other hand'. In theoretical pragmatics discourse markers have been a particular focus of interest in relevance theory where they are said to encode procedural rather than conceptual meaning.

Entailment   In logic, a relationship between *propositions*. If a certain proposition is true there are further propositions that must also be true or that follow from it; these are its entailments. 'Florence is Matilda's aunt' entails 'Matilda is Florence's niece'. The symbol '→' is often used for logical entailment, so if the proposition p is 'Florence is Matilda's aunt' and the proposition q is 'Matilda is Florence's niece' then 'p → q' is logically valid.

Explicature   A term specific to relevance theory. An explicature of an utterance is any assumption that the utterance communicates that is derived by a process of developing the linguistically encoded form of an utterance to give a complete proposition. This process of developing is guided by the principle of relevance and is specific to context. For instance, 'Mary's book is a bestseller' may have the explicature 'the book Mary is buying is a bestseller' in the context of a bookshop, but in the context of a newspaper profile of an author it may have the explicature 'the book Mary has written is a bestseller'; the genitive form is developed differently in each context. Explicatures are distinct from *implicatures*, which are also determined by the operation of the principle of relevance in context, but which can't be seen as developments of any element of linguistic form. So in the context of the newspaper profile, 'Mary's book is a bestseller' may communicate the assumption 'Mary is very rich', but this assumption is an implicature rather than an explicature.

Face   A term introduced into politeness theory by Brown and Levinson. It describes a person's social value, in interaction with other people. In producing her utterances, a speaker must take account both of her own face wants and the face wants of the hearer. There are two different aspects of face. Positive face refers to a person's desire to be liked and to be thought well of. Negative face refers to a person's desire not to be pushed around or imposed on.

Face threatening act   In politeness theory, a description of something that a speaker may need or want to say that has the capacity to damage the *face* of either the speaker or the hearer. For instance, a criticism has the capacity to damage the positive face of the hearer and a request has the capacity to damage his negative face. Speakers may choose to perform face threatening acts 'baldly' ('you look awful' or 'open this jar for me') but there are various strategies available to avoid doing so. A speaker may choose simply not to perform the face threatening act. She may choose to perform it but to do so 'off record', so as to give the hearer an apparent choice as to how he interprets what she says ('you're not looking at your best today' or 'I can't seem to get this jar lid open'). She may choose to perform the face threatening act but to do so with 'redressive action' in order to address the hearer's face wants ('I have to tell you as a friend; you look awful' or 'I'm really sorry to trouble you but could you open this jar for me?').

Felicity conditions   A term widely used in speech act theory, first by Austin and later by Searle. In general, felicity conditions are those features of a context which have to be in place in order for a speech act to be successful. For Austin, there were three different types of felicity condition: those that specified the need for the existence of certain conventional procedures and forms of words to perform a particular act, and further the need for the people involved in an individual act to be appropriate to that procedure; those that specified that the procedures were carried out both correctly and completely; and those that specified that the speaker must genuinely have the relevant thoughts, feelings or intentions. Searle used felicity conditions to define different types of speech act. His classification of felicity conditions was different from Austin's. It consisted of preparatory conditions (facts that needed to be in place before the speech act could successfully be performed), sincerity conditions (beliefs or attitudes that it was necessary for the speaker to hold) and essential conditions (what the speaker intended the speech act to be or to achieve).

Generalized conversational implicature (GCI)   A type of *implicature* first described by Grice that arises by default unless blocked or cancelled by some aspect of context. So 'I am meeting a man this evening' will normally implicate that the person in question is someone other than the speaker's husband, boyfriend, brother or father. 'Pauline was spotted by a talent scout and moved to Hollywood' will normally implicate that Pauline moved to Hollywood after and as a result of being spotted by a talent scout. Grice distinguished GCIs from *particularized conversational implicatures* which are individually dependent on specific features of context. GCIs play a major role in the work of some neo-Griceans, particularly Levinson, but have no role in the account of explicit and implicit meaning developed in relevance theory.

Grammaticality   A property of sentences; a string of words is said to be a grammatical sentence if it conforms to the rules of the language. Pragmaticists are generally interested in grammaticality because it can be distinguished from *acceptability*.

Illocutionary act   One of the three separate acts that Austin identified as being performed every time a speech act is produced. The illocutionary act is determined partly by the conventions of the language and its use in society, but is dependent also on the psychological state, or the intention, of the speaker. It is what the speaker was attempting to do when she produced the speech act or, as Austin put it, the act performed 'in' speaking, rather than simply the act 'of' speaking. 'Can you pass me my coat?' is literally a question concerning whether the hearer is able to reach the coat and hand it over, but the illocutionary act is one of requesting him to do so. Austin began an attempt to classify speech acts in terms of the illocutionary acts they performed, or their illocutionary force. The classification of illocutionary forces was a major component of Searle's subsequent development of speech act theory. See also *locutionary act* and *perlocutionary act*.

Implicature   Part of what is communicated when an *utterance* is produced in context that is not part of the literal meaning of the linguistic form used. The term was coined by Grice who drew a distinction between 'what is implicated' and '*what is said*'. It has been used in many other pragmatic theories, but often with significant differences from Grice. In relevance theory, for instance, many aspects of meaning that for Grice would have been implicatures are analysed as *explicatures*. For further discussion and examples see *conventional implicature, explicature, generalized conversational implicature, particularized conversational implicature*.

Irony   A figure of speech in which what the speaker means to communicate is the opposite or the negation of what her words literally mean. As well as communicating this opposite meaning the speaker generally communicates some attitude towards or evaluation of what she is describing. Ironic utterances are generally produced in response to what someone else has said or might be assumed to believe. If Matthew persuades Hannah to go with him on a trip to the beach, the weather turns cold and wet and Hannah says 'what a great idea it was to come here', she is not just communicating that it was not a great idea but also criticizing or ridiculing Matthew for his suggestion.

Locutionary act   One of the three separate acts that Austin identified as being performed every time a speech act is produced. The locutionary act is determined by the conventional meaning of the words used, together with an understanding of what specific reference they were intended to have. If a speaker says 'I wouldn't come here again if I were you' we can describe the locutionary act simply by quoting the words used and specifying the intended reference of 'I', 'here' and 'you', without making any comment as to whether the utterance was intended as a threat, a warning or a friendly piece of advice. See also *illocutionary act* and *perlocutionary act*.

Metalinguistic negation   A specific use of negation in which it functions not semantically to deny the truth of some *proposition* but pragmatically to object to some aspect of how a proposition has been expressed. Metalinguistic negation generally occurs in response to a previous utterance and is generally followed by a re-expression of that utterance in a different and more acceptable form. So 'There aren't several phenomenons to consider; there are several phenomena to consider' and 'Nana isn't feeling pukey; she's a little indisposed' don't reject the content of what someone else had said but are used to object to the incorrect plural form 'phenomenons' and the colloquial term 'pukey', respectively. Metalinguistic negation has been particularly important in the work of Horn who uses it to support his analysis of *scalar implicature*.

Metaphor   A figure of speech in which something is described in a way that is literally false or even absurd, but which is nevertheless meaningful because it draws attention to some resemblance or similarity. 'You are the cherry on my cake' can't be literally true; a person can't be a cherry. But it could nevertheless be said to be metaphorically true if it picks up on an analogy: perhaps that just as the cherry is the best bit of the cake, the hearer is the best thing in the speaker's life.

Mood   A property of sentences, concerned with the functions they can typically be used to perform. 'You journey by train.' is in the declarative mood; 'Do you journey by train?' is in the interrogative mood; 'Journey by train!' is in the imperative mood. Typically, declaratives are used to make statements, interrogatives to ask questions and imperatives to issue orders, but the correspondence between mood and function is far from straightforward, an issue addressed in many pragmatic theories, notably speech act theory.

Particularized conversational implicature   One of the types of *implicature* identified by Grice in his theory of conversation. A particularized conversational implicature occurs in an individual context as a consequence of the maxims of cooperation and some specific feature of that context. In one of Grice's examples, if A says 'Smith doesn't seem to have a girlfriend these days' and B replies 'He has been paying a lot of visits to New York lately', B can be taken to be implicating that Smith has, or may have, a girlfriend in New York. An utterance of 'He has been paying a lot of visits to New York lately' without the context provided by A would not have the same implicature.

Performative   A term introduced by Austin into his early work on speech acts to describe an utterance that is used to carry out an action or bring about some change. Examples include highly specialized ritualized performatives, such as 'I pronounce you man and wife' and more everyday examples such as 'I bet you ten pounds that Harry will be in detention again today'. These are both examples of explicit performatives, introduced by a first person pronoun and a performative verb ('pronounce' and 'bet'), but performatives can also be implicit. 'Please shut the door' and 'Could you possibly shut the door?' are both implicit performatives that carry out the same act: making a request for someone to shut the door. Unlike *constatives*, performatives cannot be described as being either true or false, but rather as being either appropriate or inappropriate in a particular context, depending on whether or not they fulfil certain *felicity conditions*.

Perlocutionary act   One of the three separate acts that Austin identified as being performed every time a speech act is produced. Unlike the *locutionary act* and the *illocutionary act*, the perlocutionary act is determined by the consequence or the result of the speech act. It may or may not correspond with the intentions of the speaker. If a speaker said 'You can't do that' with the intention of stopping the hearer from doing something and we are reporting on the perlocutionary act, we might say that the speaker 'convinced' or 'persuaded' the hearer not to do that thing, or instead that she merely 'annoyed' or 'irritated' the hearer.

Presupposition   If it is true that 'The grand old Duke of York has ten thousand men', then it must also be true that 'The grand old Duke of York has at least one man', because having at least one man is a logical *entailment* of having ten thousand men. But it must also be true that 'The grand old Duke of York exists'. This is not an entailment but a presupposition. The defining difference is that presupposition but not entailments are shared by the positive and the negative form; 'The grand old Duke of York does not have ten thousand men' doesn't entail 'The grand old Duke of York has at least one man' but it does still presuppose 'The grand old Duke of York exists'. This is known as an 'existential' presupposition, triggered by the presence of the definite description 'the grand old Duke of York'. Other types of expression that have been identified as triggering presuppositions include factive verbs ('The grand old Duke of York regrets marching his men to the top of the hill' presupposes 'The grand old Duke of York marched his men to the top of the hill) and temporal clauses ('Before they marched down they marched up' presupposes 'They marched down'). It remains controversial whether presuppositions are properties of sentences or of utterances, and therefore whether they should be accounted for in *semantics* or in pragmatics.

Proposition   The basic unit of logic, the content of a thought or an idea, that can stand in various different logical relations to other such ideas. When they are expressed in natural language, propositions generally take the form of declarative sentences, but they are not themselves sentences. So one proposition, 'p', might be expressed in natural language as 'roses are red', while another proposition, 'q', might be expressed in natural language as 'violets are blue'. Simple propositions such as these can be combined together in various ways to form complex propositions. So 'p $\land$ q' can be expressed in natural language as 'roses are red and violets are blue'. In pragmatics there has been much debate about whether linguistic semantics alone is able to establish a proposition expressed by an utterance, or whether further information is needed from pragmatics.

Scalar implicature   A type of *implicature* discussed in neo-Gricean pragmatics, particularly by Horn, which arise because there are various scales of semantic strength, consisting of words or expressions that are semantically related and equally lexicalized. Examples of such scales include <love, like>, <the, a> and <always, usually, often, sometimes>. An item on such a scale implicates the negation of any item to its left. So 'I sometimes eat my lunch in that cafe' implicates, for instance, 'I don't usually eat my lunch in that cafe'. Scalar implicature is controversial and is not supported by, for instance, relevance theorists.

Semantics   The semantics of a language determines the meanings of the words and the *sentences* of the language, or what might informally be called 'literal meaning'. Semantics is generally contrasted with pragmatics, concerned with the operation on meaning of features of context and language use, but there is much controversy over where the division between semantics and pragmatics lies, or even whether they can legitimately be described as separate and autonomous systems.

Sentence   A linguistic entity: sentences are strings of words that conform to the grammatical rules of a language and have a meaning determined by its *semantic* rules. Sentences are independent of any individual context of use. In pragmatics, it is usual to distinguish sentences from *utterances*, which are produced by speakers in contexts. The same sentence may be produced by different speakers in difference context; the resulting utterances will have different meanings. These differences will depend in part on the specific references assigned to deictic expressions in context (see *deixis*) but also on general features of language use such as *implicature*.

Truth conditions   In formal discussions of meaning, such as in logic and in *semantics*, truth conditions are those facts about the world that would have to be in place in order for a *proposition* or a *sentence* to be true. Truth conditions do not vary between contexts, but the truth value that they specify may be different in different contexts. So the truth conditions of 'George V is the King of England' specify that this is true in 1930 but false in 2010. In pragmatics, truth-conditional meaning is often contrasted with pragmatic meaning. For some pragmaticists, although by no means for all, semantic meaning is truth-conditional while pragmatic meaning is non-truth-conditional.

Utterance   Unlike *sentences*, utterances are produced by speakers in contexts and therefore have various spatio-temporal and physical properties.

'What is said'   Grice introduced this expression; he contrasted 'what is said' with 'what is implicated'. For Grice the expression remained rather poorly defined; it can be understood as being closely related to the conventional or literal meaning of the *sentence* uttered, with the addition of information about disambiguation of any ambiguous words and reference assignment to any referring expressions. Grice's maxims of cooperation then operate on 'what is said' in context to determine conversational *implicature*. Many pragmaticists, such as the relevance theorists, reject 'what is said' as an autonomous level of meaning. Others, like Recanati, use the expression in a different way. For Recanati, 'what is said' is determined not just by linguistic meaning but by various types of information dependent on context and determined by the application of various pragmatic principles of interpretation.

Bibliography

Adolphs, Svenja (2008) *Corpus and Context: Investigating Pragmatic Functions in Spoken Discourse*, Amsterdam: John Benjamins Publishing Company.

Ahlsén, Elisabeth (1993) 'Conversational principles and aphasic communication', *Journal of Pragmatics* 19: 57–70.

Akmajian, A. (1979) *Aspects of the Grammar of Focus in English*, New York and London: Garland Publishing Inc.

Allwood, Jens, Lars Gunnar Andersson and Osten Dahl (1979) *Logic in Linguistics*, Cambridge: Cambridge University Press.

Ariel, Mira (2002) 'Privileged interactional interpretations', *Journal of Pragmatics* 34: 1003–44.

Ariel, Mira (2008) *Pragmatics and Grammar*, Cambridge: Cambridge University Press.

Ariel, Mira (2010) *Defining Pragmatics*, Cambridge: Cambridge University Press.

Armstrong, D.M. (1971) 'Meaning and communication', *Philosophical Review* 80: 427–47.

Atlas, Jay David (2004) 'Presupposition', in Laurence Horn and Gregory Ward (eds): 29–52.

Atlas, Jay David (2005) *Logic, Meaning, and Conversation: Semantical Underdeterminacy, Implicature, and their Interface*, Oxford: Oxford University Press.

Atlas, Jay David and Stephen Levinson (1981) 'It-clefts, informativeness, and logical form: radical pragmatics', in Peter Cole (ed.) *Radical Pragmatics*, New York: Academic Press: 1–61.

Austin, J.L. (1940) 'The meaning of a word', in J.L. Austin (1961b): 23–43.

Austin, J.L. (1956) 'A plea for excuses', *Proceedings of the Aristotelian Society*, reprinted in J.L. Austin (1961b): 123–52.

Austin, J.L (1961a) 'Preformative utterances', in J.L. Austin (1961b).

Austin, J.L. (1961b) *Philosophical Papers*, Oxford: Clarendon Press.

Austin, J.L. (1962) *How to do Things with Words*, Oxford: Oxford University Press.

Ayer, A.J. (1946) *Language Truth and Logic*, 2nd edn, Harmondsworth: Pelican (1971). [1st edn London 1936].

Bach, Kent (1994) 'Conversational impliciture', *Mind and Language* 9: 124–62.

Bach, Kent (1999) 'The myth of conventional implicature', *Linguistics and Philosophy* 22: 327–66.

Bach, Kent (2001) 'You don't say?' *Syntheses* 128: 15–44.

Bach, Kent (2005) 'Context *ex Machina*' in Zoltán Gendler Szabó (ed.): 15–44.

Bach, Kent (2006a) 'Speech acts and pragmatics', in Michael Devitt and Richard Hanley (eds) *The Blackwell Guide to the Philosophy of Language*, Oxford: Blackwell.

Bach, Kent (2006b) 'The top 10 misconceptions about implicature', in Betty Birner and Gregory Ward (eds): 21–30.

Bach, Kent (2007) 'Regression in pragmatics (and semantics)', in Noel Burton-Roberts (ed.): 24–44.

Bargiela-Chiappini, Francesca (2003) 'Face and politeness: new (insights) for old (concepts)', *Journal of Pragmatics* 35: 1453–69.

Bar-Hillel, Yehoshua (1954) 'Indexical expressions', *Mind* 63: 359–79.

Bar-Hillel, Yehoshua (1971) 'Out of the pragmatic wastebasket', *Linguistic Inquiry* 11: 401–7.

Barker, Stephen (2003) 'Truth and conventional implicature', *Mind* 112: 1–33.

Barnes, Jonathan (ed.) (1984) *The Complete Works of Aristotle*, 2 vols, Princeton: Princeton University Press.

Bates, Elizabeth (1976) *Language and Context: The Acquisition of Pragmatics*, New York: Academic Press.

Beardsley, Monroe C. (1978) 'Aesthetic intentions and fictive illocutions', in Paul Hernadi (ed.): 161–77.

Beaugrande, Robert de and Wolfgang Dressler (1981) *Introduction to Text Linguistics*, London: Longman.

Bell, David (2009) 'Mind you', *Journal of Pragmatics* 41: 915–20.

Bernicot, Josie and Virginie Laval (1996) 'Promises in French children: comprehension and metapragmatic knowledge', *Journal of Pragmatics* 25: 101–22.

Bernicot, Josie and Virginie Laval (2004) 'Speech acts in children: the example of promises', in Ira Noveck and Dan Sperber (eds): 207–27.

Bernicot, Josie, Virginie Laval and Stéphanie Chaminaud (2007) 'Nonliteral language forms in children: In what order are they acquired in pragmatics and metapragmatics?' *Journal of Pragmatics* 39: 2115–32.

Bezuidenhout, Anne and J. Cooper Cutting (2002) 'Literal meaning, minimal propositions, and pragmatic processing', *Journal of Pragmatics* 34: 433–56.

Bezuidenhout, Anne and Robin Morris (2004) 'Implicature, relevance and default pragmatic inference', in Ira Noveck and Dan Sperber (eds): 257–82.

Biletzki, Anat (1996) 'Is there a history of pragmatics?' *Journal of Pragmatics* 25: 455–70.

Birner, Betty and Gregory Ward (eds) (2006) *Drawing the Boundaries of Meaning*, Amsterdam: John Benjamins Publishing Company.

Bishop, Dorothy (2000) 'Pragmatic language impairment: a correlate of SLI, a distinct subgroup, or part of the autistic community?', in Dorothy Bishop and Laurence Leonard (eds) *Speech and Language Impairments in Children: Causes, Characteristics, Interventions and Outcome*, Hove: Psychology Press: 99–113.

Black, Elizabeth (2006) *Pragmatics Stylistics*, Edinburgh: Edinburgh University Press.

Black, Max (1963) 'Austin on performatives', *Philosophy*, reprinted in K.T. Fann (ed.) (1969): 401–11.

Blake, Norman (2002) *A Grammar of Shakespeare's Language*, Basingstoke: Palgrave Macmillan.

Blakemore, Diane (1987) *Semantic Constraints on Relevance*, Oxford: Blackwell.

Blakemore, Diane (1992) *Understanding Utterances*, Oxford: Blackwell.

Blakemore, Diane (2002) *Relevance and Linguistic Meaning: the Semantics and Pragmatics of Discourse Markers*, Cambridge: Cambridge University Press.

Blakemore, Diane (2004) 'Discourse markers', in Laurence Horn and Gregory Ward (eds): 221–40.

Blakemore, Diane (2007) 'Constraints, concepts and procedural encoding', in Noel Burton-Roberts (ed.): 45–66.

Bloom Ronald, Lawrence Pick, Joan Borod, Kashemi Rorie, Fani Andelman, Loraine Obler, Martin Sliwinski, Alfonso Campbell, James Tweedy and Joan Welkowitz (1999) 'Psychometric aspects of verbal pragmatic ratings', *Brain and Language* 68: 553–65.

Bloor, Meriel and Thomas Bloor (2007) *The Practice of Critical Discourse Analysis*, London: Hodder Education.

Borg, Emma (2004) *Minimal Semantics*, Oxford: Oxford University Press.

Borg, Emma (2006) 'Intention-based semantics', in Ernest Lepore and Barry Smith (eds): 250–66.

Borg, Emma (2007) 'Minimalism versus contextualism in semantics', in Gerhard Preyer and Georg Peter (eds): 339–59.

Borod J.C., K.D. Rorie, L.H. Pick, R.L. Bloom, F. Andelman, A.L. Campbell, L.K. Obler, J.R. Tweedy, J. Welkowitz, and M. Sliwinski (2000) 'Verbal pragmatics following unilateral stroke: emotional content and valence', *Neuropsychology* 14: 112–24.

Bousfield, Derek (ed.) (2008) *Impoliteness in Interaction*, Amsterdam: John Benjamins.

Bousfield, Derek and Miriam A. Locher (eds) (2008) *Impoliteness in Language: Studies on its Interplay with Power in Theory and Practice*, Berlin: Mouton de Gruyter.

Breheny, Richard, Napoleon Katos and John Williams (2006) 'Are generalized scalar implicatures generated by default? An on-line investigation into the role of context in generating pragmatics inferences', *Cognition* 100: 434–63.

Brown, Gillian and George Yule (1983) *Discourse Analysis*, Cambridge: Cambridge University Press.

Brown, Penelope and Stephen Levinson (1987) *Politeness: Some Universals in Language Useage*, Cambridge: Cambridge University Press.

Brown, Robert and Martin Steinmann (1978) 'Native readers of fiction: a speech-act and genre-rule approach to literature', in Paul Hernadi (ed.): 141–60.

Bryan, Karen (1988) 'Assessment of language disorders after right hemisphere damage', *British Journal of Disorders of Communication* 23: 111–25.

Burton-Roberts, Noel (1989) *The Limits to Debate*, Cambridge: Cambridge University Press.

Burton-Roberts, Noel (2005) 'Robyn Carston on semantics, pragmatics and "encoding"', *Journal of Linguistics* 41: 398–407.

Burton-Roberts (2007) (ed.) *Pragmatics*, Basingstoke: Palgrave Macmillan.

Cameron, Deborah (1998) (ed.) *The Feminist Critique of Language*, 2nd edn. London: Routledge.

Caplan, David (1987) *Neurolinguistics and Linguistic Aphasiology*, Cambridge: Cambridge University Press.

Capone, Alessandro (2008) 'Belief reports and pragmatics intrusion (the case of null appositives)', *Journal of Pragmatics* 40: 1019–40.

Cappelen, Herman (2007) 'Semantics and pragmatics: some central issues', in Gerhard Preyer and Georg Peter (eds): 3–22.

Cappelen, Herman and Ernie Lepore (2005) *Insensitive Semantics: a Defense of Semantic Minimalism and Speech Act Pluralism*, Oxford: Blackwell.

Cappelen, Herman and Ernie Lepore (2007) 'Relevance theory and shared content', in Noel Burton-Roberts (ed.): 115–36.

Carnap, Rudolf (1937) *The Logical Syntax of Language*, London: Routledge and Kegan Paul.

Carnap, Rudolf (1938) 'Foundations of logic and mathematics', in O. Neurath, R. Carnap and C. Morris (eds) *International Encyclopedia of Unified Science*, Chicago: University of Chicago Press, 139–214.

Carrell, P. (1981) 'Children's understanding of indirect requests: comparing child and adult comprehension', *Journal of Child Language* 8: 329–45.

Carston, Robyn (2002) *Thoughts and Utterances*, Oxford: Blackwell.

Carston, Robyn (2004) 'Relevance theory and the saying/implicating distinction', in Laurence Horn and Gregory Ward (eds): 633–56.

Carston, Robyn and George Powell (2006) 'Relevance theory: new directions and developments', in Ernest Lepore and Barry Smith (eds): 341–60.

Chapman, Siobhan (2005) *Paul Grice, Philosopher and Linguist*, Basingstoke: Palgrave Macmillan.

Chapman, Siobhan (2006) *Thinking about Language*, Basingstoke: Palgrave Macmillan.

Chapman, Siobhan and Christopher Routledge (1999) 'The pragmatics of detection: Paul Auster's *City of Glass*', *Language and Literature* 8: 241–53.

Chierchia, Gennaro, Maria Teresa Guasti, Andrea Gualmini, Luisa Meroni, Stephen Crain and Francesca Foppolo (2004) 'Semantic and pragmatic competence in children's and adult's comprehension of *or*', in Ira Noveck and Dan Sperber (eds): 283–300.

Chomsky, Noam (1957) *Syntactic Structures*, The Hague: Mouton.

Chomsky, Noam (1965) *Aspects of the Theory of Syntax*, Cambridge: MIT Press.

Chomsky, Noam (1972) 'Some empirical issues in the theory of transformational grammar', in Stanley Peters (ed.) *Goals of Linguistic Theory*, Englewood Cliffs, New Jersey: Prentice-Hall: 63–127.

Chomsky, Noam (1986) *Knowledge of Language*, New York: Praeger.

Chomsky, Noam (2000) *New Horizons in the Study of Language and Mind*, Cambridge: Cambridge University Press.

Christie, Christine (2000) *Gender and Language*, Edinburgh: Edinburgh University Press.

Christie, Christine (2010) *Linguistic Politeness*, Edinburgh: Edinburgh University Press.

Clark, Billy (1996) 'Stylistic analysis and relevance theory', *Language and Literature* 5: 163–78.

Clark, Billy (2009) 'Salient inferences: pragmatics and *The Inheritors*', *Language and Literature* 18: 173–212.

Clark, Eve (2004) 'Pragmatics and language acquisition', in Laurence Horn and Gregory Ward (eds): 562–77.

Clark, Herbert and Adrian Bangerter (2004) 'Changing ideas about reference', in Ira Noveck and Dan Sperber (eds): 25–49.

Coates, Jennifer (1993) *Woman, Men and Language*, 2nd edn. London: Longman [1st edn 1986].

Coates, Jennifer (1998) '"Thank God I'm a woman": The construction of differing femininities', in Deborah Cameron (ed.): 295–320.

Cohen, Jonathan (1964) 'Do illocutionary forces exist?', *Philosophical Quarterly*, reprinted in K.T. Fann (ed.) (1969) 420–44.

Cook, Guy (1989) *Discourse*, Oxford: Oxford University Press.

Cooper, Marilyn (1998) 'Implicature, convention and *The Taming of the Shrew*', in Jonathan Culpeper et al. (eds): 54–66.

Coulson, Seana (2004) 'Electrophysiology and pragmatic language comprehension', in Ira Noveck and Dan Sperber (eds): 187–206.

Coulthard, Malcolm (1977) *An Introduction to Discourse Analysis*, London: Longman [2nd edn 1985].

Cruse, Alan (2004) *Meaning in Language*, 2nd edn, Oxford: Oxford University Press [1st edn 2000].

Cruttenden, Alan (1979) *Language in Infancy and Childhood*, Manchester: Manchester University Press.

Crystal, David (1981) *Clinical Linguistics*, Vienna and New York: Springer.

Cuenca, Maria-Josep and Maria-Josep Marín (2009) 'Co-occurrence of discourse markers in Catalan and Spanish oral narrative', *Journal of Pragmatics* 41: 899–914.

Culpeper, Jonathan (1996) 'Towards an anatomy of impoliteness', *Journal of Pragmatics* 25: 349–67.

Culpeper, Jonathan (1998) '(Im)politeness in dramatic dialogue' in Jonathan Culpeper et al (eds): 83–95.

Culpeper, Jonathan, Mick Short and Peter Verdonk (eds) (1998) *Exploring the Language of Drama*, London: Routledge.

Cummings, Louise (2005) *Pragmatics, a Multidisciplinary Perspective*, Edinburgh: Edinburgh University Press.

Cummings, Louise (2009) *Clinical Pragmatics*, Cambridge: Cambridge University Press.

Currie, Gregory (1985) 'What is fiction?', *Journal of Aesthetics and Art Criticism* 43: 385–92.

Cutting, Joan (2007) *Pragmatics and Discourse* (2nd edn), London: Routledge.

Davidson, Donald (1979) 'Moods and performatives', in Avishai Margalit (ed.) *Meaning and Use*, Dordrecht: Reidel, 9–20.

Davis, Steven (ed.) (1991) *Pragmatics: A Reader*, Oxford: Oxford University Press.

Davis, Wayne (1998) *Implicature*, Cambridge: Cambridge University Press.

Dijk, Teun van (1976) 'Pragmatics and poetics', in Teun van Dijk (ed.) *Pragmatics of Language and Literature*, Amsterdam: North-Holland Publishing: 23–57.

Dijk, Teun van (1981) *Studies in the Pragmatics of Discourse*, The Hague: Mouton.

Dipper, Lucy, Karen Bryan and J. Tyson (1997) 'Bridging inference and relevance theory: an account of right hemisphere damage', *Clinical Linguistics and Phonetics* 11: 213–28.

Dore, John (1974) 'A pragmatic description of early language development', *Journal of Psycholinguistic Research* 3: 343–50.

Eelen, Gino (2001) *A Critique of Politeness Theories*, Manchester: St Jerome.

Ely, R. and A. McCabe (1994) 'The language play of kindergarten children', *First Language* 14: 19–35.

Evnine, Siomon (1991) *Donald Davidson*, Cambridge: Polity Press.

Fairclough, Norman (1989) *Language and Power*, Harlow: Longman.

Fairclough, Norman (1995) *Critical Discourse Analysis: The Critical Study of Language*, London: Longman.

Fann, K.T. (ed.) (1969) *Symposium on J.L. Austin*, London: Routledge.

Feng, Zongxin and Dan Shen (2001) 'The play off the stage: the writer-reader relationship in drama', *Language and Literature* 10: 79–93.

Fludernik, Monika (1996) 'Linguistics and literature: prospects and horizons in the study of prose', *Journal of Pragmatics* 26: 583–611.

Foster, Susan (1986) 'Learning discourse topic management in preschool years', *Journal of Child Language* 13: 231–50.

Foster, Susan (1990) *The Communicative Competence of Young Children*, Harlow: Longman.

Francescotti, Robert (1995) 'Even: the conventional implicature approach reconsidered', *Linguistics and Philosophy* 18: 153–73.

Fraser, Bruce (2009) 'Topic orientation markers', *Journal of Pragmatics* 41: 892–8.

Frege, Gottlob (1892) 'On sense and meaning' in Peter Geach and Max Black (eds) (1980) *Translations from the Philosophical Writings of Gottlob Frege*, Oxford: Blackwell. [1st edn 1952]: 56–78.

Fuchs, A. (1984) '"Deaccenting" and "default accent"', in Gibbon, D. and Richter, H. (eds) *Intonation, Accent and Rhythm*, Berlin: de Gruyter: 134–64.

Fulda, Joseph (2008) 'Pragmatics, Montague and "abstracts from logical form"', *Journal of Pragmatics* 40: 1146–7.

Gardener, H.H. Brownell, H. Wapner and D. Michelow (1983) 'Missing the point: the role of the right hemisphere in the processing of complex linguistic materials', in E. Perecman (ed.) *Cognitive Processing in the Right Hemisphere*, New York: Academic Press: 169–92.

Garvey, C. (1975) 'Requests and responses in children's speech', *Journal of Child Language*, 2: 41–63.

Gass, Susan and Joyce Neu (2006) *Speech Acts across Cultures*, Berlin: Mouton de Gruyter.

Gautam, Kripa and Manjula Sharma (1986) 'Dialogue in *Waiting for Godot* and Grice's conception of implicature', *Modern Drama* 29: 580–6.

Gazdar, Gerald (1979) *Pragmatics: Implicature, Presupposition and Logical Form*, New York: Academic Press.

Gellner, Ernest (1959) *Words and Things*, London: Victor Gollancz.

Geurts, Bart (2009) 'Scalar implicature and local pragmatics', *Mind and Language* 24: 51–79.

Geurts, Bart and Rick Nouwen (2007) '*At least* et al.: the semantics of scalar modifiers', *Language* 83: 533–59.

Gibbs, Raymond (1999) 'Interpreting what speakers say and implicate', *Brain and Language* 68: 466–85.

Gibbs, Raymond (2002) 'A new look at literal meaning in understanding what is said and implicated', *Journal of Pragmatics* 34: 457–86.

Gibbs, Raymond (2004) 'Psycholinguistic experiments and linguistic-pragmatics', in Ira Noveck and Dan Sperber (eds): 50–71.

Gilbert, Anthony (1995) 'Shakespearean self-talk, the Gricean maxims and the unconscious', *English Studies* 76: 221–37.

Giora, Rachel (1999) 'On the priority of salient meanings: studies of literal and figurative languages', *Journal of Pragmatics* 31: 919–29.

Glucksberg, Sam (2004) 'On the automaticity of pragmatic processes: a modular proposal', in Ira Noveck and Dan Sperber (eds): 72–93.

Goffman, Ervine (1955) 'On face-work: an analysis of ritual elements in social interaction', in John Laver and Sandy Hutcheson (eds) (1972) *Communication in Face to Face Interaction*, Harmondsworth: Penguin: 319–46.

Goodman, Nelson. (1984) *Of Mind and Other Matters*, Cambridge: Harvard University Press.

Green, Georgia (1989) *Pragmatics and Natural Language Understanding*, Mahwah, New Jersey: Lawrence Erlbaum Associates.

Green, Keith (1997) 'Butterflies, wheels and the search for literary relevance', *Language and Literature* 6: 133–8.

Green, Keith (1998), 'A further response to Pilkington, McMahon and Clark', *Language and Literature* 7: 70–2.

Gretsch, Cécile (2009) 'Pragmatics and integrational linguistics', *Language and Communication* 29: 328–42.

Grice, Paul (1967) 'Indicative conditionals', in Paul Grice (1989): 58–85.

Grice, Paul (1975) 'Logic and conversation', in P. Cole and J. Morgan (eds) *Syntax and Semantics, volume 3*, New York: Academic Press. Reprinted in Paul Grice (1989): 22–40.

Grice, Paul (1978) 'Further notes on logic and conversation', in Peter Cole (ed.) *Syntax and Semantics 9: Pragmatics*, New York: Academic Press. Reprinted in Paul Grice (1989): 41–57.

Grice, Paul (1981) 'Presupposition and conversational implicature', in Peter Cole (ed.). Reprinted in Paul Grice (1989): 269–82.

Grice, Paul (1989) *Studies in the Way of Words*, Harvard: Harvard University Press.

Grundy, Peter (2008) *Doing Pragmatics*, 3rd edn, London: Hodder Education.

Haberland, Hartmut and Jacob Mey (1977) 'Editorial: linguistics and pragmatics', *Journal of Pragmatics* 1: 1–12.

Haberland, Hartmut and Jacob Mey (1989) 'Editorial: copp(er)ing out', *Journal of Pragmatics* 13: 817–23.

Haberland, Hartmut and Jacob Mey (2002) 'Editorial: linguistics and pragmatics, 25 years after', *Journal of Pragmatics* 34: 1671–82.

Habib, Rania (2008) 'Humor and disagreement: identity construction and cross-cultural enrichment', *Journal of Pragmatics* 40: 1117–45.

Hall, Kira (2003) 'Exceptional speakers: contested and problematized gender identities', in Janet Holmes and Miriam Meyerhoff (eds): 353–80.

Halliday, Michael (1975) *Learning How to Mean*, London: Edward Arnold.

Halliday, M.A.K. (1985) *An Introduction to Functional Grammar*, London: Arnold.

Halliday, M.A.K. and R. Hasan (1976) *Cohesion in English*, London: Longman.

Han, Chung-Hye (2000) *The Structure and Interpretation of Imperatives: Mood and Force in Universal Grammar*, New York: Routledge.

Handley, Simon and Aidan Feeney (2004) 'Reasoning and pragmatics: the case of *even-if*', in Ira Noveck and Dan Sperber (eds): 228–53.

Harnish, Robert (1976) 'Logical form and implicature', in Thomas G. Bever, Jerrold J. Katz and D. Terence Langendoen (eds) (1977) *An Integrated Theory of Linguistic Ability*, Hassocks: The Harvester Press: 313–91.

Harnish, Robert (1994) 'Mood, meaning and speech acts', in Sava Tsohatzidis (ed.), *Foundations of Speech Act Theory*, London: Routledge: 407–59.

Harris, Sandra (1995) 'Pragmatics and power', *Journal of Pragmatics* 23:117–35.

Have, Paul ten (2007) *Doing Conversation Analysis*, Oxford: Sage.

Hayes, John (1970) *Cognition and the Development of Language*, New York: Wiley.

Henst, Jean-Baptiste van der and Dan Sperber (2004) 'Testing the cognitive and communicative principles of relevance', in Ira Noveck and Dan Sperber (eds) (2004): 141–71.

Herman, David (1994) 'The Mutt and Jute dialogue in Joyce's *Finnegans Wake*: Some Gricean perspectives', *Style* 86: 505–13.

Hernadi, Paul (ed.) (1978) *What is Literature?*, Bloomington and London: Indiana University Press.

Heusinger, Klaus von and Ken Turner (2006a) 'A first dialogue on the semantics-pragmatics interface', in Klaus von Heusinger and Ken Turner (eds): 1–18.

Heusinger, Klaus von and Ken Turner (eds) (2006b) *Where Semantics Meets Pragmatics*, Amsterdam: Elsevier.

Hickmann, M (1987) 'The pragmatics of reference in child language: some issues in developmental theory', in Hickmann, M. (ed.) *Social and Functional Approaches to Language and Thought*, London: Academic Press: 165–84.

Hoey, Michael, Michaela Mahlberg, Michael Stubbs and Wolfgang Teubert (eds) (2007) *Text, Discourse and Corpora*, London: Continuum.

Holmes, Janet (2001) *An Introduction to Sociolinguistics*, Harlow: Longman.

Holmes, Janet and Miriam Meyerhoff (eds) (2003) *The Handbook of Language and Gender*, Oxford: Blackwell.

Holtgraves, Thomas (1998) 'Interpreting indirect replies', *Cognitive Psychology* 31: 1–27.

Holtgraves, Thomas (1999) 'Comprehending indirect replies: when and how are their conveyed meanings activated?', *Journal of Memory and Language* 41: 519–40.

Horn, Laurence (1972) 'On the semantic properties of logical operators in English', PhD thesis, University of California, Los Angeles.

Horn, Laurence (1989) *A Natural History of Negation*, Chicago: University of Chicago Press.

Horn, Laurence (2004) 'Implicature' in Laurence Horn and Gregory Ward (eds): 3–28.

Horn, Laurence (2006) 'The border wars: A neo-Gricean perspective', in Klaus von Heusinger and Ken Turner (eds): 21–48.

Horn, Laurence (2007) 'Neo-Gricean pragmatics: a Manichaean manifesto', in Noel Burton-Roberts (ed.): 158–83.

Horn, Laurence and Gregory Ward (eds) (2004) *The Handbook of Pragmatics*, Oxford: Blackwell.

Huang, Yan (2004) 'Anaphora and the pragmatics-syntax interface', in Laurence Horn and Gregory Ward (eds): 288–314.

Huang, Yan (2007) *Pragmatics*, Oxford: Oxford University Press.

Hurford, James, Brendan Heasley and Michael Smith (2007) *Semantics, a Coursebook* (2nd edn), Cambridge: Cambridge University Press.

Hutchby, Ian and Robin Wooffitt (2008) *Conversation Analysis*, Cambridge: Polity Press.

Hymes, Dell (1986) 'Discourse: scope without depth', *International Journal of the Sociology of Language* 57: 49–89.

Jaszczolt, Katarzyna (2005) *Default Semantics: Foundations of a Compositional Theory of Acts of Communication*, Oxford: Oxford University Press.

Jucker, Andreas, Daniel Schreier and Marianne Hundt (eds) (2008) *Corpora: Pragmatics and Discourse*, Amsterdam: Rodopi.

Karttunen, Lauri (n.d.) 'Presuppositional phenomena', Mimeo, Department of Linguistics, University of Texas, Austin.

Karttunen, Lauri (1973) 'Presuppositions of compound sentences', *Linguistic Inquiry* 4: 169–93.

Karttunen, Lauri and Stanley Peters (1979) 'Conventional implicature', in C.-K. Oh and D. Dineen (eds) *Syntax and Semantics, vol. 11: Presupposition*, New York: Academic Press: 1–56.

Kasher, Asa (1976) 'Conversational maxims and rationality', in Asa Kasher (ed.) *Language in Focus*, Dordrecht, Holland: D. Reidel Publishing Company: 197–216.

Kasher, Asa (1982) 'Gricean inference revisited', *Philosophica* 29: 25–44.

Kasher, Asa (1991) 'Pragmatics and Chomsky's research program', in Asa Kasher (ed.) *The Chomskyan Turn*, Oxford: Blackwell: 122–49.

Kasher, Asa (1998) 'Chomsky and Pragmatics', in Jacob Mey (ed.).

Kasher, Asa, Gila Batori, Nachum Soroker, David Graves and Eran Zaidel (1999) 'Effects of right- and left-hemisphere damage on understanding conversational implicatures', *Brain and Language* 68: 566–90.

Katz, Jerrold (1977) *Propositional Structure and Illocutionary Force*, Sussex: The Harvester Press.

Kearns, Kate (2000) *Semantics*, Basingstoke: Palgrave Macmillan.

Keenan, Elinor Ochs (1976) 'The universality of conversational postulates', *Language in Society* 5: 67–80.

Kenesei, István and Robert M. Harnish (eds) (2001) *Perspectives on Semantics, Pragmatics, and Discourse: A Festschrift for Ferenc Kiefer*, Amsterdam: John Benjamins Publishing Company.

Kennedy, Graeme (1998) *An Introduction to Corpus Linguistics*, London: Addison Wesley Longman.

Koester, Almut (2007) 'The performance of speech acts in workplace conversations and the teaching of communicative functions', in Wolfgang Teubert and Ramesh Krishnamurthy (eds): 232–30.

Kopytko, Roman (1995) 'Against rationalistic pragmatics', *Journal of Pragmatics* 23: 475–91.

Korta, Kepa (2008) 'Malinoswski and pragmatics: claim making in the history of linguistics', *Journal of Pragmatics* 40: 1645–60.

Lakoff, Robin (1972) 'Language in context', *Language* 48: 907–27.

Lakoff, Robin (1973) 'The logic of politeness; or, minding your p's and q's', in Claudia Corum, T. Cedric Smith-Stark and Ann Weiser (eds) *Papers from the Ninth Regional Meeting of the Chicago Linguistics Society*, Chicago: Chicago Linguistics Society: 292–305.

Lakoff, Robin (1989) 'The way we were; or; the real actual truth about generative semantics: a memoir', *Journal of Pragmatics* 13: 939–88.

Lakoff, Robin (1995) 'Conversational logic', in Jef Verschueren, Jan-Ola Ostman and Jan Blommaert (eds) (1995) *Handbook of Pragmatics*, Amsterdam: John Benjamins: 190–8.

Lakoff, Robin and Sachiko Ide (eds) (2005) *Broadening the Horizon of Linguistic Politeness*, Philadelphia: John Benjamins Publishing.

Langdon, R., Davies, M. and Coltheart, M. (2002) 'Understanding minds and understanding communicated meanings in schizophrenia', *Mind and Language* 17: 68–104.

Leech, Geoffrey (1983) *Principles of Pragmatics*, London: Longman.

Lepore, Ernest and Barry Smith (eds) (2006) *The Oxford Handbook of Philosophy of Language*, Oxford: Clarendon Press.

Lesser, Ruth and Lesley Milroy (1993) *Linguistics and Aphasia: Psycholinguistic and Pragmatic Aspects of Intervention*, London: Longman.

Levinson, Stephen (1983) *Pragmatics*, Cambridge: Cambridge University Press.

Levinson, Stephen (2000) *Presumptive Meanings: The Theory of Generalized Conversational Implicature*, Cambridge, Mass.: MIT Press.

Levinson, Stephen (2004) 'Deixis', in Laurence Horn and Gregory Ward (eds): 97–121.

Lewey. C. (1976) '*Mind* under G. E. Moore 1921–47', *Mind* 337: 37–46.

Lewis, David (1979) 'Scorekeeping in a language game', *Journal of Philosophical Logic* 8: 339–59.

Liddicoat, Anthony (2007) *An Introduction to Conversation Analysis*, London: Continuum.

Löbner, Sebastian (2002) *Understanding Semantics*, London: Hodder Education.

MacMahon, Barbara (1996), 'Indirectness, rhetoric and interpretive use: communicative strategies in Browning's *My Last Duchess*', *Language and Literature* 5: 209–23.

MacMahon, Barbara (2006) 'Stylistics: pragmatic approaches', in Keith Brown (ed.) *Encyclopedia of Language and Linguistics, vol. 12*, Oxford: Elsevier: 232–6.

Marcos, Haydeé (2001) 'Introduction: early pragmatic development', *First Language* 21: 209–18.

Marcos, Haydeé and Josie Bernicot (1997) 'How do young children reformulate assertions? A comparison with requests', *Journal of Pragmatics* 27: 781–98.

Martin, Robert (1987) *The Meaning of Language*, Cambridge MA: MIT Press.

Martin, J.R. and David Rose (2003) *Working with Discourse: Meaning Beyond the Clause*, London: Continuum.

Martinich, A.P. (1984) 'A theory of metaphor', *Journal of Literary Semantics* 13(1): 35–56.

Matsumoto, Yoshiko (1989) 'Politeness and conversational universals: observations from Japanese', *Journal of Pragmatics* 8: 207–21.

McCawley, James (1993) *Everything that Linguists have Always Wanted to Know about Logic* (2nd edn), Chicago: University of Chicago Press.

McDonald, Skye (1992) 'Communicative disorders following closed head injury: new approaches to assessment and rehabilitation', *Brain Injury* 6: 293–8.

McDonald, Skye (1999) 'Exploring the process of inference generation in sarcasm: a review of normal and clinical studies', *Brain and Language* 68: 486–506.

McEnery, Tony and Andrew Wilson (2001) *Corpus Linguistics: An Introduction*, Edinburgh: Edinburgh University Press.

Mey, Jacob (1989) 'The end of the copper age, or: pragmatics 12½ years later', *Journal of Pragmatics* 13: 825–32.

Mey, Jacob (1993) *Pragmatics, An Introduction*, Oxford: Blackwell.

Mey, Jacob (1998) (ed.) *Concise Encyclopedia of Pragmatics*, Amsterdam: Elsevier.

Mey, Jacob (2000) *When Voices Clash: A Study in Literary Pragmatics*, Berlin: Mouton.

Mey, Jacob (2006) 'Focus-on issue: intercultural pragmatics and sociolinguistics', *Journal of Pragmatics* 38: 1793–4.

Meyer, Charles (2002) *English Corpus Linguistics: An Introduction*, Cambridge: Cambridge University Press.

Meyerhoff, Miriam (2006) *Introducing Sociolinguistics*, New York: Routledge.

Montague, Richard (1968) 'Pragmatics', in Raymond Klibansky (ed.) *Contemporary Philosophy, vol. 1*, Firenze: La Nuova Italia Editrice, 102–22.

Morris, (1938) 'Foundations of the theory of signs', in O. Neurath, R. Carnap and C. Morris (eds) *International Encyclopedia of Unified Science*, Chicago: University of Chicago Press, 77–138.

Moscovitch, M. (1983) 'The linguistic and emotional functions of the normal right hemisphere', in Ellen Perecman (ed.) *Cognitive Processing in the Right Hemisphere*, New York: Academic Press: 57–82.

Müller, Nicole (ed.) (2000) *Pragmatics in Speech and Language Pathology*, Amsterdam: John Benjamins.

Norrick, Neal (2009) 'Interjections as pragmatic markers', *Journal of Pragmatics* 41: 866–91.

Noveck, Ira (2001) 'When children are more logical than adults: experimental investigations of scalar implicature', *Cognition* 78: 165–88.

Noveck, Ira (2004) 'Pragmatic inferences related to logical terms', in Ira Noveck and Dan Sperber (eds): 301–21.

Noveck, Ira and Dan Sperber (eds) (2004) *Experimental Pragmatics*, Basingstoke: Palgrave Macmillan.

Noveck, Ira and Dan Sperber (2007) 'The how and why of experimental pragmatics: the case of "scalar inferences"', in Noel Burton-Roberts (ed): 184–212.

Ochs, Elinor and Bambi Schieffelin (1976) 'Topic as a discourse notion: a study of topic in the conversations of children and adults', in Li, C (ed.) *Subject and Topic*, New York: Academic Press: 335–84.

Ochs, Elinor and Bambi Schieffelin, (eds) (1979) *Developmental Pragmatics*, New York: Academic Press.

Painter, Claire (1984) *Into the Mother Tongue: A Case Study in Early Language Development*, London: Pinter.

Partington, Alan (2004) 'Corpora and discourse, a most congruous beast', in Alan Partington, John Morley and Louann Haarman (eds): 11–20.

Partington, Alan, John Morley and Louann Haarman (eds) (2004) *Corpora and Discourse*, Bern: Peter Lang.

Paul, Rhea and Donald Cohen (1985) 'Comprehension of indirect requests in adults with autistic disorders and mental retardation', *Journal of Speech and Hearing Research* 28: 475–9.

Peccei, Jean Stilwell (1999) *Pragmatics*, London: Routledge.

Pedlow, Robert, Ann Sanson, and Roger Wales (2004) 'Children's production and comprehension of politeness in requests: relationships to behavioural adjustment, temperament and empathy', *First Language* 24: 347–67.

Pelletier, Francis Jeffry and Andrew Hartline (2006) 'On a homework problem of Larry Horn's', in Betty Birner and Gregory Ward (eds): 281–93.

Perkins, Michael (2000) 'The scope of pragmatic disability: a cognitive approach', in Nicole Müller (ed.): 7–28.

Perkins, Michael (2007) *Pragmatic Impairment*, Cambridge: Cambridge University Press.

Perner, J. and Leekam, S. (1986) 'Belief and quantity: three year olds' adaption to listener's knowledge', *Journal of Child Language* 13: 305–15.

Pope, Rob (1995) *Textual Intervention*, London: Routledge.

Pilkington, Adrian (1991) 'Poetic effects: a relevance theory perspective', in Roger Sell (ed.): 44–61

Pilkington, Adrian (2000) *Poetic Effects: A Relevance Theory Perspective*, Amsterdam and Philadelphia: John Benjamins.

Pilkington, Adrian, Barbara McMahon and Billy Clark (1997) 'Looking for an argument: a response to Green', *Language and Literature* 6: 139–48.

Potts, Christopher (2005) *The Logic of Conventional Implicatures*, Oxford: Oxford University Press.

Pratt, Mary Louise (1977) *Toward a Speech Act Theory of Literary Discourse*, Bloomington: Indiana University Press.

Preyer, Gerhard and Georg Peter (eds) (2007) *Context-Sensitivity and Semantic Minimalism: New Essays on Semantics and Pragmatics,* Oxford : Oxford University Press.

Putnam, Hilary. (1967) 'The "innateness hypothesis" and explanatory models in linguistics', *Synthesis* 17: 12–22. Reprinted in Block, Ned (ed.) (1981) *Readings in Philosophy of Psychology, vol. 2*, London: Methuen: 292–9.

Quine, W.V.O. (1951) 'Two dogmas of empiricism' in W.V.O. Quine (1953) *From a Logical Point of View*, Harvard: Harvard University Press: 20–4.

Quine, W.V.O. (1960) *Word and Object*, Cambridge MA: MIT Press.

Rapin, Isabelle (1996) 'Developmental language disorders: a clinical update', *Journal of Child Psychology and Psychiatry* 37: 643–55.

Recanati, François (1994) 'Contextualism and anti-contextualism in the philosophy of language', in Savas Tsohatzidis (ed.): 156–66.

Recanati, François (2004a) *Literal Meaning*, Cambridge: Cambridge University Press.

Recanati, François (2004b) 'Pragmatics and semantics', in Laurence Horn and Gregory Ward (eds): 443–62.

Reichert, John (1977) *Making Sense of Literature*, Chicago and London: The University of Chicago Press.

Rieber, Steven (1997) 'Conventional implicatures as tacit performatives', *Linguistics and Philosophy* 20: 51–72.

Riesco-Bernier, Silvia and Jesús Romero-Trillo (2008) 'The acoustics of "newness" and its pragmatic implications in classroom discourse', *Journal of Pragmatics* 40: 1103–16.

Romero-Trillo, Jesús (ed.) (2008) *Pragmatics and Corpus Linguistics*, Berlin: Mouton de Gruyter.

Routledge, Christopher and Siobhan Chapman (2003) 'Reading "great books": non truth-committed discourse and silly novel readers', *Forum for Modern Language Studies* 39: 1–14.

Russell, Bertrand and Alfred Whitehead (1910) *Principia Mathematica*, Cambridge: Cambridge University Press.

Ryle, Gilbert (1957) 'The theory of meaning'. Reprinted in Charles Caton (ed.) (1963) *Philosophy and Ordinary Language*, Urbana: University of Illinois Press.

Sacks, H., E. Schegloff and G. Jefferson (1974) 'A simplest systematics for the organisation of turn-taking for conversation', *Language* 50: 696–735.

Sadock, Jerrold (1974) *Towards a Linguistic Theory of Speech Acts*, New York: Academic Press.

Sadock, Jerrold (2004) 'Speech acts', in Laurence Horn and Gregory Ward (eds): 53–73.

Sadock, Jerrold and Arnold Zwicky (1985) 'Sentence types', in T. Shopen (ed.) *Language Typology and Syntactic Description, vol 1: Clause Structure*, Cambridge: Cambridge University Press: 155–96.

Sampson, Geoffrey (1982) 'The economics of conversation: comments on Joshi's paper', in Neil Smith (ed.) *Mutual Knowledge*, London: Academic Press: 200–10.

Sampson, Geoffrey (2001) *Empirical Linguistics*, London: Continuum.

van der Sandt, Rob (1988) *Context and Presupposition*, New York: Croom Helm.

Saul, Jennifer (2002) 'What is said and psychological reality: Grice's project and relevance theorists' criticisms', *Linguistics and Philosophy* 25: 347–72.

Saussure, Ferdinand de (1916) *Course in General Linguistics*, London: Peter Owen.

Sbisà, Marina (2006) 'After Grice: Neo-and post-perspectives', *Journal of Pragmatics* 38: 2223–34.

Schegloff, Emanuel (1999) 'Discourse, pragmatics, conversation, analysis', *Discourse Studies* 1: 405–35.

Schegloff, Emanuel (2007) *Sequence Organization in Interaction*, Cambridge: Cambridge University Press.

Schegloff, E. and H. Sacks (1973) 'Opening up closings', *Semiotica* 7: 289–327.

Schiffrin, Deborah (1994) *Approaches to Discourse*, Oxford: Blackwell.

Schiffrin, Deborah, Deborah Tannen and Heidi Hamilton (2003) *The Handbook of Discourse Analysis*, Oxford: Blackwell.

Scollon, Ron and Suzanne Wong Scollon (2000) *Intercultural Communication: A Discourse Approach* (2nd edition), Oxford: Blackwell.

Searle, John (1969) *Speech Acts*, Cambridge: Cambridge University Press.

Searle, John (1974) 'The logical status of fictional discourse', in John Searle (1979): 58–75.

Searle, John (1975a) 'Indirect speech acts', in John Searle (1979): 30–57.

Searle, John (1975b) 'A taxonomy of illocutionary acts, in John Searle (1979): 1–29.

Searle, John (1978) 'Literal meaning', *Erkenntnis* 13: 207–24, reprinted in John Searle (1979): 162–79.

Searle, John (1979) *Expression and Meaning*, Cambridge: Cambridge University Press.

Sell, Roger (1985) 'Tellability and politeness in "The Miller's Tale": First steps in Literary Pragmatics', *English Studies* 66: 496–512.

Sell, Roger (ed.) (1991a) *Literary Pragmatics*, London: Routledge.

Sell, Roger (1991b) 'The politeness of literary texts', in Roger Sell (ed): 208–24.

Simpson, Paul (1989) 'Politeness phenomena in Ionesco's *The Lesson*', in Ronald Carter and Paul Simpson (eds) *Language, Discourse and Literature*, London: Unwin Hyman: 171–93.

Sinclair, J. and Coulthard, M. (1975) *Towards an Analysis of Discourse: the English used by Teachers and Pupils*, London: Oxford University Press.

Smith, Barbara Hernstein (1971) 'Poetry as fiction', *New Literary History* 2: 259–81.

Smith, Neil and Ianthi-Maria Tsimpli (1995) *The Mind of a Savant*, Oxford: Blackwell.

Snow, Catherine (1986) 'Conversations with children', in Paul Fletcher and Michael Garman (eds) *Language Acquisition*, 2nd edn, Cambridge: Cambridge University Press: 69–89.

Soames, Scot (1982) 'How presuppositions are inherited: a solution to the projection problem', *Linguistic Inquiry* 10: 623–66.

Sperber, Dan and Ira Noveck (2004) 'Introduction', in Ira Noveck and Dan Sperber (eds): 1–22.

Sperber, Dan and Deirdre Wilson (1995) *Relevance* (2nd edn), Oxford: Blackwell.

Sperber, Dan and Deirdre Wilson (2005) 'Pragmatics', in F. Jackson and M. Smith (eds) *Oxford Handbook of Contemporary Philosophy*, Oxford: Oxford University Press: 468–501.

Spolsky, Bernard (1998) *Sociolinguistics*, Oxford: Oxford University Press.

Stalnaker, Robert (1974) 'Pragmatic presuppositions', in Munitz, M and Unger, P (eds) *Semantics and Philosophy*, New York: New York University Press: 197–213.

Strawson, Peter (1952) *Introduction to Logical Theory*, London: Methuen.

Strawson, Peter (1964) 'Intention and convention in speech acts', *The Philosophical Review* 73. Reprinted in P.F. Strawson (1971) *Logico-Linguistic Papers*, London: Methuen: 149–69.

Surian, L. (1996) 'Are children with autism deaf to Gricean maxims?', *Cognitive Neuropsychiatry* 1: 55–72.

Szabó, Zoltán Gendler (ed.) (2005) *Semantics vs. Pragmatics*, Oxford: Clarendon Press.

Tannen, Deborah (1998) 'The relativity of linguistic strategies: rethinking power and solidarity in gender and dominance', in Deborah Cameron (ed): 261–79.

Teubert, Wolfgang and Ramesh Krishnamurthy (eds) (2007) *Corpus Linguistics, Critical Concepts in Linguistics vol. VI*, London: Routledge.

Thomas, Jenny (1995) *Meaning in Interaction: An Introduction to Pragmatics*, London: Longman.

Thomas, P. (1997) 'What can linguistics tell us about thought disorder?', in J. France and N. Muir (eds) *Communication and the Mentally Ill Patient: Developmental and Linguistic Approaches to Schizophrenia*, London: Jessica Kingsley Publishers: 30–42.

Thompson, J.R. (2007) 'Still relevant: H.P. Grice's legacy in psycholinguistics and the philosophy of language', *Teorema* XXVI: 77–109.

Tomasello, Michael (2000) 'Do young children have adult syntactic competence?' *Cognition* 74: 209–53.

Tompkins, Connie (1990) 'Knowledge and strategies for processing lexical metaphor after right or left hemisphere brain damage', *Journal of Speech and Hearing Research* 33: 307–16.

Toolan, Michael (1998a) 'A reply to Pilkington, McMahon and Clark', *Language and Literature* 7: 68–9.

Toolan, Michael (1998b) *Language in Literature*, London: Arnold.

Toolan, Michael (1999) 'Integrational linguistics, relevance theory and stylistic explanation: a reply to MacMahon', *Language and Literature* 8: 255–68.

Tsohatzidis, Sava (ed.) (1994) *Foundations of Speech Act Theory*, London: Routledge.

Vallée, Richard (2008) 'Conventional implicature revisited', *Journal of Pragmatics* 40: 407–30.

Wardhaugh, Ronald (1998) *An Introduction to Sociolinguistics*, Oxford: Blackwell.

Watts, Richard (2003) *Politeness*, Cambridge: Cambridge University Press.

Watts, Richard, Sachiko Ide and Konrad Ehlich (1992) 'Introduction', in Richard Watts (ed.) *Politeness in Language: Studies in its History, Theory and Practice*, Berlin: Mouton de Gruyter: 1–17.

Watts, Richard, Sachiko Ide and Konrad Ehlich (eds) (2005) *Politeness in Language* (2nd edn) Berlin: Mouton de Gruyter.

Wilson, Deirdre and Sperber, Dan (1981) 'On Grice's theory of conversation', in Paul Werth (ed.) *Conversation and discourse: structure and interpretation*, London: Croom Helm.

Wilson, Deirdre and Dan Sperber (1993) 'Linguistic form and relevance', *Lingua* 90: 1–25.

Wilson, Deirdre and Dan Sperber (2004) 'Relevance theory', in Laurence Horn and Gregory Ward (eds): 607–32.

Winer, Gerald, Jane Cottrell, Tammy Mott, Matthew Cohen and Jody Fournier (2001) 'Are children more accurate than adults? Spontaneous use of metaphor by children and adults', *Journal of Psycholinguistic Research* 50: 485–96.

Wittgenstein, Ludwig (1953) *Philosophical Investigations*, Oxford: Blackwell.

Wodak, Ruth (2001) 'What CDA is about: a summary of its history, important concepts and its developments', in Ruth Wodak and Michael Meyer (eds): 1–13.

Wodak, Ruth and Paul Chilton (eds) (2005) *A New Agenda in (Critical) Discourse Analysis: Theory, Methodology and Interdisciplinary*, Amsterdam: Benjamins.

Wodak, Ruth and Michael Meyer (2001) *Methods of Critical Discourse Analysis*, London: Sage.

Xie, Chaoqun (2003) 'Review of *A Critique of Politeness Theories* by Gino Eelen', *Journal of Pragmatics* 35: 811–18.

Index